Staying the Course

Also by Robert S. Weiss

Loneliness
Marital Separation

Staying the Course

The Emotional and Social Lives
of Men Who Do Well at Work

Robert S. Weiss

Fawcett Columbine
NEW YORK

A Fawcett Columbine Book
Published by Ballantine Books
Copyright © 1990 by Robert S. Weiss

All rights reserved under International and Pan-American
Copyright Conventions. Published in the United States
by Ballantine Books, a division of Random House, Inc.,
New York, and distributed in Canada by Random House of
Canada Limited, Toronto.

This edition published by arrangement with The Free Press,
a division of Macmillan, Inc.

Library of Congress Catalog Card Number: 91-70536

ISBN: 0-449-90648-5

Cover design by Dale Fiorillo
Manufactured in the United States of America
First Ballantine Books Edition: September 1991
10 9 8 7 6 5 4 3 2 1

Freud was once asked what he felt a normal person should be able to do well. The questioner probably expected a complicated answer. But Freud, in the curt acerbity of his old days, is reported to have said: "Lieben und arbeiten."

Erik H. Erikson, *Childhood and Society*.

Contents

Introduction

This book is about men who have done well enough in their work to have achieved a place in their society that most of us would consider satisfactory. Their occupations are solidly middle-class or possibly a bit better. They own homes in good suburbs or upper-income metropolitan neighborhoods. Now aged between thirty-five and fifty-five, and at least fairly well established in a line of work, they have achieved lives to which as young men they might reasonably have aspired.

The first question to which this book is addressed is the nature of these men's lives. To answer this question I describe the activities that absorb the men's energies, the relationships that sustain their functioning (although they can also, at times, be troubling), and the goals that give their lives direction and meaning. I examine the stresses the men experience, especially at work, and how they deal with them. And I try to make evident the way the men maintain their balance and their direction despite inescapable tensions, conflicts, and challenges.

By and large the men of this study carry a good deal of responsibility at work, at home, and, in some instances, in the communities where they live. Their security and self-confidence are repeatedly at risk. To maintain their integration and direction they need resilience, and often they need, as well, support from the people with whom they work and live. I try to suggest just what such support may entail and why it is helpful.

I consider a good many narrow issues in the course of surveying the larger issues of these men's lives. While discussing the importance to men of having a secure place in a community of work, for example, I give attention to the frustration men feel when their efforts are inadequately recognized by their fellows. Now and again I suggest an explanation for the sort of stereotypic male behavior that shows up in situation comedies, such as the "fatigue display" by which men let their families know they have had a grueling day at work.

The second question to which this book is addressed is that of the internal experience of men who do well at work. How does it feel to maintain so much investment in work, to be a devoted but sometimes absent husband and father, to be a trustworthy friend but not a confiding one? If the first question asks for more or less objective appraisal of men's lives, this second question asks about their subjective experience.

Both these questions can best be answered with information provided by the men themselves. What is needed is that the men tell us how they have witnessed themselves behave in the various sectors of their lives, report to us what seemed to have been their motivations in those behaviors, and describe for us what it felt like, subjectively, to participate in the events of their lives. My colleagues and I therefore conducted interviews with a sample of men doing well in their work. In all we interviewed eighty men between thirty-five and fifty-five years of age who had what appeared to be upper-middle-class occupations and who lived in upper-income settings.

Every locality in the New England region in which our study was conducted annually prepares a Street List in which can be found the names, occupations, and ages of all residents at least seventeen years old. The information is gathered and published because it constitutes a listing of potential voters useful to voting registrars. Copies of the Street List are given free to candidates for public office and are for sale to everyone else. We obtained Street Lists for four upper-income suburbs and one upper-income metropolitan district.

We randomly chose the names of men in upper-middle occupations (managers, administrators, professionals in organizations) aged between thirty-five and fifty-five. We sent everyone whose name had been chosen a letter saying that we hoped we could interview him. We then telephoned. Thanks especially to the persuasive powers of the interviewer who became responsible for much of our recruiting, we obtained the agreement of nearly sixty percent of those living in the suburban areas, somewhat less than that of those living in the upper-income metropolitan district. In addition to interviewing the men, we interviewed twenty of the women to whom they were married. During the data collection phase of the study, two of the men divorced, and we interviewed one of the ex-wives.*

---

*As noted in the appendix on methods, five of the eighty men were pilot study respondents, and seventy-five were randomly chosen in the study proper. The quotations used in the book are drawn from interviews with all eighty respondents. The statistical analyses draw only on materials provided by the seventy-five respondents who were randomly chosen.

WHAT KIND OF MEN ARE THESE?

The men of our study were chosen because they are in job positions that are respected and responsible. In a very few instances, which we identify as contrast cases, we were misled by ambiguous occupational titles—warehouse manager, for example—and accepted as respondents men whose job positions were of lesser standing. By and large, however, our respondents are important figures in their companies or organizations. By and large they are also respected in their communities. They have nice homes in nice areas. Some have a second home in the country. Most could, if they wanted to, take an occasional winter vacation. With a few exceptions, the men are not rich, but they are comfortable.

It is an enduring theme in American literature that the men who keep the society going have been trapped by social forms and go through their lives joylessly, if stoically. In the nineteenth century Henry Thoreau offered the observation, "The mass of men lead lives of quiet desperation"[1] and, a hundred years later, Joseph Heller's *Something Happened* and John Updike's *Rabbit Redux* presented an Everyman who could serve as a case in point. Each of their central figures was successful enough—nothing extraordinary, but good enough—but nevertheless found life trying and pointless.

A related view in American literature of men who have done reasonably well occupationally is that they are limited in vision and sensitivity, yet contain within themselves a desire for self-expression and self-realization of which they are only occasionally aware. Because they so much want others to think well of them, they behave not to express their deeper feelings but rather to project the correct image. They are unaware of how they starve what is most genuine in themselves. Sinclair Lewis's *Babbitt* presents this image vividly.

In the 1950s and 1960s men like our respondents—secure, living in nice areas, doing well at work—were likely to be characterized as conformist. William H. Whyte, in *The Organization Man*, pictured them as straitjacketed into organizational styles of dress and thought. One song popular at the time had them living mechanically in ticky-tack houses, at the end of identical days drinking martinis identically dry. Their individual differences were submerged in gray flannel. They lacked the integrity or the strength to remain themselves.

But in the late 1960s and 1970s there emerged a different view of men like those described in this book. They remained men whose hair was well trimmed and whose clothes were well cut, but now this meant not comformity but rather power. These men were The Establishment. They were exploitative, especially of women, but to a lesser degree of all those less well placed than themselves. Knowingly or unknowingly they conspired against everyone not a member of their club. They were despoilers.[2]

None of these images of reasonably successful men, whether as victims or as exploiters, fit the data we collected. Our respondents rather appeared to be men who are doing as well as they can to fashion satisfactory lives for themselves and their families. They are neither passive nor ruthless; if anything, they try to be good men. It is important for them that they come through on their obligations, that they meet their responsibilities. In short, they want to be men they themselves can respect. A point that seems not to have been especially noted by their critics is that men like those of this study have standards for themselves that they are determined to meet.

For the most part, the men who are the subject of this book function well, emotionally and socially, in the work sector and in other sectors of their lives. Most of the time they are psychologically comfortable, free from painful thoughts and memories, able to relax, and able to maintain a reasonably good mood. They are able to feel good when good things happen. They are hopeful enough about the future to want to plan for it. They have enough energy for the tasks of the day. They meet ordinary social expectations.

Not all the men in the sample satisfied all these criteria all the time. Nor should this be surprising. Studies of representative samples of middle- and upper-income Americans regularly find a sizable minority to have emotional problems, generally moderate in degree. It does not seem to me inconsistent with characterizing ours as a sample of men who function well not only at work but elsewhere to report that about a third of them had at some time consulted a mental health professional because of depression, marital difficulties, or trouble with a child. One of the eighty men we interviewed regularly took medication to fend off depression. Another had been hospitalized for what seemed to have been a breakdown in ordinary judgment resembling a manic episode; we think it likely that he was diagnosed as manic by the hospital's admitting officer. Two of the men were alcoholic. A few suffered high levels of work-based stress. Several reported marital problems. Several had problems with their children.

And yet all the men showed up at work every day, where they met the responsibilities of their jobs, whatever they were. They showed up at home when they were expected (in a few cases, not quite always) and met the responsibilities of the home (again, in a few cases, not quite always). These are men who, no matter what else may be happening, stay the course. One of the concerns of this book is to explain how they are able to do it.

THE OPAQUENESS OF MEN'S LIVES

When the staff of the study read the transcripts of our first interviews, we all were surprised. The study's administrator, the interviewers, and the transcriptionist, all female, agreed that our sample must be unrepresentative. They knew what men's lives were like. They had fathers, husbands, boyfriends, male co-workers, and male friends, and these men didn't live this way. The men they knew were not so concerned about work—concerned, all right, but not to the point where their work was more vivid for them than anything else in their lives. Nor were they so unreconstructed in their domestic attitudes. Yes, sometimes they did less at home than they should, but they were not so egregiously traditional as these first respondents. And the friendships of the first respondents seemed bizarre. Imagine having a close friend whom you saw only once every six months, with whom you never had a long phone conversation, and in whom you hardly ever confided.

At that time I was the only male on the staff. I too was surprised by the early interviews. I had come to the study thinking that I was different from other men; that I was more beset by conflicting commitments to home and work, more chronically worried about my children, more vulnerable to tensions at work. I was surprised to discover that our respondents' social and emotional lives were in fundamental ways nearly identical to mine. We were, perhaps, in different lines of work, lived in households that differed in emotional climate, were different in personality, and yet the meaning to us of work, family, children, and friends, the nature of our strivings and the problems of our days—in all these ways we were much more alike than different. I went home and told my wife, "We're all cut out with the same cookie cutter."

I now realize that by our surprise at the content of the early interviews we members of the staff were demonstrating how little is actually known about the content of men's lives. I suspect that men constitute for women an alien culture, whose values and approved ways of behaving at times make no sense. (What woman has not been exasperated by her consort's refusal to ask directions when lost?) But we men seem to know each other no better: a result, I think, of our practice when with each other of playing our lives very close to the vest.

If most men's lives are opaque both to women and to other men, one consequence is that all of us have difficulty judging how odd is the behavior of the men we do know well. A marvelously astute woman, on reading an early draft of this book, said that it had helped her better understand her former husband, especially his chronic anxiety about his place in his firm. When they were married he had proclaimed his devotion to his family, but had always given his work higher priority. Only seldom had he had energy left over for the family. When his marital relationship had become stressful, and he would himself admit that it was unsatisfactory, he seemed nevertheless to be willing to settle for a stable home. All this now, she said, made sense. Once she had thought of him as neurotic; now she was willing to view him as a man like other men, though perhaps somewhat more so.

The men of this book may appear surprisingly traditional to women who believe that most men today stand ready to share dishes and diapers. The men of this book, while they "help" at home, sometimes a great deal, insist that all they are doing is helping. Another woman who read an earlier draft of the book said that the men struck her as anachronisms whose outlook was reminiscent of 1950s Ohio. They talked about their wives as if the wives were without paid employment and had full time to give to the men and their homes. Didn't the wives have careers or, anyway, paid work?

Most did. About one-third of the wives had full-time paid employment, about one-third had part-time paid employment, and only one-third were without paid employment. Among that one-third without paid employment, almost a third had regular and serious work as volunteers. Hence, less than a quarter of the men had wives who were without work obligations outside their homes.

If, despite this, the men seem to view their wives as primarily *wives*, rather than as employed fellow citizens to whom they happen to be married—well, that is the way they view their wives. For the men this view of their wives follows from their understanding of themselves as the marital partner ultimately responsible for the support of the home. They see their own work as family-relevant in a way that their wives' work is not. It follows that whatever other responsibilities they may have to their homes are secondary to the responsibility to ensure that their homes are adequately financed.

I have been told that younger men are different. That may be so. But the test is not how men of the new generation behave when they are first married. It is how they behave when they have children. In my observation there has been little change in the understandings among this younger generation of their responsibilities once they become fathers as well as husbands. They do feel that they should be more involved with their children than their own fathers were with them, but they continue to see their wives as having primary responsibility for child care. And they continue to see themselves as having primary responsibility for financing the home.

A question is raised by this study that cannot be answered entirely on the basis of our interviews: "Are these lives desirable or not?" Are these men the favored sons of our society or are they its victims? How should we feel about the lives described in this book? Should we think that men who live this way are admirable, worthy of emulation? Or should we view them with discomfort and regret?

I return to the issue of evaluation in the last chapter of the book, but I might note here my view of the men whose lives are treated here. Taking the men as a group, I admire them for their persistence, their reliability, and their determination to meet, each day, that day's social and emotional bills. I admire their stoicism, though I regret its costs. I admire their ability to make things work. Too few of them, perhaps, have goals beyond doing well at work, doing well by their children, and meeting the daily bills. Perhaps more of them might give energy to the betterment of the communities where they live. And yet even here they do the best they can, and some of them do a fair amount in their churches, their neighborhoods, and their towns. All in all, I admire them.

Others might feel that too much of their energy is devoted to their work, given their own goals, or that they sustain too much stress and experience too few times of peace and contemplation. I find it not just a defense, but a kind of explanation, that they do the best they can.

WORK, THE FAMILY, AND OTHER SECTORS OF MEN'S LIVES

Men in general, and not just the men of this study, appear to require two kinds of association to sustain themselves. The first is membership in a valued community. For the men of this study the valued community is uniformly a community of work, and their acceptance in this community is dependent on their apparent capability. In turn, their acceptance validates that they have such capability and so sustains their feelings of worth. In another society, perhaps in another sector of our own society, membership in the community that provides social place might be based on lineage, religious leadership, artistic ability, or even criminal skill. In this sector of this society it is work that matters.

Men like the men of this study experience severe distress on loss of membership in a community of work, especially if the loss appears to be a consequence of their inability to do their jobs. Just as membership in a community of work demonstrates worth, loss of membership suggests its absence. Being fired is likely to produce an almost catastrophic loss of self-esteem.

In addition to having a place at work, men require, if they are to feel their lives are complete, a partner to share their lives, with whom they can establish a home. Most men find that marriage sustains their feelings of security and in addition helps them manage the logistics of their lives. Children provide justification for their life enterprise, even more than do the goals the men pursue in their work. Furthermore, having children helps to make sense out of work, because work now becomes a means for providing for the children.

Work and family are the two sectors in which men's central emotional investments are lodged. These are the sectors to which men give most of their time and energy. Men's lives can be seen to contain a third sector as well, comprising a conglomerate of communities: kin, friends, neighbors—people who are neither co-workers nor members of the men's households. Some men's lives also contain a fourth sector, encapsulated away from their ordinary lives, centered on another woman or a series of other women.

Each of these sectors is discussed in this book, but work and family, because they count the most, receive the most space. Work is dealt with before family not because it is the more important sector emotionally but because it is the sector that is more nearly fundamental. Men find no discordance in taking a job before they have a family. In contrast, it doesn't strike them as right to have a family before they have a job or, at least, reasonable assurance of a job in the near future. Furthermore, a man who loses his family through divorce will lose only a bit of respect within the world of work, but a man who is long without work is likely to lose a good deal of standing within his family. Although work may not be the sector that matters most in a man's life, it is likely to be the foundation for the rest.

WHY STUDY THESE MEN?

Why is it important to understand the lives of men who do well occupationally? For one thing, these are the men who keep the society going. They are among the directors of the enterprises on which our society depends. Understanding their lives helps us to evaluate the costs and gratifications associated with becoming the kind of man who runs our society, the kind our society urges young men to become.

A second reason for understanding these men's lives is to provide baseline information on the nature of well-functioning lives. Men who do well at work are doing well in a critically important sector of life. They may also be expected to be doing, at the least, no worse than anyone else in other sectors. To a first approximation, they may be taken as a well-functioning population.

We have had any number of studies of men and women who are especially liable to distress, perhaps because they have suffered a loss or trauma. I have done such studies myself. As yet we have not given the same attention to men and women not identified as at special risk of distress. We need to, if only to prevent our exaggerating the extent to which members of such a population are without trouble.

Finally, we ought to understand these men's lives because these are the men with whom we live—or the men who we are. So that we can better understand ourselves and our own lives, we need to better understand them.

CHAPTER ONE

The Provisions
of Work

In responsible jobs, challenges follow quickly, one on another, all through the work day. Something must be decided, written, made, fixed, ordered, now, right now. And after that, another challenge must be addressed, and then another, until the day is over.

Consider the description of his job offered by Mr. Metzger,* a production manager.

> The whole job consists of a bunch of details. Supervising people, making customers happy, solving problems, answering their questions. I can give you an example. A customer wants to reject three hundred parts, some of them for the second time. We thought they were good. The customer tells me they are no good. And he needs them right away. So I was trying to decide if I should go myself or send a mechanic or both of us should go. And I finally decided that I was going to go until we found some more of the parts and we discovered what the problem was.
>
> Meanwhile the bookkeeper didn't come in, so I had to check the time cards. She usually fills in the payroll data for the computer. I had to do that. And I had to write a couple of

---

*Respondents' names have been changed, and all identifying information has been changed or omitted.

1

quick checks because a delivery came in. And I had to make sure that the delivery was correct.

Then I had to negotiate some prices with a customer. He wanted a reduction of five percent on a quote or else the order would go to a competitor. In this particular case we had done the job three times before, successfully, and he was interested in giving it to us if we could meet the competition's price. I said I would review what the job entailed and whether there was enough margin to give him that much money off.

Someone came in from one of our customers. He had some problems with our parts and we had to show him how our parts were good. And there were the usual problems from the shop floor: "This thing didn't come out right and what should we do about it?"

Again and again Mr. Metzger was required to act without any assurance that his response, whatever it was, would be the right one. If he sent someone else to resolve the customer's complaint, the man might fail to satisfy the customer and the customer would be lost; if he went himself, he would be unavailable to deal with whatever came up at the shop. Each challenge brought with it similar dilemmas. Yet Mr. Metzger, to do his job, had to believe in his ability to make good decisions. Only with such belief could he make decisions confidently in situations of inescapable uncertainty.[1]

Mr. Metzger maintained the self-confidence that he required, in part, by observing his own success in meeting each challenge as he moved through his day. He was reassured of his worth as he saw himself do things right. His belief in himself permitted him to take quiet pride in, for one thing, his ability to deal with clients who expected unrealistically quick delivery.

There were four jobs that had delivery problems. The customer always wants it faster than we can produce it. He wants to know what happened. I might say, "The machine broke down." Which it *did*. Maybe not the particular machine that we needed for *his* job, but a machine broke down. Machines always break down. I never lie.

The succession of challenges kept Mr. Metzger engaged with his work throughout the work day. At the end of the day Mr. Metzger might be exhausted, but if all had gone well, he would also be pleased with himself. Mr. Metzger took early retirement during the course of the study. After his retirement he very much missed the sense of worth given to him by his ability to make things go well at work.

When men are asked what makes a job a good one, high on the list of desirable characteristics is that it be challenging.[2] Jobs that are not challenging tend to be described as oppressively dull. Men work at them in a time-serving fashion, for no reason other than to pick up a paycheck.

A task that men find challenging is, before anything else, one that cannot be met through routine effort. It carries a risk of failure. Meeting it requires special skill, competence, or character and, in addition, the mobilization of attention and energy.

Men mobilize in response to job challenge because they want to come through and because they fear failing. Coming through is succeeding, with the prize of self-approbation and perhaps the approbation of others. Failing can mean trouble on the job, loss of self-respect, and possibly loss of the respect of others. Once a challenge has been met, men can feel pleasure in their performance and in the work they have done, relief that they have averted threat, and enhanced confidence in their competence. Just as mobilization is a response to the recognition of challenge, positive self-appraisal is a response to its successful resolution.

This process of response to challenge, with its mobilization and, should there be success, its end in positive self-appraisal, is as involving of men's energies as a video game is of the energies of a twelve-year-old boy. Indeed, the processes of involvement are much the same. Another man, in describing his job, said:

[It's] making decisions, having options, going one way or the other, and seeing how that works out. Finding it doesn't work out and then you see you are in a lot of trouble for making that decision. There's a sort of a thrill in doing that. Just the self-satisfaction that you can juggle fourteen balls in the air at the same time without dropping one of them. You get a lot of involvement. I really love the work.

Mr. Harris, *consulting engineer*

What made Mr. Harris love his job was its level of challenge. Mr. Harris cared about the projects on which he worked, but his excitement came from succeeding in a job that demanded all his skill, where the risk of failure was high.[3]

Of course, any work can be understood as testing a man's ability to tolerate the disagreeable, and in that sense can be challenging, but it is regrettable when the primary challenge in a job is getting through the day. Assembly-line work is demoralizing largely because engineers have done their best to remove task-related challenge. Desirable jobs challenge aspects of the man he values: skills and talents whose effective use enhances his respect for himself.[4]

If a job is insufficiently challenging, men often try to introduce challenge into it. One way of doing this is to enlarge the job's sphere of responsibility. Mr. Layton, head of an investment group in an insurance company, reported adopting this strategy:

> My philosophy is, your job is what you make it. I could have the same job, it could be very boring if I wanted it to be. But I don't think I'll ever be in a position where I'd be satisfied with just sitting there, nine to five. You owe it to yourself and everyone to make it as interesting as possible.
>
> Every once in a while I'll come up with an idea. I guess some of my ideas are far out, because I come up with some wild and crazy ones every now and then. But you have to keep throwing things out. Anyway, that is what I have done. And it wasn't long before attention was paid to some of the things that I was doing.

Mr. Turner, a partner in an industrial catering service, believed that his business had become so stable that it could run itself without him. He began to think of expansion, not to increase his income, which was large enough, but to keep himself interested in his work.

> It's less hectic today than it was years ago. But it was more fun years ago. I enjoyed the hustle and bustle of having decisions to make every day. You always had something to do. It's gotten to the point now that I don't know why I come here. But I have no place else to go. [*laughs*]
>
> We're ready to go to the next plateau in the business, to make it a little bit bigger. We've hired a couple of salespeople who are out selling for us. And we're about to make some

ventures into related fields. It keeps you busy with something to do.

You can't stay still. If I stayed still I wouldn't come in any more. I just wouldn't bother to come in. There'd be nothing for me to do. I'm too young to sit and do nothing. I don't know how anybody can totally retire. You have to do something. Everybody has to do something.

When men are able to do work that is both difficult and valuable, they have good reason to believe in their worth.

THE FANTASY SUBSTRUCTURE OF WORK

Children's fantasies are immediately evident in their play. King of the Mountain permits them to act out both supremacy and the toppling of those who would claim supremacy. Tag provides an opportunity to be a community member, fleeing the pariah, and also to be the pariah who threatens. In the work of adults fantasies are usually better hidden, and the stray thought or fugitive impulse that nevertheless escapes into consciousness is more likely to be shrugged away. But fantasies are nevertheless present.

Just as play is the work of the young, work is the play of adults. Underlying the surface appearance of pure rationality in the performance of work are, regularly, motivational dynamics of great personal significance no different from the dynamics that make children's play intense. Thus, the child playing doctor and the adult working as a doctor or medical attendant may be enacting the same fantasies of benign access to the secret places of others. Indeed, work can be a superior form of play. In children's play it is necessary to pretend the activity in order to realize the fantasy; in adult's work the activity is there in reality. It is possible for the adult not just to play doctor but to practice medicine, not just to pretend to fly a plane, but to be a pilot.

Quite regularly men's work draws energy from underlying imagery in which the men, by doing the work, act out fantasies of heroic accomplishment. In one of the memorable passages in an interview with Henry Kissinger conducted by Oriana Fallaci, Kissinger was led to describe his image of himself as a cowboy riding alone into town, where, presumably, he would confront and defeat the bad guys.[5] Other men too, when asked to tell the story of their work, are likely to have at hand a picture of their work that enhances their own worth: through their work they fend off a threat, come through against the odds, or perform extraordinary feats of skill.

Mr. Cardell is a partner in a two-man land-planning firm, most of whose clients are builders and developers. One project involved planning the use of a very large tract of land that had just been purchased for a housing development. Mr. Cardell's description of the culmination of this project suggested a comic movie of buddies on a mission.

> This was a complex, important project. My partner and his crew had prepared these maps on a crash basis. I think that they had gone four days of sleeping two hours a night apiece. And they have these four maps. And based on the four maps, I crank out four handwritten sheets of paper: That's my report.
>
> We charter a plane, jump in, fly to the site. We get there and we meet with the clients in a room and we explain to them what we're going to be telling the Planning Board. And they are delighted with the whole thing.
>
> And then there are our clients and their attorney and the Planning Board and a public audience, including some environmentalists who are defensive. And I say, "Who is going to chair this thing?" And nobody is going to chair it. So I say, "Okay, I'll chair it."
>
> And I get up and make a speech and stumble through it and there is this ability to project a certain personality that is nonthreatening. And my partner shows his maps. And everybody gets a chance to say his thing. And the goal is to get a statement on the part of the Planning Board that says they don't have any significant concerns. And everything goes fine.
>
> We go away feeling great. I kiss a client. My partner kisses a client. We jump in the car, jump in the plane, fly home. Everything is fine.

Events may not have unrolled as blithely as in Mr. Cardell's description, but as it is told the story suggests the underlying fantasy that provided emotional coherence to Mr. Cardell's experience. The events associated with his presentation, as Mr. Cardell put them together, constituted an adventure with a lot of Hope and Crosby on the road plus a dash of Harold Lloyd. The fantasy was not unlike Henry Kissinger's: Mr. Cardell flies into town (with a partner, to be sure), dazzles the waiting establishment lawyers, environmentalists, and planning board members, shepherds everyone into agreement on the plan he has brought, and then, after having set everything right, takes his leave.

Other men bring to their work still other fantasies of high adventure in which their courage or determination is tested. They may be climbing a mountain or fighting off marauders. In describing their work the fantasies come immediately to their minds as metaphors or similes.

> The uncertainty is probably exciting. It's like the guy who flies off a hang glider, climbs a mountain. It's probably analogous to that.
>
> ---
>
> *Mr. Andrade, director of a new firm*

A department manager, Dr. Sorenson, in charge of new product development in a manufacturing firm, likened a two-week-long effort to meet a deadline to leading troops in combat:

> You have some limits, some amount of ammunition available: the number of days in the time period, the number of hours in the day, the amount of skill possessed by all the people and the knowledge and strength of the individuals and so forth. And you have to keep applying those resources or that ammunition at a maximum rate and hope that all your problems succumb. You have to hope that the enemy runs out of ammunition or troops before you do. That's what infantry combat is like, if I understand that correctly. That's a firefight mentality, I guess.

These fantasies provide an emotional meaning to men's work that helps sustain their effort. Not only does their success in meeting challenge reassure them that they are capable, but their efforts are engaged in resolving issues of deep emotional meaning.

Peripheral aspects of men's jobs can gratify still other fantasies, themselves often associated with feelings of worth. A sense of magical entitlement comes with the use of a firm's credit card to obtain the best room in a hotel and the best meal on a menu. A sense of admission into wizardry can come with taking home a firm's computer terminal to keep in touch with a project. But the fantasies that really engage men in their work are the ones they enact while doing their jobs.[6]

Fantasies are important even when jobs are not what men want them to be. Men who dislike their work or its conditions can cast themselves as embattled holdouts against oppression or as martyrs or victims, or can imagine themselves retaliating against the injustice of having to do the work. Even in work they hate, men give coherence to their experience by linking it to underlying fantasy and, by the same means, can try to protect their sense of worth.

Mr. Yule, a contrast case, was foreman of a construction crew for an industrial park. He liked doing construction but disliked his supervisor and was not notably fond of the company. He was especially affronted by his boss's habit of checking on him. He reacted by asserting his autonomy in small ways—by deciding just when he would do a job, for example.

At one point Mr. Yule started on a job very early on a Saturday morning. His supervisor, perhaps because he hadn't witnessed Mr. Yule's early start, chose not to credit him with it. He approved payment to Mr. Yule for one hour less than Mr. Yule had actually worked. Mr. Yule now described his struggle to achieve justice for himself with the same pride with which Mr. Cardell had described bringing off his presentation.

> There was one instance where I and another very good worker had a job to do on a Saturday. It was a forty-eight-hour job. We went in at six in the morning and we really dove into it. We were all through by one. So we walked out at one-thirty.
>
> As I'm leaving my boss is coming in the door. So I say to him, "Hey, we are all wrapped up, the job is complete. Give us seven hours." And I walked by him, got in my car and went home.
>
> I got my paycheck and I had six hours. So I ask, "What happened? We put seven hours in." He says, "No one gave you authority to start at six." I says, "It doesn't matter that we did a forty-eight-hour job in fourteen hours?" He says, "That's right. I didn't give you authority to start at six."
>
> So I go to the Grievance Committee and I tell them this is going on and I don't like it. We set up a meeting with his boss. His boss sides with him. So we set up another meeting.

Six, seven, months, I'm tied up with meetings. It is ridiculous. And I never did get that hour.

I told my boss, "You owe me an hour." He said, "If I know you, you clipped that hour a hundred times." I said, "Yes, and twenty years from now I'll still be getting that hour back. One way or another. You would have been better off to give it to me in my paycheck." Nope. Stubborn.

They send me out to estimate a job. I say it is going to take two hours to do the estimate. I do it in twenty minutes. I go home. I go shopping. I go to lunch. I'm making up that hour. And I'll make it up for another twenty years.

Mr. Yule was thoroughly engaged at work, but by his battle with management rather than by the challenges of his job. He could hang on to his place at work—the union contract, if nothing else, would prevent him from being fired—but he felt no identification with it. He said, at another point, that he counted the days until he could retire, that he continued to work only because he needed the money. But it was not the work itself that he disliked: when he worked on his own, performing exactly the same tasks he performed for the company, he worked with pleasure and pride.

Last summer I was remodeling a friend's house. It was no prints, just do what you want, an open checkbook. And I really enjoyed doing the work. I didn't have anyone looking over my shoulder all the time.

Mr. Yule found value in work, but when it was his firm he worked for, his energies were given to ever new episodes of "I won't let them do that to me."

ACHIEVEMENT

Successful response to challenge produces only a brief boost to self-esteem. Acting out a fantasy of worth produces only temporary gratification. Most men also desire that their work make a lasting difference, that they end with something tangible to show. The hope of achievement provides them with a sense of direction, of goals. They want to know there are patients they have helped to get well, buildings they have put up, businesses they have built. They want their work to have resulted in something that will testify to the value of their efforts, that will say that they mattered, that they contributed to the world.

The kind of achievement men want would be a product of their effort, something that made their effort concrete, a tangible, external statement of their success. They do not want to retire after thirty or forty years of work and have to recognize that what they had done hadn't mattered. They want to be able to say, with pride, "I did that." An architect said, "There is no thrill like walking out on a site and seeing a building that you have designed, that you have created, going up." In a similar way, a manager can expand with pride at evidence of his department's success, a craftsman as he examines a project he has done well.

Here is a description of pride in a business achievement offered by Mr. Daniels, a broker of construction equipment. Mr. Daniel's business required bringing together suppliers, customers, and financial institutions.

> I do all the documents, I run around, and I get it all done.
> And I sit down and the lessor signs it and I get a little bit of a
> smile. And the supplier signs it and I get a big grin. And I go
> to the bank and I do it, and I get the best feeling! What it is
> like I can't tell you. It is not like anything else. It is not like
> anything physical. Not like anything sexual. It's just, "Gee, I
> did that!" There is nothing like that, the feeling.

Mr. Daniels made a great deal of money in a successful deal, and that established the magnitude of his achievement. But it was not the money itself that constituted the achievement. It was creating the linkages among the parties to the deal that turned what had been only an idea into a living thing. Then, with the deal healthy and prospering, Mr. Daniels was able to sit there, in the presence of people who mattered to him, and witness how well he had done.

A man in a very different line of work, a craftsman who worked on typewriters and office machines, reported a similar pleasure in achievement.

> When you bring me a machine that for all intents and pur-
> poses is dead and would be dead in some people's shops,
> that's a very exciting thing. There are some technicians that
> won't touch pieces with water damage because they are

fraught with all kinds of hidden problems that will occur months after the repair was made. I like it. The more damage, the better. If you are willing to pay me to do it, I'll give it a shot. And I get a great deal of satisfaction out of getting the thing right. So I do a lot of things that other people are unwilling to do. And they bring me satisfaction. It makes me feel good to know that a good job has been done.

Mr. Cox, owner, typewriter sales and service

Achievement is unquestionable testimony to worth. The demands of the job were met and met well. More than that, a product has resulted, one that demonstrates that what the man did mattered and that his efforts, even if only slightly, improved the world within which he worked.

THE IMPORTANCE OF PLACE IN THE COMMUNITY OF WORK

A job is two things at once. It is a set of tasks to be performed. And it is a position, a place, in the community of work. And just as the successful performance of the tasks of the job is emotionally important for men, so is having a place at work. Having a place at work means that the contributions work makes to well-being are secure. And having a place further reassures a man that he is good enough for membership.

If a man's place at work seems endangered, he may become both insecure and self-doubting. Mr. Moss, an account executive in an industrial consulting firm, at one point began to feel excluded by younger colleagues.

When I turned fifty or thereabouts, about three or four years ago, I found to my surprise and chagrin and hurt that somehow I was not as much a part of the staff as I had been for the first ten or twelve years I was here. There were new staff people, of course. There was turnover and there was a younger crowd—late twenties, early thirties. I wasn't invited out to lunch with everybody else. I wasn't included.

And people were giving me a hard time in some of the responsibilities that I had. I began to feel for the first time what it could mean to be ostracized on the basis of age. Nobody said, "I don't want to talk to you." But it was clear that my position was becoming increasingly isolated. I began to think of another position.

Even though the most evident of the indications of his marginality was an absence of invitations to lunch, Mr. Moss turned out to have been right to have worried. He later learned that he was at the time being considered for release by his superiors in the firm. He did not know whether the younger people had been aware of this.

Men tend to be alert to indicators of their standing even while recognizing that they may not know for sure what the indicators mean. As a result, events whose meanings are uncertain can make them anxious. Mr. Patrick, a sales manager, became upset when the president failed to include him in an informal meeting in which the firm's policies were discussed.

> We are such a nonregimented company that there's a tendency to leave people out. Fred obviously feels he is in charge, he can do whatever he wants. And he's certainly correct. But if Fred is doing something that I think I should be involved in, I don't want to be left out. I don't *like* to be left out. And it *does* bother me.

To be left out of meetings at which by rights one should be present can be construed as just one of those things or as a humiliating expression of disrespect. But even if the absence of an invitation was entirely unintentional and the discussion unplanned, the man may have reason for concern that not having been in on the discussion reduces his standing.

The proximity of a man's place at work to centers of power and authority helps decide the respect with which that man is treated. But proximity to power and authority is not fixed once and for all by an organization chart. It shifts constantly, and often its shiftings are unannounced.

REPUTATION AND STANDING AT WORK

The people with whom a man works develop a more or less shared evaluation of him, on the basis of which they will work with him happily or avoid him, defer to his opinions or ignore them, want to be identified with him or want others to know they are not among his associates. This is the man's reputation.

Men begin developing their reputation almost immediately upon joining a work group. An engineer, Dr. Bentwood, for example, was still new in his firm when he was asked to identify a machine problem. Overseas clients were complaining that the machines malfunctioned in their shops, yet all the machines had been tested by Dr. Bentwood's firm before being shipped and all had functioned properly at that time.

Dr. Bentwood studied some returned machines and located a plastic element that seemed too rigid to work properly. When he checked machines about to be shipped, he found the element adequately flexible. It occurred to him that the machines, when shipped in the freight compartment of a plane, were subjected to extreme cold which could affect the physical characteristics of the plastic. A bit of experimentation convinced him he was right. He redesigned the component of which the plastic element was a part. He asked the head of the fabrication department to produce components following his design so that they could be put in machines about to be shipped. The head of the fabrication department said he was understaffed and couldn't afford to put a man at Dr. Bentwood's disposal. Dr. Bentwood went to higher management.

> Well, to make a long story short, he was told to try it out. It did work. It was a save. It was dramatic. I looked very good. He looked very bad.

The incident produced two sets of assessments. Dr. Bentwood was seen as ingenious and potentially an important contributor to the firm. The head of the fabrication department was seen as unimaginative, maybe even obstructionist.

Dr. Bentwood was asked to trouble-shoot another malfunctioning machine. Again he found a way to fix it. Now he was seen in the firm as almost magical, capable of turning failure to success single-handed.

But reputations are always being amended. A co-worker who has a significant experience with someone, positive or negative, will report on it to others and so modify the person's image. Someone doing badly will have a major success, which is widely recognized in the firm, or a former Golden Boy will trip up, and everyone will know.

Mr. Masters, an engineer in a consulting firm, decided at one point to take a chance on a colleague with a spotty reputation. The result of his experience with the colleague was then passed on.

I had been warned about Les, but I had never tried him and I figured I got along with him well. He was entertaining and personable. And he wasn't doing very well at the company, and it would be good to give him a chance rather than taking other people's word. And I needed help. In any case, I thought that it would be a good thing to have this guy work with me. I thought he would make a contribution.

So I asked Les to visit the client with me and evaluate the kinds of machine tools that they use. Les is supposedly expert. We conducted the visit and I stayed down there another day. Someone else was joining me to do some other work and Les was coming back to the home office. I asked him if he could write what he saw. I said, "Please write if there is something in the marketplace that is better than what they are using. And why." And he said he would.

I expected that when I got back on that Friday—this was a Tuesday—I would have my memo. But what I got when I got back was someone came to me and said, "I need Les, could you please wait until next week for him to give you the report?" I said yes, I could wait.

I got nothing from him. He didn't deliver. And when I determined, after a certain number of weeks, that I wasn't going to get anything, it was not so much that I was angry at him for not delivering—I could put in some extra work and do it myself—I was more concerned that he had charged me for something that he did not deliver. It's a question of getting nothing for something. Literally thousands of dollars diluted, removed from your budget, and getting nothing in return.

Mr. Masters now entered the event of Les's failure to deliver in Les's invisible dossier. He did this by returning to the friend who had warned him against Les and reporting that Les had behaved as predicted.

I talked with the original person who said that I would regret asking Les to participate. I just described the situation as best I could, as objectively as I could. He thought the guy was a parasite. That was the original reason that he suggested to me that I not use him in the project.

If Mr. Masters's friend were again to be consulted about Les, he would have another item to report. And to the extent that Mr. Masters told still others in the firm that Les had failed to come through (his anger at Les would make this likely), Les's unfavorable reputation would spread.

Reputations are especially likely to be affected by performance when the tasks are visible, demanding, and critical to the well-being of the firm: Casey-at-the-bat tasks. For just this reason, such tasks are apt to foster a very high level of effort.

Dr. Sorenson, the director of the development group who thought of a crash program as combat, said of his two weeks of nonstop effort that being able to come through for the firm had made the experience a good one. At the time it had been grueling, but everything he and his group did had counted, not just to themselves but to the company as a whole. Their successfully meeting their deadline had resulted in acknowledgement by the firm's president of the group's value to the firm.

> This particular crisis was constant, nonstop: decide this, decide that; push this, push that; do this, do that. Go to bed late, get up early. Drag yourself through one more tired day. [*laughs, then sighs*]
>
> You don't even have time to stop and think to yourself that isn't it nice that I have something that everything I do every day, all day long, is important to somebody? I thought of it more often from the point of view of resenting, why is it that there isn't five minutes out of any day that I feel I have to myself? But that's certainly a whole lot better than sitting around wondering whether anybody cares at all about what's happening or what I'm doing.
>
> I've had work experiences where for extended periods of time it was perfectly clear that it didn't make a bit of difference to anybody whether I even showed up. And that's the most debilitating kind of work experience I've *ever* had, to be sitting around, not obliged to do anything at all. That's very, very destructive to your ego and your self-image.

Dr. Sorenson felt guilty, after the deadline had been met, for having passed along to his staff the pressures that had been put on him. One of his subordinates had become seriously ill during the interval of nonstop work, and Dr. Sorenson worried that he had been responsible. Even so, the experience had been gratifying. What he had done had been important. He had come through, and his coming through had been recognized.

Reputations matter. Should there be a forced reduction in the firm's staff, those of questionable reputation are most likely to be seen as dispensable. Dismissing them would be less disruptive to the organization than dismissing someone more highly respected. They are more likely to be without allies, and their dismissal is less likely to make others feel, "That could have been me."

The head of a planning firm, Mr. Gilman, described firing a man whose reputation was generally poor. It was important to Mr. Gilman, in his account of the firing, that it was not he alone who thought the man a burden.

> The only guy we've fired in the last two and a half years, he never could get his priorities straight. I told him when he left that we had tried very hard to get him to focus on the fact that ten years from now he could be a department head or he could be the office gossip. And it would be nice to walk around the office and not find him at the coffee machine or talking with the secretaries or having his feet up on the desk reading a magazine.
>
> I said, "I'm not talking about me alone. I'm talking about all the management in this organization. The only comment they have is that it doesn't seem to be working, that everybody tried very hard to suggest to you that it might be good for you and this firm if you worked a little bit more. And you didn't. You ought to be earning the money you are paid. If you're not, we ought to get someone who will.

After Mr. Gilman fired the man, Mr. Gilman's secretary said that he had done just the right thing. There was consensus in the office that the man should be let go.

EVALUATION, FORMAL AND INFORMAL

Many firms require periodic formal evaluations of their members. That can be an occasion when men's reputations—with the boss, at least—are made known to them.

Men justifiably become anxious if they are told they are suspect in any way. Any attribution of weakness, no matter how mild or how deeply buried in an otherwise positive report, can provide a reason for being passed over for an assignment or a promotion and, ultimately, for being identified as dispensable. Any negative element in the formal evaluation is, therefore, reason for worry. Indeed, men who have received a negative assessment can wonder if it means that they are already on their way out. Why else would the person evaluating them be willing to wound them and so make them less effective? Why else would he risk their enmity? Might not the negative assessment be part of a case being built against them so that they can be more easily dismissed?

Mr. White, an insurance executive, received a formal evaluation that contained a single negative appraisal. A month after the evaluation, this one negative element occupied his thoughts.

> I was surprised when my boss rated me low on leadership. Okay, I'm a low-keyed guy. But I didn't think my leadership was that lacking. I really feel that if he had gotten feedback, if the people who report to me had been asked what *they* thought of my leadership, I would have gotten pretty high marks. In a crowd, or under some circumstances, I might not seem like a leader because I tend to be quiet. I don't speak out in a group very often. Maybe that's how he measured.

Since receiving the evaluation, Mr. White had silently rehearsed arguments in his favor. Now he defended himself to the interviewer as he had not been able to defend himself to his supervisor:

> Over the years almost every organization I have ever become associated with, I have ended up in a leadership role. Two years after I joined a civic organization, one hundred twenty-five members, I was elected vice president. I think that shows something. Just about everything I've gotten into, it has turned out I've seemed to move up to being in a leadership role. So I don't think my leadership is that bad. I am a low-keyed leader.

Not long after the "leadership lack" evaluation, Mr. White's department underwent reorganization. Some of the men with whom Mr. White worked were reassigned. Others were told to leave. Mr. White was told that he would remain with the firm, but he stopped receiving assignments. He became extremely anxious.

This guy I was supposed to be working for would not deal with me. For a three-month period nothing was happening. I would go to work and I would walk around looking for things to do. It was a very strange feeling. This went on for three months. You can say, "Well, that sounds great, no responsibilities and full pay." But boy, that was eating me up inside.

The time in limbo ended with Mr. White's appointment to an important administrative position in which he would report directly to the chief executive. The new job was gratifying, but after a few months there was another change. While retaining the same responsibilities, Mr. White was told to report to a department head—a man younger than he—rather than to the chief executive. In effect, he was moved one level farther out from the center of the organization. The move toward the periphery was a demotion in organizational placement.

I felt I was a key part of the organization. I never really thought I was indispensable, but I thought I was a key person. Now, even though I have the same responsibilities, I just don't feel as important a person. It erodes my self-esteem, my self-evaluation. I don't feel as indispensable as I felt I was.

I try not to let it bother me. I think I cope, not letting it bother me, just going ahead. I have a spirit of responsibility and I think I fulfill it. I provide excellent service where I need to, where the job entails it. But I guess I don't feel part of the organization as much.

If positive reputation sustains, negative reputation burdens. Mr. White was now required to accept that others saw him as someone who had lost standing in the firm. A few months after the interview in which he had said "I try not to let it bother me," Mr. White took early retirement.

The view of a man held by his superiors is of such great importance to his security that even without negative assessment the absence of positive evaluation from the superiors can be worrisome. Then it can be of value to the man to learn that the absence of positive evaluation has no special significance; it happens to everyone.

I really haven't had a negative evaluation. But my boss is the kind of a person who doesn't give you that much positive feedback. Well, positive feedback is important. I know I like to get it. It makes me feel good. But very rarely will he say, "I think you are doing a good job." That used to bother me, because I felt, "Gee, maybe I'm not doing a good job and he is not saying anything." But then I talked to other group leaders. They said, if he doesn't say anything, it means everything is going okay.

Mr. Ryder, department head, optical engineering firm

Formal evaluations occur once a year in those firms that have them at all. Informal evaluations occur constantly in every firm. At work everyone is always on trial. It is hard to relax—though the appearance of relaxation may be useful, for it suggests self-confidence—because every performance yields an assessment to those who witness it. Within meetings, mutual evaluation is a constant subtext to the official agenda. A comment is listened to not only for its manifest meaning but also for its indication of personal stake, self-perception, and comfort or discomfort. The speaker's fluency in advancing a position is rated. Some watch the watchers and make assessments of others making assessments: "I think the way that Harry argued with the client, he lost points with Jim."

Often without being aware that this is what they are doing, men take notes on who has power and who is knowledgeable, who has inside information and who has sound intuition. They appraise alliances and enmities and the nuances of people's feelings about each other (which is why office romances so rarely go unnoted). They are exquisitely alert to indications of others' appraisals of themselves, and so they speculate, sometimes obsessively, about what it means that an assignment was or wasn't made to them, or that a supervisor did or didn't ask them for a report, or that a colleague was or wasn't deferential in a meeting. It can matter enormously to a department head if a chief executive met on an elevator is friendly.

The closeness with which men observe each other, especially if they are linked as supervisor and subordinate, is suggested by the comments made by Mr. Layton, the executive in an insurance firm, about a subordinate named Hank. Mr. Layton was intently observant of Hank's performance at work.

Hank is a very confident guy, but he is not cocky. He was going to pay a visit on a potential client and he came to me and he said, "Would you mind coming along?" I said, "Not at all." As it developed, there were questions raised that he was unprepared for, which I responded to. And when we got through the meeting he said, "I'm just so glad that you came along with me. I'm glad I thought to ask you to come."

He distinguished himself in my mind, the way he handled everything. He was confident in doing the whole process, but at the same time—it is a small thing—but afterwards he distinguished himself just a little more because he said, "I'm just so glad you were there." He could admit that he had problems. You don't find that too many times. That is my problem with some of the other people, that they will go and jump into something, hell or high water. You can get burned that way.

I left about 6:15 tonight; he was still there. And I said, "Hank, are you sure you don't need a hand?" He said, "No. I have it all under control. No problem."

Hank is one of those people that you take an instant liking to. And it is not just style. He is in there digging. He is trying. If he is not working on his own stuff, he is helping someone else on something else or trying to learn something else. And that certainly has made quite an impression.

Undoubtedly Hank, aware that he was being evaluated by Mr. Layton, intended to ingratiate himself when he brought Mr. Layton to meetings and then thanked him for his help. It is likely he was aware of the good impression he would make by remaining late in the office. But what did it matter to Mr. Layton if his judgments were being manipulated? If Hank was actively attempting to gain Mr. Layton's approval—and was able to do so successfully—so much the better. Mr. Layton was aware that Hank could use friendliness manipulatively. He witnessed Hank's careful courtesy toward members of the the publications group and recognized that it was motivated at least partly because Hank wanted their help. Mr. Layton approved.

People in Publications can kill you if they don't like you. Sometimes all it takes is a "Thank you." When somebody just saved your hide, let them know it. It doesn't take too much to say, "Thanks, that was a super job you just did." Don't tell them that unless they did it, but if they did it, by golly, let them know. It makes a big difference. The next time you want a favor from them, you've got it. Hank has that nature. Hank is the type of guy that if somebody comes through for him, he will thank them. And the people in Publications are breaking their tails for him. He'll just come in and say, "Can you help me?"

Mr. Layton was prepared to act on his appraisal. He felt confident that trusting Hank would turn out all right.

I'm giving Hank client responsibility. I have confidence that he can do the job and that he's not going to fumble and embarrass himself and create problems.

The primary reason for all the evaluation that occurs in the world of work, formal and informal, is the critical importance of performance. It is essential to many men, if they are to manage their own participation in their firm intelligently, that they have a sense of how others manage theirs. But there may also be an aesthetic component in men's alertness to each other's performance. Observing each other perform under pressure can be a kind of spectator sport.[7]

RECOGNITION AND EMBLEMS OF WORTH

Recognition is positive evaluation formalized and, often, made widely known. It puts all those to whom it is directed on notice that those authoring the recognition think well of the person recognized. Its effect on a man's reputation is powerful. Recognition enhances a man's security and further establishes him as worthy of respect.

Recognition is inherently in limited supply. To recognize everyone would be to recognize no one in particular. In consequence, recognition of one man can make others feel undervalued. Absence of recognition when recognition would have been appropriate may be felt to be too significant an omission to be mere oversight. And so men are likely to feel injured if they fail to receive appropriate recognition, and doubly so if they see someone else get credit for what they believe is their achievement.[8]

Mr. Linnell, an account executive in a large architectural firm, had helped organize a successful seminar program. A memo was later distributed praising the program and Mr. Linnell's partner, but not Mr. Linnell.

> I did a lot of the work, worked very hard, to set up a special seminar that we held here. It was a new type of venture for the firm to get involved in. And it was very successful. And there was a written memo, from people who really should have seen my contribution, that gave another guy the lion's share of the credit without mentioning me at all. I wouldn't put myself ahead of this other guy, but I would put myself close behind him in terms of credit for the thing. But it didn't look that way.
>
> I thought about saying something, but in that kind of a situation it just would look egotistical. And it wouldn't do any good. It would have more negative effects than it would have positive effects in terms of getting credit. Because anybody who was involved in the thing could see who had done what. And the written memo, in and of itself, wasn't going to be the only thing that formed their opinion about who had worked on it and who had done good work on it. It was unfortunate, but it wouldn't have done any good to make noise about it.
>
> I was disappointed. I felt underappreciated. I was anxious about how I was viewed and what the implication of that was for my long-term situation here.

Negative recognition is as much an assault on the security of a man's place at work as positive recognition is a strengthening. Mr. Davis, a manager of quality control in a manufacturing firm, was sitting in a meeting chaired by his superior, daydreaming a bit, when he heard the superior criticize the quality control group for the costs it was imposing on manufacturing. Immediately following the meeting, Mr. Davis asked his group to collect all the quality control records for the preceding months so that he could demonstrate to his superior that pieces had been sent to scrap only if they had serious defects. Even so, the message to other managers was clear: Mr. Davis did not have the boss's backing.

A tangible form of recognition is the firm's equivalent of medals and honors: the perquisites, privileges, and organizational benefits that are in short supply and so are given selectively. As is true for other forms of recognition, emblems of worth enhance men's security in their place and strengthen their feelings of worth.

Emblems of worth, like other forms of recognition, are inherently comparative. As one instance of this, when an organization moves people from one building to another, the distribution of offices becomes a statement of relative worth. Even if the offices were supposed to be distributed randomly, having a better office might be interpreted by a visitor as implying higher standing, and men would, for that reason alone, try to defeat the random assignment. And it is hard to believe offices would ever actually be distributed randomly.

Mr. Ward, a service manager for a large organization, became responsible for the assignment of offices when the organization expanded. Other managers then campaigned with Mr. Ward for a desirable office. Mr. Ward saw it as a matter of "ego," of wanting validation for inflated ideas of self-worth. Mr. Ward said:

> There are only so many good offices in a building. And if you have a lot of people with large egos—well, it's very difficult to put a large ego in a small office. That's basically the problem. Everyone wants windows and everyone wants high-ceilinged offices and they don't want partitions and they want two square feet more because that means that they're two square feet better than someone else.

Men who have modest offices are unlikely to be considered important but unassuming; they are more likely to be seen as unimportant. Office space is universally interpreted as an emblem of worth, and its message, even if unintended, will almost certainly affect the man's confidence in his place in his firm, the way he is treated by others, and his self-confidence and resilience in response to challenge. It is likely, in short, to affect how he feels about his job and how well he does it.

In addition to the size of an office, emblems of worth include its furnishings, whether it has a corner view, whether it is on the executive floor, and whether it is protected by its own secretarial desk, with a self-assured secretary serving as gatekeeper. Emblems of worth also include company credit cards, company cars, and access to the executive dining room and washroom. They encompass everything having to do with access to the firm's resources and amenities, including the right to take off for an afternoon or come in late or leave early. And they include, of course, title and income.

Indeed, title and income are the ultimate emblems of worth. Title indicates centrality and power. It stipulates who should defer to whom. Although the standing indicated by title may require validation in the way men actually do their jobs, it generally holds up. Income constitutes the individual's share of organizational profit. Obtaining a larger share than others indicates either greater bargaining power, greater worth, or both.

Within the firm, income is a statement of relative organizational worth. At home, income translates into goods and services, the necessities of life. Mr. Bentley, a highly successful manager, noted the difference between his and his wife's understanding of an increase in his salary:

> At some point, when the new fiscal year had begun and I'd find out what my pay would be, my wife would always try to figure out what that meant in terms of could she do this or do that. Whereas payment, for me, is sort of a measure of how well you're doing.

Income validates positive assessments. Words may mislead, but money, as Sydney Greenstreet said in a memorable line, is coin of the realm. Mr. Masters, for example, noted:

> There is a formal evaluation, a performance review, that is done once a year. The last time, my boss approved everything that I had been doing. One of the words that he used on the form, a comment on my performance, was "superb." As far as he was concerned there were no limits to my growth. It was a very positive review. The only problem was, what would the salary increase be? Talk is cheap. Although I can live fine on the money that I make, it is nice to be recognized, and the way that is conventionally done is through money.

Men cannot judge the organizational meaning of a raise in income, or of a bonus at the end of a year, until they know what others have received.[9] One mid-level executive received a sizable Christmas bonus, but only when he discovered that he had done better than most of his peers could he feel pleased.

> Today is the day that we get the annual Christmas bonus. You get a bonus and it is just a number. And you feel around and

get a sense of whether it is a relatively high or a relatively low bonus. The bonus I got was very good.

Mr. Linnell, account executive, architectural firm

An executive who receives a less-than-adequate pay increase, given the increments others are receiving, is likely to feel inadequately valued.[10]

The company hadn't been doing very well in the past year, so there were certain guidelines that were established for salary increases. I think our section averaged eight percent. I was given a ten percent raise. To look at it in one way, I was rewarded. But a person who hasn't done *anything* useful got an eight percent raise. Two percent doesn't amount to a whole lot. That two percent certainly isn't going to identify me as being much better than this other person.

Mr. Michaels, middle-level manager

Men who own businesses need not concern themselves with their standing in the firm. Ordinarily, however, their communities of work extend beyond the boundaries of their firms. They include other company heads, entrepreneurs, bankers, suppliers, and large customers whom they meet for lunch or at parties and, if they are doing really well, with whom they serve on boards and committees. Appraisals of worth also occur in this larger community of work. A man can feel pleased with himself if he is doing better than those with whom he compares himself.

As Veblen observed, one way for a man to gain the respect of others is to demonstrate that he has earned a great deal of money. Conspicuous display of the kind Veblen described might today be thought tasteless, but the wish to be seen as a winner persists. Men who have done well are likely to make it known. In any event, the men know it themselves, and there is satisfaction in this.

When asked what satisfactions he got from the money he earned, Mr. Foster, a partner in a firm that manages mutual funds, said:

I don't know. I like to live well. I like to travel, like to have my boat and my house. That's important to me. The money, as much as anything, it's a measurement. It's the chips by which the game is played. They could give us something else and if they gave it to us, we would all be happy, knowing that we won.

In the world of work, money measures how well a man is doing. It does this a bit differently for the man on salary and the man who is independently employed. For the man who earns a salary, income is a statement of how much he is valued by his firm. For the man who is independently employed, it is a statement of how effective his efforts have been. But for both it is the basis for feelings of worth and of security in place.

In one important respect income is different from the other contributions work makes to men's self-esteem and security. It is negotiable outside the workplace. Quite apart from income, satisfactory work provides men with the sense of worth and of place that together provide a foundation for their participation in the other sectors of their lives. It is in addition to this that work gives them the income they need to maintain themselves and their families in the wider society.

CHAPTER
TWO

The Importance of Work

What would go wrong with a man's life were he simply to walk away from work? Is work essential as a basis for self-esteem and security?

The answer is, it depends. It depends on whether the man is old enough to be honorably retired or is still in the age range where working is what a man does. And it depends on what else, besides working, there is in which he could invest his energies, especially whether he has available to him a different valued community—a religious community or a voluntary organization—that offers not only membership but also a mission that would give meaning to his life.

Few men in the age range in which men expect themselves to be productive—the age range of the men of this book—can find another basis for self-esteem that serves as well as valued work. Furthermore, place at work is critical for establishing place in the larger society. To judge the social position of a man just met, we ask, as soon as good manners allow: "What do you do?" In response, men provide job titles. Young men perhaps may supply the name of the firm for which they work, if that carries more weight. And a man whose occupation is truly impressive—a neurosurgeon, say—may choose modestly not to name it, although he will keep it in mind, as a poker player might his hole card. But these are variations on the theme; in general, occupational title locates a man's social place.

So closely linked are social place and what a man does at work that a man without adequate work will tend to withdraw from social life and may question the legitimacy of his functioning as a husband and father.[1] The distress produced by an absence of adequate work diffuses everywhere within a man's life.

Representative samples of American men have been asked, in several studies conducted over the past thirty years, whether they would go on working if they did not have to work for a living. Nancy Morse Samelson and I used the following phrasing in a 1955 study: "If by some chance you inherited enough money to live comfortably without working, do you think that you would work anyway or not?" Eighty percent of the men who responded said yes, they would keep on working.[2]

The percentage of men who said they would continue to work did not vary greatly by the kind of work they were doing. It was not much higher among professionals and managers than among those whose jobs were monotonous or low in status, closely supervised, unpleasant, or dangerous. And though few assembly-line workers or laborers said they would go on working at the same jobs if they had the money to quit, most said they would go on working.

Asked why they would continue to work even if they didn't need the money, only three percent of men said that it was because they enjoyed their work. Most said they needed something to do. They wanted to keep occupied. Yes, they could watch television or take long walks or build an addition on the house. But none of these are occupations in a social sense, in the sense that provides place in the society.

One of the men we interviewed for the present study, a contrast case of a special sort, actually did not have to work to earn a living. Mr. Taylor's family had been wealthy for several generations, and when Mr. Taylor was still an adolescent his grandfather had died, leaving him a large trust fund. From then on Mr. Taylor was able to live well on its income alone. And he did.

Mr. Taylor had been a good student at prep school, an honor graduate of his Ivy League college, and successful as a graduate student in a field that was both intellectually demanding and glamorous. But despite possession of an advanced degree, he was unable to find an acceptable job.

I felt I was going to go and get a fine job and work hard and become a really productive member of society. I was very confident. I had several good things in line. I was offered one position which, if I look back on it now, I probably should have taken. But it was a lesser position than they'd advertised. I said, "Look, I'm sorry, I'm not interested in the lesser position. I came here for the one that you advertised." And then it was a long period without a job.

As time went on and Mr. Taylor remained unemployed, he became desperate for a job. Undoubtedly, had he not had his trust fund he would have found work in another field. He could have gone into a building trade; he had done much of the work required in remodeling his home. But as things were, Mr. Taylor preferred to continue to look for work in his field. And yet positions in his field were scarce. In addition, employers may have been put off by a résumé without substantial employment: at first only a year without employment after leaving school, but then two years and, every year, one year more.

Mr. Taylor lost confidence in himself. His efforts to find work became sporadic.

It wasn't like all of a sudden somebody walked up to me and said, "Oh, by the way, you are no longer employable." That's not the way it happened. It was a slow, steady erosion of confidence, of that feeling of positiveness.

Mr. Taylor turned to psychotherapy.

The psychiatrist couldn't deal with the fact that I had enough money that I could make my own choice. He felt that that was robbing me of the necessity and that that was the problem. What he thought was I didn't really want a job, I wanted to be a coupon clipper. And that was just totally wrong. Not having a job was eating me up. It was destroying me from inside. And it still does, to a great extent.

Mr. Taylor resented the thought that he would be content to be a coupon clipper, a member of the idle rich, a noncontributor. Perhaps Mr. Taylor should have described himself as an investor. That might have done the trick, if he could have convinced himself that it was a valid occupation. But he had given years to training in another field, and he would not relinquish that investment in self.

Mr. Taylor was not actually idle. He had done all the contracting for remodeling his house and much of the actual labor. But that wasn't a contribution to a larger enterprise, nor was it work in the field in which he had trained. Before the remodeling was completed, he had lost interest in it.

Mr. Taylor gave a good deal of time to volunteer work, especially as a member of the Board of Trustees of a local charity.

> I have outside activities. I'm on the Shelter Board and I put in a lot of time, more time than my wife likes, on the telephone. But you have to look into yourself for the rewards rather than toward a job situation in which you accomplished a goal or got a big bonus, or things like that. You don't get those kinds of returns.

Mr. Taylor found volunteer work helpful but ultimately unsatisfactory. Although his contributions as a volunteer were valued, he was not a full member of the community of work. He lacked the place that would have been his had he been employed. One indication of his lack of place was that he had no obligations; other people did not count on him. Had he received income from his work, he would have had responsibilities. He would, to begin with, have been expected to show up. But as it was, people at work had to be ready to do without him.

As a volunteer, Mr. Taylor was removed from the usual organizational rewards and penalties, from promotion, salary increases, and bonuses. But that meant he was a nonparticipant in much of the life of the organization. Furthermore, the recognitions of worth that are so important to paid members of an organization were unavailable to him.

Nor did service as a volunteer provide a basis for occupational identity. It is an inadequate response to "What do you do?" to say, "I'm on the Shelter Board," or "I help raise money for charity campaigns."

> You have to cast away what is, in our society, a major element of self-definition. You have to throw that out the window and say, "Well, I'm not going to be a lawyer, fireman, Indian chief, whatever." The loss of that is something that I suppose you have to grieve to some extent.

Mr. Taylor envied the other men in the loose network of friends and former fellow students who served as a sort of reference group for him. He felt like an oddball, a man without a place.

> I went to dinner last night and there were a bunch of people who I had been to school with or who were associated with

the school. And I'll never lose the pain of thinking, "My God, here are all these people walking around who have good jobs and are working in these various places. And I so much wanted this. And I just didn't seem to be able to make it happen for some reason or other. And that is very painful.

In short, though income without work will enable men to sustain themselves materially, it leaves them unable to sustain themselves socially. Perhaps, if a man's contemporaries are also without work, he may find a place in a community of the leisured—though this is far from certain. But when a man's contemporaries are workers, to be without work is to be marginal. And insofar as a man's feelings of worth are based on his valuation by others, worklessness leads to feelings of worthlessness.

Feelings of worth prove difficult to bank. A man can obtain respect for what he did in the past, yet no longer count. There is, perhaps, solace in the feeling, "I used to count." But this translates poorly into feelings of present worth. Feelings of worth depend most on the man's place among his fellows in the present, not on what his place was in the past.

Mr. Draper, in his early fifties, had been a production manager responsible for whatever happened inside his shop. He had been in charge of scheduling, output, and shipping—everything inside the shop. The firm's president, who had been its founder, was responsible for sales, financing, advertising, and marketing. Mr. Draper owned fifteen percent of the firm's stock; the president and members of the president's family owned the rest.

One year the firm's sales failed to meet expectations. Foreign competition had been severe and was threatening to become worse. Mr. Draper and the firm's president agreed that it was time to get out. A Midwestern holding company offered to purchase the firm. They accepted the offer.

The purchase agreement stipulated that Mr. Draper would remain as production manager, with the title of vice president and an increase in salary. But within weeks Mr. Draper discovered that his recommendations were ignored by the new owners.

When we were autonomous, we were pretty much a two-man team, the president of the company and myself. Now that we are a subsidiary of a parent company I am the vice president in charge of this division. So it sounds like I've been promoted. Which in a sense I have. But in truth I've got a manager in the central office that I have to report to, and I never had a person over me.

You've got to understand, there's nobody in my subsidiary that has more responsibility or a higher rank than I have. But the man from headquarters is really the guy who controls the purse strings. And there are people at the headquarters that make it difficult for me to make decisions and move on my own. It's a helpless feeling.

Mr. Draper began getting headaches. At home he was irritable and withdrawn. He complained to his wife about his work. His wife urged him to quit. It turned out he didn't need to. He was fired.

They really didn't need me on a continuing basis. My role was to help them through the transition. I had a big fancy title, but I really was a fifth wheel. And I was about to approach them and say, "I really don't think you need me any longer," and I got a visit from the corporate vice president. He had decided that where the company was having problems and they were cutting back, that I had become overhead that they could not justify. The meeting was very brief, very friendly.

The purchase of Mr. Draper's stock by the holding company had made him wealthy. He no longer needed to work to meet his bills. For a while he enjoyed what was essentially an early retirement. But after two or three months things started to go wrong. Mr. Draper began to feel marginal to the social life around him. Having relinquished his place in his former company, he began to feel he was losing his place in his network of friends.

Most of Mr. Draper's friends were businessmen and managers he had known for years. Now his situation was different from theirs. He was no longer active in work; they still were. And when he protested that he was looking for a business to run, his friends seemed not to believe him or, worse, not to care.

I was under absolutely no pressure in terms of finances. Emotionally, however, you get to feel a little bit useless. After a period of, let's say, five or six months, you begin to think that probably people are looking upon you as kind of lazy, not sincerely out looking for a situation. And you get to feel a little bit embarrassed among your peers, your friends, your relatives, because you are not gainfully employed.

Nobody ever came to me and said, "Hey, Draper, you're a phony. You really don't *want* to work." But you tend to conjure these things up in your mind, that that's what everybody's thinking. So you begin to get yourself worked up a little bit on what others think about you and your situation. And that puts a certain subtle pressure on you.

Mr. Draper's work had sustained an identity as an effective businessman, active and responsible. Without work, the identity of businessman no longer had any basis. So who was he?

It relates to image. I like people to think well of me. I don't want to be anything less than I have been, which is a doer, a very responsible, dependable person. I like that image. And I like the idea of creating something and making a contribution to a decision-making process and seeing something good come from it. That kind of success has been very gratifying.

At home another problem developed. Mr. Draper was neither sick nor on vacation, and yet there he was, around the house all the time. To be sure, his search for another business opportunity took him out of the house from time to time. But there was no guarantee that he would find anything. And in the meantime his wife thought he was around entirely too much. She reacted more and more with the complaint, "I agreed to 'for better or worse,' but not to 'every day for lunch'."*

Tension started to develop with my wife because I was getting in her way or she wasn't getting out of my way, depending on how you looked at it. Or I was using her telephone. Those were just casual comments at first. But after about six months those casual comments had real bite to them. And

---

*It isn't only managers who have problems with extra time at home. When a program of four-day weeks was introduced into Detroit industry men began to refer to their extra day at home as their "Honeydew day"—as in "Honeydew this" and "Honeydew that."

they would be coming every day. She'd make comments to her girlfriends that Bob is still home.

Men's wives sometimes object if the men become overabsorbed in their work. But they can object, too, if at times when the home by rights should be theirs, when other men are out doing the work of the world, their husbands have not left the home but instead remain under foot.

After eight months without work, Mr. Draper bought a business in a field not too distant from the one in which he had previously worked. Once again he could participate with his business friends in discussions of work. He no longer had to suffer his wife's querulousness. As an owner, he could count on the respect of his employees. He could once again present himself to his friends and family as someone who mattered. When we last talked with Mr. Draper, he was happily busy.

Membership in the community of work is ordinarily established quickly, with a few forms, a brief speech of orientation, a few introductions, and the assignment of work tasks and of a place to perform them. Membership in the community of work can be lost as quickly—"Please clean out your desk"—although the ceremonies of departure can also include a series of farewell parties marked by testimonials and gifts. No matter; once departure has occurred, the person no longer belongs. A return to the office a week after fond farewells will bring surprise and an awkward, "What brings you back?"

To be without work is bad enough. To be without work because of one's own failure is worse. To have been fired, whether the firing was justified or not, is to have been cast out from the world of work, rejected as undesirable. Loss of social place is then not accidental, not something everyone regrets. On the contrary, it was intended. The others at work didn't want you. You weren't good enough.

Mr. Green, a project supervisor in a firm in the transportation industry, was fired. He had known he was having problems of some sort with his boss. He had not known how severe the problems were.

This happened a little over two years ago. I joined a very large company and thought I was doing well. The division manager happened to be one of the sons of the owning family. He had very little experience in the work we were doing. He was a man in his mid-thirties, a liberal arts education. And we went through a period of a number of weeks where he said, "Gee, I've got something to discuss with you." And we tried to work out a time. He couldn't make it in the morning when the job started. He had a long drive. I said, "Why don't you come up some afternoon, we'll have dinner and we'll spend the evening?" "Oh, yeah, I'll give you a call."

Well, the only call I got from him was, "Come into the office tomorrow." And when I came in the office, "Carl, we don't need your services any more."

I was shocked. I couldn't believe it. He couldn't give me a good reason. I think what it was, he made commitments that he couldn't get the company to do and he was using me as a scapegoat for the promises the company couldn't execute.

They actually treated me fairly well in the sense that I got two months' severance pay and I had been there less than a year. It wasn't that I lost any income. But I was really hurt. It really feels bad not to be wanted. I consider myself fairly intelligent, fairly experienced, with good expertise in my area. I feel I'm smarter than the average person, that I can do things quicker and better than most of the other people that work around me. It was just disconcerting. I felt bad.

Mr. Green is a resilient, capable person. As he described it, his life now became filled with pain. He questioned his worth to others, and hence his intrinsic worth. His loss of work was distressing to his wife, and so he questioned himself as a husband. Losing his work because he was not good enough, no matter how he tried to reject the appraisal, burdened every sector of his life. It brought with it the accompanying fear that no one would want him and that there was no place for him in the world of work.

We went through a trauma, both my wife and I. That, I guess, was probably the most emotionally draining single event that my wife and I have suffered through together. If I was not able to get a position at another firm that could employ me in the position that I wanted, it would mean compromising, working in a lesser position for a lesser company and getting a commensurate decrease in salary. Or perhaps not even being hired because they feel I am overqualified for the position that is available.

For nine weeks I envied people having to get up and go to
work every morning. I was really hanging by my thumbs. I
just had to hope that there would be a job out there, that
somebody out there wanted me.[3]

A man without work—Mr. Taylor, Mr. Draper, and Mr. Green are
examples—not only misses work's activities and engagements, but also
feels marginal to society, uncertain of his identity, doubtful that he can
elicit the respect of strangers and doubtful that he is entitled to that
respect, without assurance of worth. This is true whatever the reason
the man is without work, but may be especially true when the man
believes that others may see him as at fault.

Just because effective functioning in the sector of work is essential
to the lives of men like those of this study, problems in that sector are
devastating to them. For them, functioning well in work is fundamental
to functioning well everywhere. Younger men, still exploring themselves and their worlds, can see stable respectability as something to be
achieved in the future. And some men in the age range of the men of
this study may have been led by disappointments at work to find a place
in a community more marginal to the workings of our society. But to
have a place in the social world of stable families and people who count,
it is necessary to have work.

UNSATISFACTORY WORK

Unsatisfactory work can be as demoralizing as the absence of
work. The difference is between being without membership in a
community of work and having membership, but in a position that does
violence to one's self-conception.

Mr. Webb, a contrast case, was in his mid-thirties, in charge of
returns for a large department store. Before taking the job in the
department store he had managed a store selling sports equipment.
When that store closed, he spent four or five months looking for another
managerial job. He had thought, when he accepted his present job,
that it would lead to something better. So far it had not, and he no
longer believed it would.

Mr. Webb hated his work. So far as he was concerned, the problem was the work, entirely. But it isn't at all evident, in his account,
why he believed he would be able to move from the back of the store to
a management office. Maybe he was misled; maybe he misled himself;

maybe he lacked some quality necessary to better employment. Whatever the explanation, he and his work were not made for each other.

In Mr. Webb's view, his work offered demands without challenge. He had a lot to do, but no discretion in doing it. He felt himself underutilized. And he had absolutely no investment in the outcome of his work.[4]

> Carriages filled with damaged merchandise are sent up, which I have to take care of. Send the merchandise out to repair or for credit or throw it in the compactor and get rid of it somehow.
>
> I have no control. I have to get everything signed by the manager of the department that I'm throwing out or sending out. If I wanted to ship something out I would have to get permission to return to vendor before I could package it, put a packing slip in the box, and get it ready for shipment.
>
> Stationery has three different vendors who come to the store and service us. How am I to figure out what belongs to which? This one might belong to one company, that one might belong to someone else. To me pens are all the same. I'll dump the whole thing. It doesn't matter to me.

The tasks of Mr. Webb's job were repetitive and seemingly endless. The sequence of challenge, resolution, self-approval that is so effective in engaging men in their work was here absent. The only challenge Mr. Webb found in the job was just getting through the work, and there were times when there was too much for that to be possible. Then Mr. Webb's sense of frustration might lead him to attack the job.

> You don't see any end of it. One carriage I can deal with, two I can cope with. Three? When we go up there after a weekend, I don't know how many carriages are going to be up there, but it could be three or four or five.
>
> During the Christmas season I would clean out three or four carriages and another three or four would come up. I would take one and just shove it against the wall. Just fling it against the wall. It made a great sound. The assistant sales manager used to catch me doing that and he'd say, "Listen, you'd better cool it."

Mr. Webb's pay further established that his work was of little value.

> You get paid a pittance of what the corporation heads are getting. The corporate heads get five hundred thousand dollars a year, plus little perks here and there. And jerks like myself are being paid minimum wage or a little bit more. I know there is no justice in the world, but this is ridiculous.

Accompanying Mr. Webb's alienation from his work was marginality to the workplace community. Mr. Webb believed that others at work did not respect him. To defend himself from misuse he was quietly uncooperative.

> Any time something needs to be done or moved, Returns gets a call. Like we don't have enough to do in the back room or upstairs, we don't have enough to do checking the warehouse, we have to run around the entire store to move tables and everything else. I don't mind it sometimes, but sometimes, after a while, it's really ridiculous.

> I am suspicious of their ulterior motives. I think that some people like to have power. They feel they can ask any one of us in shipping to do anything that they want. I quietly think to myself, I'll do it, but I'm not happy about doing it. I do it very reluctantly.

> One lady is a sales manager for cosmetics and she thinks that she has all the power in the world. She just comes up and says, "Listen, I want you to put up some shelving." And if you refuse, she'll run upstairs and write you up and get you fired or suspended for a couple of days. So you say, "I'll be over in a second. I got to finish putting this thing away. I'll be over in a second." You play it cosy.

An unemployed man would think it impossible to marry and accept responsibility for a family. Mr. Webb, too, thought it impossible to marry. Actually, he and his girlfriend would have been able to pay their bills if they had married; they were already paying their bills while living separately. But how could Mr. Webb assume responsibility for a family when his job was so low-level, his income so small and his prospects so poor? Another man in the same job, more optimistic or with lower expectations, might have seen things differently, but for Mr. Webb, given his understanding of his job, marriage was impossible.

> My girlfriend keeps complaining that we should get married. And when my sister visits she says I have to get married, it's wonderful. It probably is wonderful. But not now. Maybe a couple of years, but not now. I couldn't afford it. Not on what I get from my job. They have some big deal where they give you a week's pay if you get married. Would they give me a raise? Of course not. Would they give me a more important job? So at this point it's ridiculous to even think about it.

Perhaps there was more opportunity in Mr. Webb's job than he was able to see. Perhaps he should have had more faith in his future, in the eventual availability to him of acceptable work. But as it was, Mr. Webb's work diminished, rather than augmented, his feelings of worth. Mr. Webb's experience suggests that although men's work, more than their activities in any other sector of their lives, tells them their social worth, the message is not always sustaining.

WORK AS A GREEDY INSTITUTION

With work so important to their well-being, and with competent performance and a reputation for competent performance (not necessarily the same thing) so important to their place at work, men generally give work as much time and energy as it requires—and that can be a very great deal. They work hard not because they are forced to by close supervision but because they want to.[5]

> I think to work hard is the only way I know how to work. And to be a success, I think, is what it is. To be recognized. To be patted on the back by everybody.

> But I think one of the reasons that I work so hard is that the work is interesting. And the combination of things that I do for work, probably not many other people do. And for that reason it is seductive. It keeps you asking for more. The phone rings and someone asks you if you can do something. And you say, yes, I can do it, and they say, when? And I can do it soon. Because the work is interesting.

For me it is just wanting more. Wanting to do more interesting work. And constantly trying to learn things that I don't know now. Or exceed my own capabilities by trying to learn something and doing whatever it is that I learn, applying that knowledge. I think that is it. It is seductive. And I really am trying to make a contribution to something.

Mr. Harris, consulting engineer

Actually, it is difficult to determine just how much time men give to their work, because it is often hard to decide when men are working and when they are not. Is it work when men thumb through trade journals during commercial breaks on television? Are they working if, while apparently at leisure, they are actually mulling over how to design a part or conduct an experiment? The head of a small firm went skiing with his wife partly to gain distance from a troubling personnel problem and, while making his way down a slope, developed the strategy he would use to resolve it. If he had given the same thought to the problem while in his office, he unquestionably would have been working. Was he working while coming down the ski slope?[6]

Some men, to be sure, wall off their work concerns when away from the workplace. These are generally men who feel abused by their jobs, or are required to do work they cannot abide. And yet these men too carry their work with them, as a weight they are determined not to notice.

On the other hand, not all the time men are at the office or in the workplace is devoted to activities that would ordinarily be considered work. Bouts of work are punctuated by passages of banter and gossip. Meetings to discuss shared responsibilities are warmed by friendly talk. Nor is the work day necessarily entirely spent at work: Many work settings permit men to escape for an hour's shopping, a couple of hours at the dentist's, or the remainder of an afternoon to take home a sick child from school or ferry a well child to an after-school activity.

Some men give themselves to work more easily than others. It is not entirely chance that decides which men find their way into work that requires, and rewards, investment, and which into work that is alienating, where a time clock or a watchful boss is necessary to keep them on the job. Those for whom working and being successful have always been core elements of identity are more likely to move into jobs that require investment in work. The best predictor of success in later life is working hard as a youngster.[7]

Men who are their own bosses are likely to give their work as much time as they can wrest from the demands of home and social life. This can be both because they want to and because they must. Often, if they are to succeed, they have to work very long hours.

Mr. Brewer had always worked hard. When we talked with him, he owned a small but growing catering service. He had been in business for two years. On some days he devoted all his waking hours to his work—and did so happily.

We're up at five o'clock in the morning to make sure that the invoices are ready. By seven-thirty we have our coffee vans going out to whatever sites we have contracts with. They are back by ten and we set them up for lunch.

I keep very tight records. I know where the trucks are going today, who is working on what truck. I know on a daily basis how we are operating and what it is costing us.

I spend morning hours, from five to nine, doing the managerial paperwork. From nine to five I may be on appointments, I may be out.

Mr. Brewer is married. His wife sometimes took his telephone calls and sometimes helped him with the books. Because they had adolescent children, Mr. Brewer tried to be home by six for the evening meal. After that he returned to work or work-related sociability.

I belong to a lot of organizations, which really helps in a situation like this. Here in town I'm into the politics. You name it and I'm around somewhere. Because we feel strongly that, I would say, ninety-five percent of our business is in this town and the towns right around. And I'm known in town. If people want to check on me, they can get a personal reference.

Other evenings I'm working. We have branched out into the home area. We'll do anything you want. Parties, receptions. We did an after-theater party. We brought in all the knives, spoons, brought in all the ice, the setups, the food. We set the bar up. As soon as the guests arrived, they were being served. And as soon as we were told, "Close it off," we took everything with us. We got home eleven o'clock, twelve o'clock.

Mr. Brewer had good extrinsic reasons for working so hard. His position in his community depended on the success of his business. He had moved to his present community to take a job as manager of a branch office of a national firm. (Another part of his story is told in Chapter Nine.) When he left that job to open his own business, his invitations to social gatherings dropped off. He thought the reason was that people weren't sure how he would do and didn't want to be embarrassed by him if he were to fail. His business succeeded, and the invitations resumed.

But more than social acceptance kept Mr. Brewer engaged with his work. He enjoyed running a good operation and having it recognized by clients as good. When a customer referred new business, that wonderfully confirmed his worth. He found challenge in keeping his crews working well. He described with contempt a competitor whose men he saw taking a midmorning coffee break by the side of the road. His income, already much more than he had expected it to be when he began the business, validated his worth as an entrepreneur and reassured him that he was going about his work in the right way.

Mr. Brewer was also aware that it all could easily slip away. He knew that without constant vigilance his service could go bad or he could be underbid by competitors. He knew he would always lose customers just because of the vagaries of client relationships and that he must always be searching for new ones. Of course he would give his work whatever time he could. The rewards for doing so were great, as were the penalties for not doing so.

But men in salaried work may also feel dissatisfied with the amount they can accomplish in the "normal" nine-to-five work day. They too may use evening time to meet what they perceive to be the demands of their jobs.

> The way I experience my job is that there are always more things to do than I can possibly do. I'll come in with a plan for what I'm going to be doing that day and if I'm lucky I'll get through sixty percent of that. I'll finish a day, reflect on the things that I haven't done and that I need to do and I'll develop a work list for myself. In that work list I'll include some things that I'll do at home.

> *Mr. Reynolds, design engineer*

Men may feel that they cannot do their jobs properly in the "normal" nine-to-five day or that they can do their usual assignments in the normal day but special assignments—a yearly budget, a proposal, a business plan, a talk to colleagues—require evening time or weekends. These special assignments occur regularly.[8]

In almost all engaging jobs a policy of not working extra hours means leaving tasks unfinished. Men who adopt such a policy risk limited accomplishment, inability to take pride in achievement, diminished respect from colleagues, and vulnerability to a reputation for not doing their share. This means that any limiting of work hours can give rise to a kind of free-floating anxiety. One man, a business manager in an educational institution, was determined to be with his family at dinner rather than still behind his desk, as were many of his colleagues. As it was, he worked more than a forty-hour week and often took home a full briefcase. Despite this, he was acutely uncomfortable about the way his "early" departure might be seen by others.

> I have found in a general managerial job like this that it has no boundaries in terms of anything. You never finish. And the stress that you feel is the stress of setting limits, particularly in a culture in which few others set limits on themselves. To set limits on oneself in this organization goes against the organization's culture.

> I can get away with not doing a certain amount of work. Half of what I have to do probably I could not do and it would not be particularly recognizable. It does not cost me in terms of unmet expectations by my bosses. In part that is because I make sure to get what I think is the top-priority stuff done so that it looks good.

> The toughest thing for me is the stress of not being able to manage in a way that I don't feel guilty about. It is like when you are in school and you can always study more. Well, it is the same thing. You could always do more. I could work every night until ten o'clock at night and work Saturdays and Sundays both and it wouldn't all go away. I would not get caught up. I literally would not get caught up. And you have to make choices. And that is another whole stress dynamic, how you make those choices.

> I consider eating dinner with the family an important part of every day. I go home at the same time every night. I may take work, but I go home.

But I have a lot of anxiety about being able to say no to the work and live with it. And that comes out, I can see it coming out, in unrelated ways. Everything from getting upset in traffic to being nasty around the house.[9]

Mr. Craig, high-level administrator

Because the rewards of devotion to work can be substantial and the penalties of sloughing it off severe, work can be, in Lewis Coser's phrase, a greedy institution.[10] No matter how much time and energy men give to it, there will be more to be done. The attractions of doing well and the fears of doing badly may well be great enough to lead men to want to do as much as they possibly can.[11]

The term "workaholic" implies that men devoted to work are pathologically addicted to it. This seems usually to be mistaken. Yes, work can be an escape. It is possible to find relief at work from tensions in other sectors of life; indeed, work requires compartmentalization and vigilant inattention to everything that could distract a man from the problem at hand. But it isn't as though work so alters men's physiological states that unless they have a work fix they experience withdrawal. The gratifications of jobs well done and of solid achievement are many and real. Furthermore, work is absolutely essential to the social functioning of men and to their emotional lives as well. Although it would be regrettable if a man had nothing else in his life, it is perfectly possible for men genuinely to find work more enlivening than anything else.

And yet, with nothing else in his life, a man might well find that his work loses its meaning. Work is important for men's lives partly because it provides a foundation for everything else. But if there is nothing else, then work is a foundation still waiting for a structure. If immersion in work were to prevent men from functioning as husbands, fathers, and participants in the wider community, that would be irony indeed.

CHAPTER THREE

Work Stress and Its Management

INCIDENCE OF STRESS

That men want jobs that are challenging, as we have seen, means that they want jobs in which there is a significant possibility of failure. They also want their performance to be witnessed, so that their successes will be recognized—which increases the stakes. The constant risk of failure in a high stakes situation makes stress almost inevitable. And indeed, men regularly find that their work produces stress.

Stress at work occurs when men mobilize their energies and attention to deal with challenge, but to no avail. Instead of meeting the challenge and then experiencing relaxation and the self-approbation of a job well done, the men continue to struggle with the problem and so remain mobilized.

The mobilization of energy and attention is not in itself stressful. It is mobilization that persists beyond the time the task should require, beyond the work day itself, defeating every attempt at relaxation, that constitutes stress. Stress is a state of mobilization that persists intolerably long.[1]

There are four ways in which persisting mobilization commonly expresses itself. At the lowest level of mobilization men remain preoccupied with the stress-inducing development even when away from their work. More intense or protracted stress is expressed also in irritability; any new demand seems more than can be borne and must be fended off. At these two levels mobilization may not be apparent

45

unless the man is asked to attend to something new. A higher level of stress expresses itself in the visible symptoms of restlessness and tension. At a still higher level sleep disorders occur: The man cannot get to sleep at night or awakens at three in the morning and cannot return to sleep.

The lowest level of stress expression, preoccupation with work, occurred so frequently among the men we talked with that it was accepted by most of them as part of daily life. The next higher level, irritability, was reported by eighty-four percent as having resulted from events at work during the preceding year. Being fidgety, tense, or nervous was reported by seventy-seven percent. Sleep difficulties were reported by fifty percent. It would seem nearly universal for men like our respondents to have at least one experience of work stress beyond the level of preoccupation during a year. About half might be expected to have at least one bout of a quite high level of work stress.

Yet even this probably understates the incidence of stress produced by work. Men's wives say that their husbands systematically underestimate how often they are tense or irritable as a result of their work. It may be that the state of stress is one of those conditions that, like loneliness, isn't much remembered once it ends. One man, the owner of a small business, responded in this way when asked about early waking:

> Probably once every couple of months I might wake up in the middle of the night and start thinking of something: a problem, never about good things or a project I might want to do, always a problem. And I might toss and turn for a while.

> Most of the time they are money issues. I would say that is the issue maybe a hundred percent of the time that I wake up during the night. I need a hundred thousand dollars tomorrow to pay the bills. I don't *have* the money. I'm *going* to have it in two days. But I have to send checks out today. Well, we'll send the checks out today and when the bank calls up I'll manage it. I'll tell them, "Hey, listen, I needed to send out the checks. Cover the checks for me and we'll have it set in a day or two." I have a good banker. He'll take care of it for me.

> It might happen, maybe, five or six times a year. No, not even that much. Three times a year. My guess is I haven't

had one of those nights in the past three months. Maybe one. I must've had one. I think I remember having one.

Mr. Brock, independent businessman

If sleepless nights cannot be recalled with certainty, lower levels of stress expressed in tension and irritability are even more likely to be forgotten soon after they happen. Furthermore, men may attempt to hide from themselves how severe the stress they are experiencing is. Some men report that they were surprised to witness themselves displaying stress symptoms at a time when they were convinced they had everything under control. The head of a medical training program, himself a physician, said he sometimes imagined he had handled a potentially tense interview with great aplomb, only to be corrected by a post-interview ulcer spasm.

Some men actively try to maintain an appearance of being in control, no matter how they feel inwardly. Dr. Davis, a department head in a large manufacturing firm, appeared to the interviewer to be entirely relaxed. This presentation of self seemed habitual with him; he mentioned that his co-workers thought he had an enviably easygoing approach to his work. Nor did he see himself as under stress. Nevertheless, he frequently experienced early waking as an expression of work-based tensions.

On occasion I'll wake up at two or three in the morning with my mind going and then I can't get back to sleep. I guess if things at work are really stressful that happens a couple of times a week or something like that. Other times I might go for weeks without it happening. Maybe on the average it is once a week, once every two weeks, something like that. . . . Usually it takes me by surprise.

It appears that sooner or later every man in a position of responsibility will encounter problems in his work or in his relationships with co-workers that are for a time intractable, but whose resolution is nevertheless required. Taking all our materials together, I would guess that most men we interviewed experienced irritability or symptoms of still more severe stress between once a week and once every two or three months. A few of the men we talked with had work that sent them home every evening needing a drink to relax. A few, in contrast, insisted that they never brought home work-based stress. But most men seemed to experience persisting mobilization that gave rise, at the least, to irritability, not daily, but fairly often.

A number of factors affect how frequently men are under stress. Personal resilience makes stress less likely, as may effectiveness at work. Position helps, too: The owner of a firm may be less likely to experience stress than someone reporting to him—he doesn't have a boss to worry about. Yet there is no sure defense against stress. Indeed, that it will happen is almost certain, given work that is sufficiently challenging.

One man, Mr. Hayes, the very effective owner of a firm selling health plans and pension plans to industry, had successfully weathered a dozen business and familial crises. One day, without forewarning, he learned that one of the underwriting firms he used was canceling a program he had been selling to a corporate customer. He was suddenly faced with the likelihood of substantial financial loss.

Mr. Hayes's reaction was typical of him. Instead of succumbing to dismay he was mobilized by the challenge. He decided to try to persuade the customer to buy a different package, one that would provide similar, although not identical, coverage.

> I'm looking at a company that pays me three hundred thousand dollars a year premium. The parent company called me this morning and said, "We're not writing that kind of program any more." That's it. See you later.
>
> So I'm trying to say, "How can I save it?" I'm not sure I *can* save it. But I'm going down to Poughkeepsie [the customer's headquarters], and I'm going to sit with the accountant and the owner and I'm going to see what I can do to keep things going. That's the sort of a challenge that you like to think about. That's fun, in a way.

At this point Mr. Hayes displayed no indications of stress. He was concerned about his potential loss of income, but not so focused on it that he could attend to nothing else. Nor did he seem especially tense.

But Mr. Hayes did not make the trip to Poughkeepsie. When he called the chief financial officer of his customer company, he was told not to come. Now he did display symptoms of stress.

> This guy in Poughkeepsie gets me irritable. When I think about it I wake up, four o'clock in the morning, thinking, "How are we going to solve this? What's going to work?"

Mr. Hayes prided himself on his resilience. But his helplessness in the face of impending business loss led even him to sleepless nights.

SOURCES OF STRESS

The stress produced by men's work has two primary sources. One is the threat of failure produced by the difficulty of the tasks to be done. The other is the threat to the man's place in the community of work produced by hostile or uncooperative co-workers. The interpersonal problems are ordinarily the more disturbing.

Men also report a third source of stress, frustration produced by workplace impediments to getting the job done. The level of stress to which such frustration gives rise is rarely more than moderate. But now and again a needed employee will call in sick or a missing signature will prevent a purchase order from being processed and the job will become more difficult than it should be.

Finally, stress may have a fourth source: Men may impose stress on themselves even in the absence of challenge or conflict or frustration. There has been much discussion of the idea that some men are prone to stress because competitiveness, distrust, or hostility leads them to want to achieve a great deal quickly.[2] Among the men we interviewed for this book, however, there were few such "Type A" individuals.[3]

To be sure, a few men seemed unusually prone to perceiving threat at work, and so may have been especially likely to be embattled. And a few seemed at times to push themselves into persisting mobilization in pursuit of goals. One of the latter, Mr. Linnell, an architectural firm account executive, at one point reported stress symptoms stemming from anxiety about not his current position, but one that he only hoped to attain.

Two or three weeks ago I was putting together a test market campaign for Washington, a city that I have worked in and lived in before. It looked like there might be an opportunity for me to go down there as a sort of provisional office manager to upgrade the office. That would be a great opportunity for me. So I was very keyed up about making sure it got done right. The kind of thing that even if I try to think about something else as I'm falling to sleep, I may wind up with my thoughts coming back to that in the middle of the night so strongly that it wakes me up.

Because Mr. Linnell's was a mobilization in which failure would not cost him his present place, he woke in the middle of the night energized by schemes for achieving success and not damp with the cold sweat of fear. Perhaps mobilization driven by ambition is as physically wearing as mobilization driven by threat, but it seems a preferable experience.

Problems with required tasks, problems with others, and frustrations in the workplace seem to occur with about equal frequency. Of the seventy-five men whose interviews were coded, forty-one percent linked stress symptoms to task difficulties, forty-eight percent to relationships at work, and forty-eight percent to frustrations encountered in getting the job done. Only sixteen percent gave evidence of stress stemming from the way they approached their work.

As an example of stress stemming from the challenges of the job we might consider a story told by Mr. Bentley, an account manager in a firm that provided direct mail magazine subscriptions and billings. Within weeks after Mr. Bentley was hired he was given responsibility for an account in which the client firm was unusually demanding. Mr. Bentley was still making his way through back correspondence when he was told to expect an appraisal team from the client firm. The team would include two men who were experts in the computer management of mailing lists.

> These two guys who are heavy computer technocrats were coming by, and I know that they will be interested in our computer ideas. I come from a creative services background, and I don't know a damned thing about hardware or software. And here they are coming for two full days and I am brand new on the account and I don't have a clue about how I am going to get through this deal and actually impress them. Plus they were coming out of a relationship with another guy who designed the whole operation and was very close to them.
>
> I was worried. I really was. I didn't know how they would react to being told, "This is your new guy and he doesn't know a damned thing." So I was scared. And I was in during the weekend trying to figure out what to do, desperately trying to figure out how to position myself so that they will think I am of some value to them.

Mr. Bentley did hit on a solution. He defined himself as the client's representative within his company, and described his duties as ensuring that his firm would be responsive to the client's needs. He then brought in his firm's computer specialist to talk about the computer work.

The result was as successful as Mr. Bentley could have wished. He was told by representatives of the client firm that they preferred his approach to that of the previous account executive. They also let others in Mr. Bentley's firm know that they were pleased with him. Mr. Bentley was exhilarated.

Problems with others are capable of producing a higher level of stress than Mr. Bentley experienced, and their resolution is less likely to cause feelings of exhilaration. Nor are they easily avoided. Every relationship at work has its potential for tension, friction, and conflict. Supervisors may be hostile or subordinates disloyal; colleagues and co-workers may become rivals and enemies; clients may prove hard to please, become contentious, or simply disappear. Forty-three of the seventy-five men whose interviews were coded had bosses, and of these sixty-one percent described at least one incident of conflict or misunderstanding between a boss and themselves that gave rise to stress. Fifty-six percent of those who had subordinates described at least one incident of conflict or misunderstanding that was stress-provoking. Forty-seven percent of those who had peers reported at least one stressful occasion involving a peer.

Relation-based stress seemed most likely to occur where there was intermeshing of responsibilities, as in a partnership or a relationship with a boss or subordinate. Such stress seemed most regularly severe when the stress-provoking relationship was with a boss. Hostile or dishonest subordinates, though they could make work a trial, did not threaten the security of the man's place at work. And although a hostile business partner could rival a hostile boss as a source of severe stress, it might prove possible to separate from the partner without separating from the workplace as well. A hostile boss cannot be managed, avoided or escaped.

Mr. Reynolds, head of the design department in a manufacturing firm, reported to a man who was by reputation a bully.

Sometimes when Cal is stressed and under a lot of pressure he'll beat me around the ears a little bit. Threats. "Why the hell don't you do what I want you to do? Why the hell do you do it your own way? I don't need you. I need somebody here who is going to do what I want."

I feel with Cal it is kind of like riding a tiger. We had a shouting match once. I said, "What I think I hear you saying is, if it doesn't increase profits, it doesn't count. If it doesn't show on the bottom line, it doesn't count. Hell, not everything immediately shows on the bottom line." And he got absolutely pissed! He slammed his hand down on the desk and said, "That is enough of that! I don't want to hear any more of that!"

It reached the point of him going to Lorimer, who is Vice President of the Division, and saying, "I want this guy off the job." Lorimer told me pretty much verbatim what Cal had said. I offered to move into some other job, but Lorimer said, "Don't worry about it." He said, "No one could do the job you're doing better than you are doing it. Don't take it seriously. It will work itself out." But I was deeply hurt. And I was angry. I was angry because I knew I was doing a good job and I knew that he was wrong.

I went through a period of about two or three days of feeling stressed. Beat up. I knew that because of the way I felt, and also my gastric juices started to work. I was telling myself on the one side that who I am is more important than what I do. But on the other side I was forgetting that wisdom and wondering if I was really worth anything at all.

I kind of came back in balance after three or four days, with the resolve to show the bastard by continuing to do a good job. And if he wants me off the job he is going to have to do something more.

Mr. Reynolds's conflict with his boss continued for two more weeks. Then, quite suddenly, Mr. Reynolds returned to his boss's favor when an executive in another department commented positively on the quality of Mr. Reynolds's work. But Mr. Reynolds's feelings of having been misused persisted.

We never talked about it, but in our interactions after that I noticed he was more conciliatory. And we just kept working together, and a little while after that, I think a couple of weeks after that, he said something like, "I really think we work well together."

I felt pretty good about his saying that. I also had some cynical feelings. "Why did we have to go through this whole thing to get here?"

Despite his boss's gestures of conciliation, Mr. Reynolds thereafter distrusted him. When men successfully meet stress-provoking difficulties in their work, it is common for them to experience a surge of self-approval. But a man who believes he has been misused by someone with whom he works, like a skater who has fallen through the ice, is thereafter wary.

Being the boss oneself does not prevent relational stress. Many men have sleepless nights because of a dishonest, disloyal, or disagreeable subordinate. The man feels betrayed, yet may be reluctant or unable to fire the subordinate. The subordinate has been with the organization too long to be fired; or it would be embarrassing to admit that the subordinate had been permitted to get away with so much; or it isn't all that clear that the fault is the subordinate's; or the subordinate might bring suit; or the man considers himself to be someone who helps others, not someone who hurts them. Men who have subordinates they would like to replace may find themselves in conflict not just with the subordinates but also with themselves.

Mr. Westin, director of a venture capital firm, discovered a bookkeeper embezzling. He had the power to fire her, but the decision was hard to make.

Our bookkeeper has been with us for five years and has a pretty close relationship with a lot of people in the company. She happens to be in her mid-fifties and single. Work is her life. But she made a serious error in judgment regarding personal finances and company finances. She wrote herself a check. The auditors found a check written to her for eight hundred twenty-five dollars.

I confronted her and asked her what the eight hundred twenty-five dollars was for. That was on a Friday, and she denied knowledge of it. On Monday she chose to share what had happened. She said, "I lent some money to someone else and they didn't pay it back. I don't know why I did it." And then she said, "It was only once. I've never done anything like this in my life. Can you give me a second chance?" And she said, "I really did intend to pay it back."

Mr. Westin believed strongly that his firm was like a family and that he was responsible for the well-being of its staff. What the book-keeper had done was thoroughly wrong, but might not firing her be too severe a punishment? She was contrite, she claimed she had never done anything like this before, and she seemed sincere when she said she intended to return the money. On the other side, Mr. Westin felt that his responsibility to the firm required that he fire the woman. Some of his management colleagues might well say he should turn her over to the police.

> As I wrestled with the decision, I easily could have gone on either side. I knew I could live with the act as a one-time event by somebody who for a variety of reasons got a little mixed up. I could have convinced the auditors, convinced my partners, convinced everyone else in the company who needed to know, that she made a mistake and that we should take the risk, which I think would have been relatively minor, of it happening again.

The first two or three nights after Mr. Westin learned that there had been an embezzlement, he could not sleep. Throughout the episode he was preoccupied with it. Still, once Mr. Westin identified the issues he had to deal with, his level of mobilization never seemed as high as, say, Mr. Reynolds's had after he learned that his boss wanted him fired. Although being the person in control does not prevent stress stemming from relationships, it does seem to limit its intensity.
What finally made the difference for Mr. Westin was that when he had confronted the bookkeeper, she had lied to him.

> It was rough, emotionally. There was a real wrestling with the complexity of the emotions, and trying to sort through which is the one I want to ride with. What swung it for me was that she lied to my face. When I asked her, "What is this about?" she had said, "I don't know." I decided I couldn't live with five years of building a relationship with someone who chose to directly lie.

Mr. Westin fired the bookkeeper. He provided her with severance pay, told her he would guarantee a loan if she needed it to repay the money she had taken, and assigned a secretary to her to help her write her résumé. He also wrote a letter of recommendation for her in which he said that under supervision she could be a good employee. With the incident resolved, he discovered that the uninterrupted mobilization had taken its toll.

> I was sad, telling her she had to resign. Sorry it had to happen. That kind of meeting is going to be tough. The more you care about the person, the more you care about the concept of the relationship of the individual to the organization, the more difficult it is going to be. And there's that judgment saying back up, you're wrong, change your mind while you still have a chance. There was a little of that there.

> How it affected me, I guess, was that I had constant-level stress. I was thinking of it a fair amount of the time. Right now I would say I am feeling worn down, tired, not really sharp. I am probably feeling a little off, physically off just a little bit.

Even relatively low-level stress, if it persists long enough, can drain a man's energy. Higher levels of stress can have more serious consequences, as will be shown in the next chapter. Although some amount of work stress is inescapable, a general problem men have at work is to keep that amount to a minimum.

PROBLEM-SOLVING AND COMPARTMENTALIZATION

Men deal with potentially stressful events at work by trying to respond to them rationally. The path of action they then decide on may be no less uncertain than if they had chosen it on impulse, but at least they can be reassured that the way they arrived at it made sense.

Mr. Forge, a manager of a mutual fund, said it was in the nature of his business for things to go wrong. Asked to describe such an occurrence, he said:

> You might have owned four thousand shares or five thousand shares of stock you bought at twenty dollars. You pick up the

phone and you hear it stopped trading at fifteen dollars and indications are that it is going to open at ten or twelve.

The interviewer asked, "When that happens, how do you respond?" To which Mr. Forge replied:

Badly. "Oh, my God!" But you try to deal with it. You try to find out why it happened. Then you figure out what your options are.

There are only three choices. You can sell, buy, or hold. You pick one and you live with it.

This is a model of the strategy men use in dealing with potential stressors. It is an extension of the way they would deal with any challenge: Analyze the problem so that you know what is at stake; identify the options; choose the best one. This is the strategy of "problem-solving."

When confronted by an unanticipated threat, men are likely to react emotionally, to be startled at first and then to want to correct the situation impulsively, before taking time to think. This emotional response must be suppressed, because otherwise it would impede a dispassionate, rational appraisal. And so Mr. Forge described his first reaction, the reflex utterance, "Oh, my God!" as responding badly. It was being emotional rather than engaging in dispassionate analysis.

The first step in problem-solving is the collection of information, as much as possible in the time available. As Mr. Forge put it: "You try to find out what happened." Ordinarily the problem neither justifies nor permits postponing response, and so the decision will have to be made on the basis of the information at hand.

What decisions are possible? The options must be identified. This was Mr. Forge's next step: "You figure out what your options are." In Mr. Forge's line of work the options are clear-cut: sell, buy, hold. Men in other jobs might not have a limited list immediately available; indeed, their skill in problem-solving might be based on their ability to invent options.

Finally, a choice must be made from among the options. In Mr. Forge's words, "You pick one . . ."

Men generally believe that decisions made this way are rational. The approach replaces a planless thrashing around for a solution with a systematic procedure: collect information, identify options, choose. Even if the decision to which the process leads is mistaken, the process can be defended as correct. Indeed, men accountable for their judgments, such as middle-level managers, may adopt a problem-solving approach just because it is defensible.

Beyond this, problem-solving routinizes the management of dilemmas. Where there can be no certain best solution it provides a method for coming to a choice.

Yet problem-solving is not the only way in which men come to decisions. A second way of dealing with challenge might be named "entering the problem," to distinguish it from "problem-solving." It is the process by which decisions of unusual importance are likely to be made.

If Mr. Forge were to have been offered an attractive job at another firm, he would have wanted his response to be based on more information than was immediately available. He also would have wanted to explore how he *felt* about a possible move as well as to have added up the pluses and minuses. He would have taken more time than the problem-solving approach permits. He would have slept on the issue. He would have talked to his wife, perhaps to a friend, and he would have listened to himself as he talked. He might have tried to imagine himself in the new job and then have examined how this made him feel. He would have tried to *enter* into the decision rather than treat it as external to himself.

The more usual demands that make up a job cannot be treated this way, because it is too costly in time and effort and too taxing emotionally. As was seen in the first chapter, men's work tends to be constructed so that challenges follow closely one on the other. Mulling a problem over, getting a feel for it, entering into it, are luxuries that cannot often be afforded in the ordinary packed work day. Most of the time, decisions have to be made now. Problem-solving is then an alternative to acting on impulse.

But let us return to the observation that despite the use of problem-solving, the man usually cannot be certain that the decision he came to was correct. Whether Mr. Forge decides to buy, sell, or hold, it may turn out that the decision was mistaken. Nevertheless, he must be able to give full attention and energy to the next task in line.

This requires that once problem-solving is complete, Mr. Forge must put the issue out of his mind. He must be able to suppress his continuing concern; as Mr. Forge put it, "You live with it." A term for the process is compartmentalization.

A man who has compartmentalized his persisting uncertainties about a decision will remain aware, in one part of his mind, that the decision may go sour. But he will fend off that awareness so that he can give his full attention and energy to the problem at hand. That is what it means to live with a decision.

This is the second part of the strategy men use to deal with potentially stressful developments at work. Having chosen what seems the best of the available options, they compartmentalize any lingering uncertainty. They do not second-guess themselves; indeed, they do not permit themselves to give further attention to the problem. On some level they may remain aware of it. They may have a sense of discomfort that would be allayed if they were learn their resolution had worked out; but they refuse to attend to the discomfort. They keep their attention free for new concerns.[4]

Compartmentalization is not denial. There is no repression of uncertainty, such as might express itself in a blank incomprehension were it to be referred to. Raise the issue—"Remember the so-and-so problem?"—and the man is immediately alert, with total recall of the decision and its uncertainties: "Yes, did something happen?" But the man will not raise the issue with himself. Instead he sets the issue aside so he can get on with other things.

One man, describing his disdain for reviewing decisions already made, said, "I like to spend my time thinking about things I can change." He went on to say that he had learned early in his business career that there was no profit in getting involved in "Coulda, woulda, shoulda." Make your decision and get on with it. Don't look back.

Yet compartmentalization has its costs. In order not to think of something, it is necessary to fend off associations, impressions, feelings that would lead in the wrong direction. Men must patrol their perceptions to make sure that the worries they are warding off do not break through. The effort can absorb energy. In consequence, although compartmentalization is necessary if men are to do their jobs, it can result in their feeling tense and depleted at the end of the day without knowing exactly why.

Because men who are in work whose level of uncertainty is high may not allow themselves to recognize their tensions, they can be surprised when they overreact to a minor provocation. To their dismay, they see themselves behave with childish bad temper, perhaps suddenly blowing up—and only then do they realize how tense they have been. For most men, this happens only occasionally, but for some men in some kinds of work, it is a distinct problem.

Mr. Cooper is an independent professional, head of a firm that creates convention displays. Sometimes, when he has several projects at once, he is under pressure to have each one completed by the convention date. He is frequently under stress, and often not aware of it.

> I have a quick temper, to the point it gets ridiculous. It concerns me enough that I have gone to a psychiatrist. I'm very quick-tempered. I'll be set off like a bonfire just like that. It happened in the office the other morning. I just flew right off the handle. I didn't want to. This psychiatrist that I saw told me that I put things into drawers. And then all of a sudden I put so much in the drawer that it springs open, and that's it.

As the next chapters suggest, compartmentalization can also be a problem at home. Preoccupation and irritability whose sources are unacknowledged can make men unsatisfactory as supportive figures. And though it could be helpful to the men to talk about their day with their wives, so much anxiety may lurk just outside their awareness that they may prefer to keep it all under wraps. But being unwilling to talk about issues of central emotional importance can make for a chilly domestic climate.

On the other hand, an inability to compartmentalize carries with it severe costs. Mr. Wundt, owner of a firm that supplied equipment to professional offices, was asked by a customer to replace a machine part that had broken. Mr. Wundt believed that the part had become worn as the machine was used and that its replacement was a matter of normal maintenance for which the customer should pay. Nevertheless, to retain the customer's good will, he agreed to provide the part without charge.

> The part broke down because he had used the machine for a thousand hours. There's no justification for us replacing it. He ought to buy it. But he's a good customer. It's a thirty-dollar part. I can't get into a hassle with him over a thirty-dollar part. I'm going to give it to him. It's actually one of the account clerks who talked with him, and I told the account clerk to give it to him.

So far, so good. Mr. Wundt had identified his options, weighed them, and decided on one of them, in good problem-solving fashion. The issue should now have been closed. But it wasn't. Mr. Wundt could not follow his problem-solving with compartmentalization.

I can't forget about it. I know that's the right thing to do. But I can't get it out of my mind. Because he is a sharp operator and I know he is taking me and I hate it.

Mr. Wundt could not now give full attention to new issues, because he continued to obsess about the decision he had made. It may be worth noting, incidentally, that Mr. Wundt not only suffered from second thoughts but blamed himself for suffering from them: "I know that [forgetting about it] is the right thing to do." Men's belief that compartmentalization is the right way to deal with persisting uncertainty makes them criticize themselves if they fail to achieve it.

PERSONAL MYTHS

We have seen that one way men give emotional coherence to their work is by linking the work to imagined dramas or fantasies of which they may be only glancingly aware. An element in these dramas is always a characterization of themselves. Some men picture themselves forever fighting against odds, others picture themselves moving from exciting adventure to exciting adventure, still others picture themselves forever being frustrated just when they are about to win. These understandings of themselves, their histories, and their fortunes constitute personal myths. Men express these personal myths when they tell the story of their lives and, often, in the way in which they respond to threat.

The different implications of men's personal myths for their treatment of potentially stressful situations is exemplified by the reports of two men, each threatened with business failure. It would be understandable if someone contemplating bankruptcy displayed preoccupation, irritability, and all the rest of the stress syndrome. Yet one man reacted in this way and the other did not.

Mr. Pollock, with two partners, had opened a small manufacturing firm. He soon bought his partners out, at their request. He then overexpanded, ran into problems associated with being insufficiently capitalized, threw a great deal of personal money into the business, and nevertheless headed toward business failure.

I went into business with some friends, had partnership problems, made some poor investments, ended up working long, long hours, lost my shirt. Lost every goddamned cent I had, plus another hundred and fifty thousand. Lost everything. And I was working eighteen hours a day.

Mr. Pollock's view of himself—his personal myth—was of a man beleaguered, fighting vainly against odds, constantly prey to ambush. He spoke of customers, including people he had thought of as friends, who had delayed paying him what they owed him in the hope that his business would fail and they could avoid paying him entirely. He saw himself as having been deserted by his partners, his former friends, everyone. His stress level was extreme.

I went without any income to my family for almost six months. The mortgage was in arrears. I was just paying the interest on it. Hadn't paid a bill in six months. My mother was bringing us food packages.

And to go from making a pretty reasonable living—not having an abundance of dough, but spending it freely—to being in that situation was difficult to accept. I had some nights where I would just lie in bed and cry.

Another man whose business also faced bankruptcy, Mr. Turner, said that he had never lost a bit of sleep. Indeed, Mr. Turner found the fight against bankruptcy to have been exhilarating.

Mr. Turner, with a partner, owned an industrial catering service. They regularly had to meet bills for food, space, transportation, and, of course, staff. One of their bigger customers declared bankruptcy without paying them the money they were owed. Mr. Turner and his partner then were unable to pay their own bills.

It got to be touch and go. I couldn't pay suppliers, and if you can't pay suppliers, you don't get what you need, and if you don't get what you need, you're out of business.

It was fun. Everything I did mattered. I'd get up in the morning and know I have to do it right today or I'm out of business. I wasn't scared. What's to be scared about? If I go out of business, I have a real estate business I can go into.

In contrast to Mr. Pollock, who saw himself fighting alone against hopeless odds, Mr. Turner saw himself engaged in an exciting adventure. To be sure, Mr. Turner's situation was not exactly the same as Mr.

Pollock's. Mr. Turner was successful in avoiding bankruptcy. Unlike Mr. Pollock, he was not battered by a succession of small defeats. In addition, Mr. Turner had a partner who worked with him, whereas Mr. Pollock's partners had deserted him. And yet it seems likely that their personal myths to some extent created their realities.

In at least one respect, each man seems to have distorted his real situation. Mr. Pollock, who described himself as endlessly beset, actually had a job waiting for him whenever he wanted it: his old position in the firm he had left when he went into business for himself. Ultimately he returned to that job. Mr. Turner, who described himself as never really at risk, because he had a real estate business to go into, would have had to build that real estate business from scratch. He had a real estate license, but there was no business waiting for him.

In their personal myths, Mr. Pollock was confronted by a world barren of resource, while Mr. Turner always had something else to call on. Mr. Turner's optimism was a resource that helped sustain him, a resource Mr. Pollack did not have.

SUPPORT AT WORK FOR MANAGING STRESS

Much of the threat in potentially stressful developments at work is directed at the security of the man's place. Often the immediate threat is not that he will lose his formal position but that he will be embarrassed, will be shown up as inadequate or incompetent, and so will lose both informal standing and a measure of security. But that can be threat enough.

To the extent that men believe that their position and standing are not at risk, they will see less threat in potentially stressful developments. The backing of others at work, especially of powerful or influential others, can be reassuring.

"Support" is anything people receive from others that helps them to keep themselves going or to get what they want.[5] Most work situations provide members with a good deal of support. Men at work ordinarily can count on superiors and peers and subordinates to augment their efforts, react to their ideas, give them advice, and sustain their confidence by recognition and respect. In addition, work situations provide the reassurance of emblems of worth, including status, salary, and office space. There is support, too, simply in belonging to a work enterprise and being accepted by a group with the power to produce income for its members.

Just as other people are the most important sources of stress, so they are the most important sources of support. For a man not at the top of a work structure, the most important of the other people, for support as well as for stress, is his boss. This is the person who gives him assignments and evaluates his performance, who decides his rewards and, often, is able to decide his continued membership. Having a boss's support, being able to count on him as an ally, fosters self-confidence both by encouraging the man to believe in himself—he has the boss's assurance of his worth—and by enhancing his sense of security in his place.[6]

Dr. Tripp, head of a research group in a drug firm, had the sort of relationship with his boss, Dr. Gregory Aylmer, that most men would consider ideal.

> I find my relationship with Greg to be very rewarding. He has done some important work and he's got a good reputation. He's an established figure in the field, with all the experience, and I came wet behind the ears. And as time has gone on, he essentially has been referring to me publicly, as well as just between the two of us, as his colleague. Which makes me feel very good.

> We have skull sessions, very informal skull sessions, and there have been a few times where I have said, "Let's do it this way," and Greg has said, "You know, that is a good idea!" And I've come up with the idea. Other people may have had it, but they didn't voice it.

> It's a great feeling when you've been accepted. I feel good about the way he looks at me. I think he sees in me what I see in me, what I consider my own worth.

The relationship with his boss enhanced Dr. Tripp's security in place, because he believed that insofar as it was in Dr. Aylmer's power to keep him on the job, he would be kept. Since Dr. Aylmer was highly respected in the firm, his backing was especially valuable. In addition, Dr. Aylmer's respect for his work enhanced Dr. Tripp's sense of worth; a man of importance in the firm and in the field thought well of him. Having Dr. Aylmer's support reduced the extent to which Dr. Tripp felt threatened by the uncertainties of his work.[7]

There may have been something more in Dr. Tripp's relationship with his boss. Dr. Tripp noted that Dr. Aylmer was "somewhat of a father figure." Insofar as transference elements stemming from Dr. Tripp's early relationship with his father were elicited by his relationship to Dr. Aylmer, Dr. Aylmer's approval would be the more important emotionally.[8]

Men do best if the superiors on whom they are dependent for support appear to them to be strong and reliable. Dr. Sorenson, the head of a development group, was at one point threatened with the closing of his department. He recognized that his subordinates' security required that he continue to appear confident that the department would survive, though he actually had no such assurance.

> They try to interpret my face when I walk in in the morning. So you have to somehow project the same, regardless of all this stuff going on up in the front office. You have to try to keep them focused on the tasks to be worked on and assure them that everything is okay.

In general, it is up to the boss to foster in subordinates a sense that, as Dr. Sorenson put it, "Everything is okay." Men require for their security not only that their boss be allied with them but that he seem to be in control.

While bosses' support is understood as conditional on competent performance, men may expect unconditional support from subordinates. Men who have subordinates want two distinct contributions from them. They want the subordinates to be competent so that the subordinates can assume part of their workload. They also want the subordinates to be committed to their aims, perhaps even to them as individuals, because then they can count on the subordinates not only for acceptable work but also for the additional assurance that comes with alliance.

Men can feel diffident about admitting to the importance of a subordinate's loyalty. One man, a store owner, talked a great deal about needing to be confident of his employee's honesty. But he seemed to be concerned about more than just the money in the till, although of course there was that as well. An honest employee can be thought of as on your side; a dishonest employee is clearly working against you.

Mr. Bernard, who managed a chain of wine stores, was candid about wanting the personal loyalty of people with whom he worked closely.

I just fired my secretary last week. She was a very willing worker. Nice person. But I always felt that every time I asked her to do something, it was too much, like she sort of resented my asking her to do things. I would sort of tiptoe into her room and say, "Could you please type this letter?"

It was just never a good relationship. I never felt like she liked me. There was no ability to feel warm about each other. I don't think she ever said, "I really like this man, I really want to help him." It was much more, "Well, I'll be here until I find something better."

When it came time to move my office I could have chosen to take her with me and let go of the person who had been working at the front desk. But I actually used it as an opportunity to let her go, because I just wasn't happy with the relationship.

The value Mr. Bernard put on personal commitment does not seem unusual. Recall that Mr. Westin, in the story of the employee embezzlement earlier in this chapter, made up his mind to fire his bookkeeper because when he finally confronted her she lied to him, and that seemed to him a betrayal of their relationship. Mr. Bernard kept on a bookkeeper who had made some unsettling errors because she was unquestionably loyal.

There was this situation last week in which my bookkeeper made a five-and-a-half-thousand-dollar adding mistake. That is a serious mistake. It was a report she prepared for a partner in one of my stores, and he questioned me on it and I had to go back and check and find out what had happened. And I then had to go back to him and say my bookkeeper had made a five-and-a-half-thousand-dollar adding mistake. That is not the kind of thing that bookkeepers are supposed to do.

I don't think she's a great bookkeeper. But I hold on to her because she works hard and she is loyal and she understands the business. And I think the relationship works well. She has been loyal to me. She's hung in there through some tough times. And I don't have the energy—or the desire—to start replacing her.

If his bookkeeper were hopelessly incompetent, then despite her loyalty Mr. Bernard would replace her. Loyalty, support, and emotional contributions in general do not make competence unimportant. But loyalty matters a lot.

A few men have someone working for them whose primary responsibility is to provide support. The subordinate—usually, although not always, a woman—is responsible for contributing to the enterprise of the man for whom she works in whatever way might be useful. The job title of this subordinate might be "administrative assistant" or "assistant to the manager."

When Dr. Brown, a hospital administrator, accepted his present job, he brought along his administrative assistant from his previous job.

> There is a door between our two offices. The only time we close the door is if she's on the phone privately or I'm on the phone privately or she has a meeting privately or I have a meeting privately. Or even if it wasn't necessary to be private, we sense that the individual would like privateness. But other than that it's open all the time.

> Probably for the hospital our relationship works well. Probably, on most things, Linda would tend to go the road of least resistance, more the road of what she thought would make most people happy, cause the least amount of confrontation, achieve the greatest consensus. And probably, on most things, I would prefer to go the way my conscience or my gut dictates. My feeling is that they hired me to do leadership. The balance that she brings is that she undoubtedly smooths off the rough edges.

Relationships with subordinates who have these very general supportive responsibilities of necessity become informal and close. Mr. Bernard said:

> The first seven years I worked in this business I had a right-hand assistant who worked very closely with me, doing just about everything I needed to support me. She was fabulous. We had a kind of semi-love relationship. We were never lovers. We just really appreciated each other, really took care of each other. If one of us was sick we'd send flowers. There was a relationship which was not just a work relationship. Because when you are putting sixty hours a week in with somebody, she is like a close friend.

Relationships with subordinates cannot provide men with the support for feelings of security that can be provided by a respected boss. But subordinates, in addition to sharing the man's workload, can help a man sustain his belief in himself and in the validity of his enterprise.

Partnerships can function in the same way and, even better, provide someone with whom responsibilities can be shared. Men sometimes describe partnerships as similar to marriages. If the partnership is working well, then, as in a marriage, each partner can count on the other's support. Each can offer the other a listener who cares about the shared enterprise and understands the issues that might arise. Burdensome responsibilities can be traded.

Mr. Wundt, whose problems with compartmentalization were described earlier, at a later point brought in a partner. The arrangement worked well.

> My partner has one area that he is responsible for and I have a different area that I'm responsible for. I have confidence in him and he has confidence in me. And he's a sounding board and I feel comfortable in dealing with him in that respect. I feel very comfortable that he is going to do a really good job. That takes a large burden off of me.

Mr. Wundt's business grew, and he and his partner decided they needed additional space. Mr. Wundt, as the partner in charge of store administration, took on the chore of looking for the space. But after a week or so the searching and negotiating began to feel oppressive. He asked his partner to take over.

> Fine, no problem. He goes off and he does it. In that situation there was something that I started out being responsible for, and it had gotten to the point where I just sort of couldn't take it any more and I gave it to him, and he was willing to accept that. Sometimes it works the other way around. He will say, "So and so's been calling twice a day, he wants this, he wants that. And I'm just not getting anywhere with him. Would you take over?" So it works the other way around.

In every partnership, working so closely together means that differences of opinion that in another relationship might be shrugged off become emotionally significant. Here, too, a partnership is like a marriage. Mr. Wundt continued:

> In certain situations he can become very upset and antagonistic. Something comes up and he sort of blurts out, this is how it has to be done, one hundred percent. Twenty-four hours later, it is a completely different thing.
>
> I accept that this is the way he is. It took me a little while to figure it out. Now I say, the next day, "Why don't we get back on this issue we were talking about yesterday and let's see if we can get a little closer to resolving it." But sometimes it's tiring, and I forget to do it.

Partnerships augment resources and diminish risk. Yet partnerships also reduce freedom of action and require division of rewards. And partnerships seem to go sour at least as often as the marriages they resemble. When they work, they are invaluable as defenses against stress. When they do not, they become sources of stress themselves.

MANAGING RESIDUAL TENSIONS

Men's resilience and their supportive relationships may prove inadequate to the stressors with which the men must cope. Their day might have been frustrating. They may have made decisions about which they now feel uneasy. Often men arrive home still tense. Yet, to protect compartmentalization, they must avoid anything that would remind them of work. One answer is hobbies.

> I'll get irritable. I go home and I just won't feel like talking. Sometimes I'll bury myself in the boob tube. Then I raise plants. That's one of my hobbies. I have banks with lights in my basement that I grow plants under. I'll go down and I'll start futzing around with them, cleaning them, things of that nature. I raise a garden in my yard. It's a form of therapy. Or I'll go read. That's usually the effect of a substantial amount of tension or pressure. I might bury myself in a long, involved, very pulpy book. It may not be one that will ever be considered a classic, but it is something I will bury myself in. I also don't read one book at a time. I usually have three or

four of them floating around the house, something that's rather deep and something that's very pulpy. That's one way of dealing with it. Go into a fantasy world, play with your fantasies. I do that by reading. Other people will do it by, I guess, TV or something like that.

Dr. Tripp, experimental psychologist

Hobbies, with their absence of time pressures and inaccessibility to criticism, are safe activities. Television or reading can provide a fantasy world that can help sustain compartmentalization. Important in any such distraction is that there be nothing to trigger the anxiety and pain that lie just beyond the fringe of awareness.

Some men are troubled by the physical tension that is one expression of persisting mobilization. One form of remedy is chemical; alcohol seems, within our sample, the drug of choice. One man in the sample described himself as alcoholic. Another said he was not, but his wife reported that he was physically distressed when unable to obtain his usual 6:00 P.M. Scotch. Several others included alcohol use within a ritual of unwinding at the end of the day. Other men found sports or jogging effective; while engaged in the activity there was distraction; afterward there was a bit more distance from the day's problems. Dr. Brown, whose relationship with his assistant was described previously, used jogging as a time to indulge fantasies of aggression and revenge:

I jog five or six times a week. Jogging just seems to work out the unhappy things. Maybe it is realizing that you can fantasize at your most hostile and that you are not going to do those things once you are done with your run. But on my jogging path I work out all the angers. There is the quietness and the solitude of the running. And there is the pounding, the pain, the discomfort that lends itself to thinking over unhappy things. I'm nastier during that time, almost always, compared with what I'm ultimately like. It is me at my nastiest.

Dr. Brown, medical training program administrator

Drinking and jogging can meet similar needs for the management of residual tensions. The side effects of jogging would seem preferable.

A CASE STUDY OF STRESS AND
ITS MANAGEMENT

Mr. Bentley's successful resolution of the problem of gaining client acceptance was described earlier. Because he had done well in his first months with his firm, he was assigned to one of the firm's biggest accounts: a publication with a strong regional following. He was to divide responsibility for the account with a somewhat older man, Andy. Both would report to Curt, a vice president of Mr. Bentley's firm.

Mr. Bentley thought that the publication could do well nationally and that trying for a national market would require only a slight change in editorial emphasis. He did not know that there had been many discussions within the client firm about going national and that the leadership of the firm had decided that its identity depended on staying regional.

Soon after Mr. Bentley was assigned to the account he, Andy, and Curt flew to the city of the client's headquarters, where they were to meet with the client's top management. While at their hotel Mr. Bentley mentioned to Andy and Curt that he thought it might be a good idea for the client to go national.

> The two guys that I worked with, Andy and Curt, I believe this to this day, really kind of set me up. They said, "You should really propose that," knowing darn well that it was going to get shot down and be torn apart.

At the meeting with the management of the client firm Mr. Bentley was asked whether he had any thoughts about their business strategy. He said that one idea had occurred to him and that he had developed a plan for its implementation. And he sketched out how moving to national distribution could be accomplished.

> I didn't have the experience to really be able to distinguish whether or not this was a good idea, so I said it haltingly, because I didn't have confidence to really do it from conviction. And I kind of realized halfway through what I was saying, this is not going to work. Maybe I read it in the faces of the people. I suppose it was like a comedian with a bad joke. Everybody started squirming.
>
> I just sort of kept on talking mechanically and I condensed it as much as I could so I could sit down. And I remember sit-

ting down and saying to myself, that was awful. I felt like a fool. I felt just dreadful.

One company guy, very sarcastic, said, "Well, I'm sure your idea may have some merit." And this other company guy was very condescending and he said, "Well, Sam, I'm sure once you gain a little more experience in this field you'll realize that that idea wouldn't quite apply to this particular situation." A real putdown.

I thought, Gee, why did they set me up? Why did they do this? It was rotten. I would never have done that to them, the bastards. But I also realized you've got to be pretty desperate to do this crap. And I realized, you don't do this unless you're scared of me.

That insured that as far as this client was concerned, which was the company's most important client, I'd never have any credibility with them. From that standpoint it probably was more or less what Andy and Curt wanted.

That night I didn't sleep very well. And after that there were some sleepless nights.

Mr. Bentley's colleagues had now proved to him that they were enemies. But their tactic had been successful. Mr. Bentley's place in his work community had become vulnerable. Mr. Bentley's first response was to reassure himself of his worth and so provide himself with a basis for optimism and self-confidence.

I said to myself, I'm certainly more honest than you are. My intentions are better. And the company was right to hire me because they can't run an organization with people like you.

Mr. Bentley then sought an ally. Here his record of early success may have helped.

I went to Jerry Hallowell, who was one of the founders of the company and a senior guy. We sort of got along: I enjoyed him and he obviously enjoyed me. And I felt that he and I could be friends. I just sort of did it impulsively. I just went to him and I said, "Look, Jerry, I don't have a mentor here and I don't think I'm going to survive if I don't have a mentor. So I hope you don't mind, but you're the one." And he said okay.

Mr. Bentley told the senior figure whose alliance he had obtained what had happened, not to express his hurt and outrage, but in order to problem-solve. Here is the problem; what's the best way to deal with it? The two discussed the situation dispassionately. They agreed on a solution. The senior figure had the power to implement it—although not immediately.

He said I ought to get out of that situation. And eventually he got me assigned to a different team.

Mr. Bentley now went to Andy, the colleague who had done him in, and said that they should go their separate ways. Andy could have full responsibility for the magazine account and he would give his attention to other accounts. But though Mr. Bentley could limit his work with Andy, he could not avoid working with Curt, the vice president to whom he reported. He therefore did what he could to repair that relationship.

I sort of worked on it with Curt. There was something about Curt that I did like. And Andy was really the guy that set me up. So with Curt I just said, well, if I just keep on plugging, we'll get along eventually. And we did.

When I first came into his department, I represented a threat. But the more he got to know me, the more he began to realize that I wasn't a threat. Because I'm not a threat to people. I've never stepped on anybody or tried to supersede anybody. And I haven't done it with him.

Mr. Bentley succeeded in repairing his relationship with Curt. This was a success comparable to the one described earlier, where he had worked out how to position himself for the visiting team of computer experts. But instead of the exhilaration he had felt after the earlier success, he had little pleasure in having met this challenge. Even though he successfully repaired his relationship with Curt, he would never again trust him. Some months later, after he had been reassigned, Mr. Bentley said:

Curt and I get along very well now. We're good friends. But as far as he is concerned, it will always stay with me. I'd never work with him.

Until his reassignment Mr. Bentley felt he had to be constantly on guard as he worked in the same department as a colleague who had encouraged him to blunder, and as he reported to a boss who had let it happen. Yet he was able to maintain himself in that situation for the four or five months before his transfer was arranged. More than that, he had come out of the situation with a senior figure as an ally and a strengthened reputation for handling difficult situations well. Asked how he had managed all this, he said:

It was tough. But I don't think you do these things that consciously. When I talk about it now, it sounds like I had this plan and I worked it out and I did it by sheer will-power. But that's not the way it happens. I don't think I would've been able to say, "Well the way I'm gonna deal with this situation is to do this and this and this." I think it's sort of deep down inside, what you do.

"It's sort of deep down inside . . . " What does this mean? What was it that was "deep down inside"? For one thing, Mr. Bentley maintained a personal myth in which he was able to do what he had to do to surmount adversity. Associated with this myth was a proto-scenario of what had to be done: Succeed well enough to gain the respect of peers; make your peace with authority; ultimately, achieve security and position by demonstrating your worth.

When my parents sent me to boarding school, very strict English-style boarding school, and I walked into the school, I was sort of scared and a little surly with what was going on. And I was immediately made to wear my pants backwards for having my hands in my pockets. So I started out feeling pretty miserable.

They had sort of a pretty intense lacrosse league. And I didn't know how to play lacrosse. But I am pretty athletic. And lacrosse, it's an awful lot will power, I think. And if I decide to go for something, I'll go for it, really go for it. So I made the lacrosse team.

Then the school had a school captain who was the senior boy in the whole school, and he ran the school under the tutelage of the faculty. I don't know how conscious it was, but I've done it every time. I decided if I run the school, then I won't have problems. So I became school captain. That's how I dealt with that. And all my life I have done that.

This is a powerful myth of winning through. The strategic program associated with the myth—win the respect of peers and the rest—was available to Mr. Bentley when he was confronted at work with what could have been a career disaster. Mr. Bentley had no need to think through a strategy to deal with his situation, because it was already part of him. That he could implement it well was a credit to his interpersonal skills, his resilience, and, perhaps, his luck in having at hand a senior figure who would agree to back him. But his personal myth told him what to do.

A SUMMARY STATEMENT

Men function well at work not by escaping stressors but by managing them. They manage them by using the strategies of problem-solving and compartmentalization and by faith in these strategies, by reliance on support, and by a variety of techniques for distracting themselves and for inducing relaxation. Even so, most men are likely several times a year to have a night's sleep interrupted by worry about work and much more often to come home tense and irritable because of problems on the job. Their stress-management devices serve to keep the levels of stress they experience within tolerable bounds; nevertheless, now and again the devices fail.

CHAPTER FOUR

Unmanaged Stress

What happens to a man when the challenges of his work are unyielding regardless of his effort? What happens when he is enmeshed in what seems to be an unending conflict? In either case threat persists, so he must remain mobilized. And yet he cannot remain mobilized indefinitely.

He may give up. He may decide that success, no matter how much he wants it, is unattainable. The tasks are too difficult, or the conflict unwinnable. Whatever it takes to come through, he does not have it. There is no point in continued effort. He loses hope. He becomes *depressed*.

Or he may accept that success is unattainable but, instead of losing faith in himself, may withdraw his investment in what had been his goals. He stops caring and, because he no longer cares, the prospect of failure no longer frightens him. He just wants to get away. He is *burned out*.

Or neither of these processes occurs to interrupt the man's mobilization. The man is resilient enough, resourceful enough, and determined enough to continue to struggle. He may regularly have problems sleeping; nevertheless, he is at it again the next day. His stomach may be chronically upset; he takes antacids. Small muscles may begin to display tremors or tics; he shrugs them off. He remains mobilized until, sooner or later, *a physical system gives way*. If he is lucky, the system that fails will not be cardiovascular.

The immediate expressions of stress are preoccupation, irritability, tension, and difficulties in sleeping. The longer-term consequences include depression, burnout, and somatic disorders.[1]

75

DEPRESSION

Depression occurs when men lose hope of a successful outcome and believe the fault lies in themselves. Then continued mobilization appears pointless; no matter how hard they try, they are not good enough.

Many men in challenging work sooner or later experience at least brief depression.[2] The following story is presented in some detail to suggest the way in which a business crisis can first produce stress and then, as loss of hope in this one venture produces loss of confidence in the self, can lead to depression.

Mr. Daniels is a broker of equipment used in the construction industry: cranes, earth movers, and the like. Firms that have equipment sitting idle come to him to find other firms to whom they can lease the equipment. Mr. Daniels then arranges for the firm that owns the equipment to obtain the entire amount of the lease from a bank, giving that firm operating capital. The firm that leases the equipment then will make a monthly payment to the bank, reimbursing the bank for the money it provided the owning firm and also paying interest. Mr. Daniels receives a commission from the owning firm. Everyone wins.

A deal that appeared at first not much different from any of dozens of other deals Mr. Daniels had arranged unexpectedly went sour:

> This guy told me his company had bought construction equipment for which they paid one hundred fifty thousand dollars and, because their business had changed, they couldn't use it. But he didn't want to sell because he would have an investment tax recapture issue. When you buy a piece of equipment you are entitled to deduct ten percent from taxes. But if you don't keep that equipment for five years, the government comes along and recaptures the tax credit that you took. So I could see that on one hundred fifty thousand dollars of equipment, if he took a fifteen thousand dollar credit, selling was a problem.
>
> So he asked me would I remarket it for them? And I asked him, if I could bring seventy-five thousand in cash for a three-year deal on the equipment, would he consider that doable? And he said, "Yeah, that would be fine."

Mr. Daniels had three men working with him in his office as junior partners. One of them questioned the new client's trustworthiness.

This guy is a very rough man, lacking in formal education, but very successful. The first day we saw him, one of the guys that works for me asked, "Do you think you've got enough of an understanding to do business on a handshake?" I was absolutely confident that the guy was okay. I didn't think of it for a nanosecond. "He's okay. I can tell this guy wouldn't try to blow anything by me."

After some effort Mr. Daniels located a lessee for the equipment. It was easy, then, to arrange for the bank loan that would permit the lessee to give Mr. Daniels's client the entire rental up front.

From the day I first saw the guy until last week, I was focusing more and more time and energy on his transaction. Everything else that came in was delegated to somebody else. It got to the point where I was almost full time on it. I took ads in trade papers and I spent a lot of time calling on people. Finally I found a company in New Jersey that was willing to do it. I found that through another broker, who I had to cut in for a couple of thousand bucks.

There was a lot of bringing everything around and getting it ready to go. I went to my attorneys, I had meetings with my bank. I called the guy and I outlined the deal for him. He said, "Okay, get it to me in writing and let me run it over with my finance people." So I worked that night and put together a two-page summary of the transaction and I gave it to him.

I was pretty pleased with myself for doing all this. Then in a matter of thirty-six hours, it crashed.

Throughout the deal Mr. Daniels had been carried along on a wave of ebullience. He had admired his own adroitness in creating the deal and recruiting the players. But then Mr. Daniels discovered that the deal was fundamentally flawed, and he would have known it from the beginning had he followed good business procedures.

When I had my first meeting with the bank on this thing, two or three weeks ago, they said to me, "Did you do the lien search yet?" I said, "No. I believe the guy." I knew I

> was going to do it. It's something you have to do. But I
> wanted to believe the guy, so I did.
>
> Thursday, I was looking for an excuse to go have lunch with
> somebody downtown. And I thought that along the way I re-
> ally ought to do a lien search on this thing. It was kind of my
> excuse to go downtown. And I went in and I did it. And it
> appears that the guy really doesn't own the equipment. He
> had a group of investors buy the equipment and rent it to
> him. He doesn't have title to the equipment at all.

Mr. Daniels's client apparently hoped to obtain a large amount of
money as prepayment for the rental of equipment he didn't own. He
would then have the use of this money as a sort of interest-free loan. He
could also use it to pay off his own loan and, in addition, make a small
profit, since Mr. Daniels had obtained a higher rental for the equipment than he was himself paying.

Now that Mr. Daniels was aware that his client didn't own the
equipment, he realized that the deal he had planned was impossible.
The bank could not take the equipment as collateral. But rather than
accept failure, Mr. Daniels searched for another way to write the deal.
The client could not lease equipment he didn't own, but he might be
able to contract with the New Jersey firm for the work for which his
equipment was to be used. It would be a different deal, and a less
profitable one, but something might be salvaged.

> Even if the guy isn't the owner, it isn't the end of the world.
> There are ways around that. It makes it a bit difficult that he
> lied to me, but we still could have done something. The deal
> might have gotten skinnier, but we could have worked some-
> thing out.

Mr. Daniels gave himself an evening to mull over what had
happened. He planned to call his client the following day, Friday,
because he wanted the revised deal agreed to before he left for the
weekend. That weekend he planned to serve as one of several judges of
a sailing race.

The next day, calling from home, Mr. Daniels did indeed reach
his client.

> I had a list of three or four people I was going to call and I
> started making the calls. And I got a call from this friend,

Forrest. Forrest and I go back a long time, to when we were kids. We went to prep school together and we went to college together and we have been good friends for a long, long time. And he called and said, "Look, it's Friday night, can you meet us?" And he named this bar where we meet from time to time. I told him I had to get up at five the next morning and I wasn't up for a big night, but we'd come down around five o'clock.

Finally I got hold of this guy. I just told him, point blank, "Maybe I didn't tell you this, but you are going to have to assign the equipment to the bank." He started yelling and screaming. Totally unreasonable. I said to him, "We're not going to get anywhere with you hollering and yelling." And the guy threatens me with physical harm! I thought, God, I'm not used to things like this. No one has threatened me since about high school and then it was some kid that didn't mean it.

That precluded the possibility of us doing anything further together. And I kept thinking, what if I told him that I knew he didn't own the equipment? What if I told him I caught him? I wanted to give the guy enough room to walk through the door. But what I did was I put him in a position where he felt there wasn't a way out. And I just got blown away by that reaction.

On hanging up the receiver, Mr. Daniels discovered his composure had been shattered. His thoughts and feelings were totally engaged by what had occurred, and yet he could not make himself think systematically about it. He could not do what he was ordinarily good at, work out a strategy. His mind seemed to skitter, panic-driven, searching for a way out. Nor could he think about anything else.

I was stunned by the whole thing. I wasn't concerned that the guy was threatening me. I didn't take it as anything more than hot air because he was hot under the collar. I'm sure he's not sending his friends in the mob out to get me. But at the same time it was a very uncomfortable feeling to have a man say that to you.

Right after that a fellow who works with me called me on something else. We got some machines in inventory right now and he's sold some of them. And he was telling me so I would take them off the list and not offer them to someone else. It was important, basic stuff. But I was so upset that I couldn't listen to what he was saying to me. My head was going ninety miles an hour on this other thing. I'm saying, "Okay, we deliver the eleventh," and repeating the whole thing to him and never hearing a thing he said. Or at least not recording it. It's on pass-through.

In the meantime I forgot all about the fact that we were supposed to go to meet Forrest. I was sitting in the den trying to figure this whole thing out and the phone rang and Forrest is saying, "Hey, we've got two seats we are saving, one for you and one for Betty, and we're feeling kind of lonely." I had forgotten all about meeting them, I had gotten so involved with this thing.

Mr. Daniels told Forrest that he wasn't up to sociability at that moment. He stayed home and tried to watch television. He was able to get to sleep at his usual hour, but he woke around three A.M. and remained awake until he had to leave for the boat race at five.

The impact of the incident on Mr. Daniels's self-esteem had been severe. He spent the evening of the first day of the boat race with an old sailing friend. That helped a bit:

Saturday I was busy all day with the regatta. And I had more on Sunday. I saw an old friend Saturday night, and I had dinner with him. Wells has a tremendous ability to relax me. I can relax better with him than with anybody outside of my wife. I'm extremely fond of him. I would do anything he asked me to do for him. And I think he'd do the same for me. We went up to his hotel room about eleven-thirty at night, and we were sitting in there laughing over nothing until about two o'clock.

I didn't even mention this whole thing. At one point, toward the end of dinner, we were having a cup of coffee and he asked me, "How's business?" I was having a nice time and I really didn't want to even bring it up and go through it all. Because there's no point in it. It wasn't going to do any good. I really wanted that to go away, to be gone. So I just said, "Oh, it's okay. We're doing all right."

Mr. Daniels did not confide in his friend. To do so would have interrupted the compartmentalization he was barely maintaining and would have required him to go through it all again. Too, he would have had to reveal to his friend that he had been a bit of a fool. This would hardly have benefited his battered self-esteem. He did, however, reassure himself that his friend remained an ally, someone on whom he could count. There was a sympathy between them that was affirmed by sitting around and laughing over nothing.

Mr. Daniels returned home Sunday evening. He was now depressed: Not so depressed that hospitalization was in order, but enough to be reluctant to return to the challenges and interactions of work.

> I got home and Betty tried to tell me there will be another one, not to get too wrapped up in this, not to let it be too damaging. But usually I kind of look forward to going back to work and here I felt bad that it was Sunday night.

> We were supposed to go to a party. I just couldn't. I told Betty, "Look, if you want to go, go ahead. But I can't." She said, "The hell, you want to sit home and mope? Go ahead. I'm going to go." So she went anyway. And I preferred that.

> There was a good movie on television. I kind of got into the movie and enjoyed it. Then, when the movie was over, I wasn't tired, because I'd taken a nap. I was lying in bed and I was thinking, for the first time in I can't tell you how long, I didn't want to go to work. And when you do what I do, if you don't want to go, you just don't. That hurt. It fed on itself in an uncomfortable kind of way. I thought, "Well, maybe when you get up in the morning you'll feel more like yourself."

Things were no better the next day.

> I got up this morning and Betty had to go somewhere and I had to get the kids fed. So I was running around the house. And I thought, "This is good. You're all right. Go get 'em." Within a half hour I was all hunched over and moped out again. It's been like that all day. I was mopey all day.

The symptoms of depression contrast sharply with the symptoms of stress. Stress is persisting readiness to deal with threat; depression is the suspension of readiness because hope has been lost. Instead of mobilization there is torpor, instead of tension there is flaccidity, instead of vigilance there is withdrawal.

> I'm a very social type of person and I usually love an afternoon get-together. This afternoon I didn't even get off the couch to go out. I somehow felt I let myself down, like I could have avoided this.

> I didn't want to go back to work this morning. I think the reason was because when I got to work I had to face it again. I had to explain it to the other people who were working on other parts of the deal.

> I had to make a business development call this afternoon. I love to call. I can usually get myself pumped up and go in there and do it. But I couldn't get myself up. And I wouldn't have been able to get myself in the men's room and give myself one last pep talk before I go in there. My enthusiasm has gotten dampened. I've lost that "Let's go!" type of stuff. I've been walking around for four days with my tail between my legs.

Again and again Mr. Daniels's thoughts returned to the deal. Try as he might, he could not come to terms with his management of it. But only if he could assimilate his failure to the self in which he was confident, so that both together made sense, could he function as he had. As it was, his attempts at recovery of his former self-concept continually foundered on the painful memory of his gullibility and carelessness.

> I've got to call my attorney, I've got to call my banker, I've got to call the Jersey firm to let them know that the deal isn't going to go together. I didn't do anything about it today. I've got to tell all these people that I'm not going to deliver on what I said I could deliver on. I don't like it. It doesn't sound like fun.

> The guy said if I could bring him such and such we would have a deal. I went out and I went through all this effort and expense to do it. And then to get there and it is dead in the water! I'm back to nowhere. I've got nothing of significance going. I have to start all over again. I have done all this work

for naught. And what I thought was going to be my next success, so to speak, has been rudely taken away.

If I had positioned myself properly from the beginning, this wouldn't have happened to me. I guess if the truth be known, at least half of my displeasure is caused not by the fact that the guy tried to screw me, but that I let myself get screwed. I can blame myself for it. I should have known better.

Because Mr. Daniels had lost faith in himself, he could not work. But at least he was no longer under stress. That was over.

I really thought I had this thing pulled together, and all of a sudden I caught the guy. He doesn't know he's been caught because I never let him know, but he knew he was in a corner. And instead of coming out in a reasonable fashion and saying, "Hey, I prefer not to do business with you," he just took out at me. I'm very upset by it. I can't get it out of my mind.

It's done. I can't see any way to salvage the thing. I'll get over it and I'll learn something from it and I won't do it again. I won't make that kind of commitment again on an intuitive feeling that, "Yeah, I'm going to be all right with this guy." But it's always easy when you look back.

This whole thing makes me feel really crappy about myself. I don't think I did anywhere near my best. And it's terrible because it spills over. Like going out on that call this afternoon. I felt like, hell, I'll probably just screw this up anyway, so don't bother. Really self-degrading stuff.

Things like this make me feel beat. They make me feel like I lost. And that's hard for me, because it makes me feel poorly about myself. I'm mad at that guy, I'm mad at myself. It just runs me down.

Mr. Daniels's depression, though mild, shared with instances of chronic depression the symptom picture of lassitude, withdrawal, self-deprecation, unrelenting self-criticism, and, of course, distress and despair. It differed from chronic mild depression in only one important respect: Mr. Daniels was sure the state was only temporary. Whereas in chronic depression there is likely to be unmitigated hopelessness, Mr. Daniels believed that it would take only a success or two to restore his belief in himself and he would then be as good as he had ever been.[3]

> To get out of this I'm going to have to put a deal together, to pull one off and get it done properly, all the damned holes filled in. The thing that will get me pumped up again will be doing it properly. And then I'll say, "Well, yeah, see? You can do it."

> I know this will pass. I imagine that in a month or so I'll be able to look at it and chuckle. We'll see.

Mr. Daniels was right in his assessment. A month later he was again functioning well. The deal in which he had been taken in was history (although he would still wince when he thought about it), and he had new projects that now mattered more.

Mr. Daniels's depression actually made an important contribution to his well-being. It interrupted a mobilization that no longer had value since it could never have brought about success. Continued mobilization would have pointlessly maintained Mr. Daniels in a state of stress in which he was anxious, irritable, and tense, where he was preoccupied during the day and unable to sleep through the night—a state that would only have worn away at his resilience. When stress was replaced by depression, Mr. Daniels's mobilization was at an end and in its place was total, albeit despairing, relaxation.

There is a second way Mr. Daniels's depression may have had value. The discomfort and self-deprecation Mr. Daniels experienced forced him to reassess his goals. He was forced to reconsider whether they were attainable and whether they were worth attaining. As it happened, his conclusion was to continue in his line of work but to manage it better. He might equally well have decided to move on to something else. Depression, because it is unpleasant, because it prevents action, and because it induces a questioning of the self, forces men to reconsider their commitments.[4]

Depression as a response to failure, in someone who is not characterologically given to depression, tends to be self-limiting. After a while men emerge from this sort of depression, determined to persevere in the direction they had been taking—as was true for Mr. Daniels—or prepared to set off on a course that seems more promising.

BURNOUT

Withdrawal of investment in work, together with what might be symptoms of depression except that self-deprecation is muted, has been characterized as burnout. As in depression, there is a loss of commitment to work and to the achievement of its goals. There are also fatigue, a sense of being burdened, and an inability to summon the energy work requires. But there is less repudiation of the self as inadequate and less generalization of a sense of inadequacy beyond the work situation. Instead there is a sense of the work as pointless and ungratifying.

Mr. Wundt, before he took in his partner, had been dealing with a staff problem for at least a year. His assistant manager, an older woman, had been disturbingly contentious, making work unpleasant for everyone, including him. But she had been with him since he had opened the business, and he was determined to retain her.

The assistant manager did not want to work overtime herself, and she discouraged Mr. Wundt from asking others to work overtime. Meanwhile, orders were being sent out late. Customers complained. Mr. Wundt began coming in evenings and weekends to catch up. Without warning, he was required to submit to a tax audit. Two days were lost to work on the books. Now Mr. Wundt began to feel overwhelmed.

> The last two weeks have been extremely busy, long and tiring and sort of draining. Very, very hard on me personally. A number of business-related problems came up, all together at the same time. Just a lot of things that needed to be done just weren't getting done. They weren't being resolved as quickly as they should have been. And although you may not particularly want to work late into the night and on weekends, you work late into the night and on weekends just to get those things off your back. You end up physically tired.

> I feel under a tremendous amount of stress and pressure. I feel really tired. I feel emotionally exhausted and physically exhausted. I don't want to deal with other people and their feelings and their emotions or my emotions toward them. If you are upset about something or distraught or unhappy, I really don't want to know about it. At another time I would like to know what you are upset about, why you are distraught or unhappy. Right now I don't care.

I don't want to work as much as I do. Partly it is a sense of responsibility. Over the last few years, and more so the last few months, and still more so the last few weeks, I have just felt more and more physically and emotionally drained. I just feel that I want less and less to do what I'm doing.

It's just that things have been difficult and I'm tired of the difficulties. I'm sick of the burdens.

The extent to which burnout is a state distinct from depression, rather than a form of mild depression, is difficult to say. Very occasionally, however, men report states in which they do not so much feel unable to meet the demands of their work, but only that they are sick of the demands. This, too, can interrupt persisting mobilization.[5]

PHYSICAL SYMPTOMS

What happens when, because of commitment or ambition or the demands of the situation, men cannot withdraw their investment in their work and continue in their efforts despite stress?

Mr. Bartlett, who had moved from a profession into public service, had accepted a government position in which his first task was to overhaul an ancient and costly program. Despite its inefficiency, the program provided jobs and income for influential people, and changing it plunged him into conflict. Mr. Bartlett said:

My real task was to topple the old order and to prepare the way for change. The problem that I was faced with was to wrestle control away from what you might call the old guard. The fellow that ran the system, when I arrived, had been there for twenty-seven years. He and some commercial agencies and some other people had a nice relationship. There was nothing illegal going on, but they did their business to their benefit, not necessarily to the system's benefit. And they wanted to run it like they'd always run it, with the deals they had always made.

The first thing we did was reduce the employment level. That was stressful for everybody. There's nothing easy about downsizing an institution. Then we made a run at the guy who was running the system. Some of the top administrative people sided with him, and some sided with us. Most sided with him. To get control we had to change the rules to eliminate his position.

It was a big battle. I didn't have enough experience to really know what I was doing. I was too naïve, believed much too strongly that people would do the right thing if they saw that it was the right thing to do. I hadn't been in this kind of battle before. It was tough! I made a lot of enemies.

We were at the height of the crisis regarding the future management of the system. I was spending long hours and all that, at the expense of my children and my wife. And I was under attack. Basically it became apparent that the old structure was going to go. And part of that equation was that I was going to go too.

I had a heart attack. It was out of the blue. There was no warning. There was nothing to prepare me, or anybody, for that kind of an experience, to come so close to death.

I didn't have the physical characteristics that would predict a heart attack. I didn't have high blood pressure. I wasn't overweight. I didn't smoke. I exercised vigorously. There was nothing on the physical side of my makeup, other than maybe to some degree a Type A personality, that would have accounted for it. I associate the heart attack with the job.

Some of the physicians I consulted agreed that it could very well have been stress that caused the heart attack. Nobody knows.

Mr. Bartlett's wife was also convinced that his heart attack had been produced by the stress of his job. She said:

If Gene just hadn't been in that job crunch, he wouldn't have had a heart attack. The week of the heart attack Gene was describing to me in detail the situation that he was in and he kept saying, "This is the most unhappy week of my life. I'm so unhappy! I'm so unhappy!" I saw him strapped on the rails and saw the train coming and just didn't know what to do. In retrospect, he should've quit. But that was an option we never thought of.

A job situation in which he was assaulted, if only verbally, by enemies and was without any collegial support brought Mr. Bartlett under severe stress. Although he would ultimately turn out to have won the battle, in that he had set in motion a process that eventually forced his opposition from office, the persisting high level of stress appears to have been too much for his heart.

In Mr. Bartlett's case the physiological system that gave way under stress was critical to his continued life. It is too bad we don't come equipped with unneeded structures like electrical fuses that fail early and so protect our more essential structures. Or perhaps we do. Perhaps depression and burnout constitute fuselike neurological linkages that shut us down before we sustain life-threatening damage.

EARLY WARNINGS

In two instances men reported having acted on early warnings that stress might lead to physical damage. Each man needed a medical authority to justify letting up.

Mr. Viner was a financial analyst with a marketing firm. He had been hired by a man with whom he got along but that man was moved to another position, and someone with whom he did not get along became his boss.

> Early on what I was doing was accepted highly. But then my boss was moved aside and a guy came in who became my boss. He and I had a few conversations, and I knew right then that there were going to be difficult times ahead. Our relationship was difficult almost immediately. And it got worse.
>
> As a manager he was an absolute disaster. He was not people-sensitive. He could not give advice and counsel. He was a dictator, a bull. I saw him running roughshod over several people around me. And he was crude. He had a million one-liners, most of which were filthy. He told them in the company of women. To me, for that kind of conduct, he should have been fired. But he really couldn't care less.
>
> He threw a lot of baloney. And I found that to be difficult to accept. I felt I had my reputation on the line, my reputation with the people who worked for me and the people whom I

worked with. I would not do a shoddy job just for the hell of it.

It got to a point where I couldn't even speak to him. That was constantly a tense period for me. There was no letup. I just went through the motions everywhere. It was very, very difficult. I had never gone through a period like that in my life. I was a nervous wreck. It showed in irritability, sleepless nights, all the normal things that go along with it, that you hear about.

It got so difficult that I became physically ill. I had extensive tests taken. I had high blood pressure. My doctor felt that I really should get out of the situation. And I had a friend that I played golf with who is a cardiologist, and he indicated, after a long conversation, that I had a fairly high stress level and that I really ought to move. That really iced it. Two friends independently told me I should leave that job.

Mr. Viner gave notice. Almost immediately his stress symptoms abated. There was nothing more his boss could do to him and nothing more to fear. His skills were good enough, and people with his skills were enough in demand for him to feel confident that he would soon find something else. His agreement with his boss permitted him to remain at his firm until that happened.

There was no immediate pressure on me to walk the street, because my performance was such that he really couldn't do that. Once I decided I was moving and my boss and I discussed it, I was pretty much at ease.

Another man, when he was just beginning his company, exhibited the usual array of stress symptoms and, in addition, stomach pain and occasional headaches.

I went to see our doctor and he said, "Ron, what's wrong?" "Well, I got some pain in my stomach." He says, "Sit on the table." So I did. He says, "There is nothing wrong with you. Here's eight pills. Take two a day, until they are gone." And he says, "Now, tell me. You got any problems at home?" I say, "No more than anybody else." He says, "You got any money problems?" I say, "No more than anybody else. Trying to meet everything and do what we're supposed to do and everything. There's a couple of guys who owe me quite a bit of money. I just can't seem to get it. But we're working on it."

He says, "You're worrying about it at night, aren't you? Take that pill now. You go home and go to bed. Tomorrow morning when you get up, you go out that front door and you let your wife handle everything at the house. That is what your wife's for, to handle everything at the house. You go in the office and you work in the office until you quit. I know you work late, you always did, but when you leave that office door, leave that office work there. Because from six o'clock, when you leave it, until eight o'clock the next morning, you can't do a thing about anything anyway, so why let it eat at you?"

By God, I did that. And I have never had a pain since. I just relax at night. No matter what time you get in, you throw everything out of your mind until the next morning, because there isn't a thing you can do.

Mr. Graham, owner of small business

The doctor, among other things, recommended to Mr. Graham that he stop trying to control everything at home and at work and that he compartmentalize more effectively. But how valuable it is to have a doctor say, "Stop trying so hard." It goes against the grain, among effective men, to walk away from challenge. Believing they have what it takes to win through and staying with challenge no matter what, are much of what makes them effective. How can they give up, even though they should, and retain their belief in themselves? Only if the reason they are giving up is that it is doctor's orders. Mr. Viner gave special weight to his friend's advice because his friend was a physician. The authority of the physician permits a man to withdraw from a stressful challenge without having to feel he has quit too quickly.

It may be men with the strongest commitments, whose belief in themselves is the most resilient, who are the most vulnerable to damage to their health. They are fortunate if someone they respect, whose recommendations they feel they must rationally follow, tells them when enough is enough.

CHAPTER FIVE

Bringing Work
Stress Home

When a man is under stress, with whom could he better talk, from whom could he better seek understanding and comfort and counsel, than his partner in life, his wife? Yet most men take the advice given to Mr. Graham by his physician: Don't bring home work's worries; when you leave your office, close your door on the day's problems. They try not to talk about their work's lingering uncertainties at home. Instead they have a drink, read, watch television, play with the kids, or join their wives in preparing the evening meal. They keep work's worries safely walled away.

> When something goes wrong at work there's nothing at home that can solve the situation. I go home and talk about something else. Just try to get everybody laughing and myself laughing too, to just forget about the crap, because you come back to that the next day. There's nothing they can do about it. There's no sense in talking about it. So you say, "Well, what happened to you today?" Because it's more comfortable to talk about what's going on at the house. Because the house is in a lot better shape than I am most of the time.

> *Mr. Eggert, middle-level executive*

I always leave the business at the office when I go home. Always. When I leave the office, that's it. It really is. I don't know how I do it, but I do it. In the fifteen minutes it takes

me to get from office to home, that's it. I just put it out of
my mind. I don't even think about it. I don't like to relive
my business life blow-by-blow when I go home. I did it once
already.

Mr. Turner, partner in small business

To be sure, not all men compartmentalize the problems of work,
and most men have intervals in which, whatever their normal policy,
they share work concerns with their wives. But most men, most of the
time, are reluctant to do so.[1]

One reason men are reluctant to talk to their wives about their
work concerns is that such talk would dissipate whatever compartmentalization they are maintaining. The men would then become accessible to the anxieties of unresolved challenges and the pain of questionable actions or judgments. They would be prey to all the discomforts
lurking in the periphery of their thoughts.

Furthermore, home should be a refuge, a haven from the assaults
of the world. People apologize when they call a man at his home to talk
to him about work. And they should: Work worries are an intrusion into
the home. Some men want to safeguard their refuge.

There are still other reasons men keep their work worries to
themselves. Often a man will feel that just as it is his wife's part to deal
with home and children, it is his part to deal with work. And just as it
would be unfair for his wife to want him to take over child care, it would
be unfair for him to ask his wife's help with his work.

Mr. Hayes, head of a small business, explained in the following
way why he limited his discussion of work problems with his wife:

I have this client who is in financial trouble that I didn't
know was going to be in financial trouble. He owes me a lot
of money. And I can't get it straightened out. I told my wife
what the problem is, but there really isn't anything she can
do. This is a business matter, and that's the way it is.

I suppose it helped to talk about it. I was probably looking to
vent a little steam. Sally was sympathetic. Understanding. But
it's not her job. It's my job.

I try not to burden Sally with too many problems. If I have
something that's really bothering me, I'll say, "This is a pain
in the neck," or something like that. She'll say, "What're you
going to do about it?" And I'll say, "Well, this is what I think

I'm going to do about it." Period. That's all. I don't think a wife should be too concerned about what's going on. A wife has her own problems to worry about.

Some men avoid telling their wives about work difficulties because they believe their wives are too easily upset. Telling their wives about a difficulty at work would only make their wives anxious. Then the men would have two problems where before they had one.

Finally, there is the issue of self-respect. It can feel like an admission of incompetence, weakness, or immaturity to have to bring your problems home for your wife's help. You ought to be able to manage them yourself. Mr. Bartlett, now the business administrator of an academic institution, put it this way:

I don't tend to share small problems, like a problem at work. If it's something that troubles me a little bit, I had an argument with somebody or I did something that wasn't high quality or I was criticized, or whatever, that might take me a little while to come to grips with, I don't run home and start talking about it.

Men sometimes seem to feel that asking for their wives' support would weaken their confidence in themselves. It would demonstrate that they weren't up to handling their work by themselves. And suppose they did ask their wives for help, what if they then were to see doubt in their wives' eyes, along with solicitude? If that happened, they would have the burden of reestablishing their wives' belief in their competence. Much better not to disturb their wives' belief in them in the first place.[2]

However, men's embargo on news of work extends only to its tensions. Men who regularly compartmentalize their day's problems will be happy to report in detail the day's triumphs. Just as doing badly at work represents failing the marital partnership, doing well at work is a contribution to the marital partnership they are likely to want to have recognized. Telling their wives of a success, or even complaining of a job's demands in a way that demonstrates their mastery of their craft, is a way of strengthening their wives' belief in them.

Dr. Stevenson, a physicist who was among the first to move laser technology from laboratory to factory, often discussed his ideas with his wife. Although she had some technical background herself, she rarely understood his discussion fully; nevertheless, he felt reassured by her admiration, even though it might be uncomprehending.

> Sometimes I talk something I'm working on through with Kitty and sometimes I don't. But if there's anybody I talk things out to, it's her. I will try pieces out on her. Especially when I get some neat insight that really works out well, I'll try to bedazzle her with it.

Some men are so involved with their work, so enthusiastic about it, that they bring the enthusiasm home, like a gift. Mr. Abbott, a high-level technician, would come home late from his job still excited by the project on which he was working and wake up his wife to talk. His wife did not always take kindly to the role he expected her to play.

> You're so wound up, you get home, you don't want to go right to bed. Catherine's not sound asleep because I haven't got home. Or I'd get home at three in the morning and she's asleep and all of a sudden she wakes up and says, "You're home." And I'd start talking to her. I would tell her what's going on and what we're doing. And the trials and tribulations, the hard parts or the difficult parts of the job. How we combat it and how we get out of problems. And, naturally, where we ate or the kind of food they brought in. Catherine says a lot of times I talk too much about the company. She doesn't want to hear it. She says, "I'm bored! Talk to *me*."

Actually, Mrs. Abbott may have been imprecise in suggesting that her husband was not talking to her. Talking to her was exactly what Mr. Abbott was doing: talking to her to impress her and elicit her admiration and at the same time extend the high his work had produced. What Mr. Abbott was *not* doing was interacting. He wanted his wife to listen passively, a captive audience for his animated description of occupational adventure. What Mrs. Abbott wanted was to be talked *with* rather than *to*.

Indeed, when men become so caught up in their work that they think—and talk—of nothing else, they risk turning their wives off. Their wives cannot possibly care as much about their work as they do.

Mr. Cooper, the head of a firm that creates convention displays, was often under stress. Equally often he was totally absorbed by the creative challenge of his work. Adding to this challenge was an unpredictable cash flow and the constant need to obtain bank loans against accounts receivable. Mr. Cooper's preoccupation with his work was so great that work tended to dominate his conversation. His wife said:

> I have always known what was going on with him and his work. He talks about it all the time. It is foremost in his mind. He spends hours going back and forth about how he ought to approach one thing or another, how he ought to finance something, how he ought to plan something. He is consumed by his work. You start a conversation on X and you end up being back to his work: What am I going to do, where should we go, and so on. And there is a lot of tension. I think I have withdrawn to get away from the constant obsessing.

It should be noted that although Mr. Cooper fretted about his work to the point of obsession, he did not present himself to his wife as incompetent. Worried, yes. Often short-tempered. But at bottom thoroughly competent. Mr. Cooper, like other men, did not want his wife to think he was unable to do well in the world of work.

Still, men do not want their wives to think they do their work effortlessly. On the contrary, although men are ordinarily unwilling to talk about the stressful events of their work if doing so would interfere with compartmentalization, they are often willing to talk about how hard their day was and entirely willing to display their fatigue.

Fatigue and stress convey different messages about men's relationship to their work and their families. Weariness implies a long, hard day at work motivated by determination to provide for the family; stress implies challenges not fully met. Weariness implies selfless devotion; stress is more questionable. Weariness is an honorable affliction that justifies grateful attention; stress suggests being overmatched by the job.

In consequence, a man who tries to leave his worries at the office is entirely willing, on arrival home, to provide a display of fatigue that, although genuine, is also theater: a halting walk to the front door, a deep sigh on dropping his briefcase in the hall, a tired groping for a hanger for his coat, an utterly depleted collapse into a chair.

Despite themselves, men under stress also give evidence of their stress. They are preoccupied and so unable to give full attention to the family life around them. They respond to reasonable requests with irritation because they feel their resources have already been overextended. They need their wives' indulgence but cannot explain why. At night they are likely to have problems sleeping. They may drink a beer or a glass of warm milk or stay up watching television. Nevertheless, they have trouble getting to sleep or they awaken in the middle of the night and cannot return to sleep.

Men are often aware that, despite their best efforts, they have not been able to leave their troubles behind when they leave the office.

I'm sure I have brought stress home from work. I don't think that it happens that frequently. I try to lock it in the drawer at night, to maintain some separation. But I'm sure there are times when I come home and it's because of something that has happened at work that I act differently. I may be a little shorter with the kids. Or I have even said to the kids, "Look, I'm in no mood for any of your horsing around tonight. Just tread lightly. Don't push it tonight." I warn them ahead of time.

Mr. Orcutt, middle-level manager

I try to isolate my work problems from my family. With mixed results. Once in a while I bring them home, to the real detriment of my family life. Usually I don't. Usually I'm a little happier or a little sadder at night, depending on whether the day went a little better or a little worse. But I can certainly think of some examples, hopefully not more than one a year or two a year, where extreme frustration has found its way into my doing unnecessary yelling at my family, or acting in an extremely crotchety manner to build family stress where it shouldn't have happened.

Mr. Metzger, production manager

A situation that is perfectly normal and next to nothing—something happens with a kid—I may go into a tailspin over it. I might boil up or boil over. Norma will then fly up and say, "You are not treating them fairly." And then it will come out that at that particular point I was up to my eyebrows with the damned business and I just wasn't relaying that. In fact, I was keeping that in. Or I would wrestle with a problem to the point of I would be eating supper and interacting with the kids and gradually tune out and disappear. I would be physically there, but I would just be out of it.

Mr. Cox, owner of a small business

Men sometimes are aware that they have not succeeded in their attempts to hide their stress from their wives. For example, Mr. White, an executive in a large insurance firm, after a few months in which he had tried to hide from his wife his quite high level of stress, learned that she had been able to read the signs right along.

The story, beginning with an evaluation that criticized Mr. White's ability to lead, is told in the first chapter. Not long after the evaluation, Mr. White's firm disbanded his department as a cost-cutting measure. For three months Mr. White had nothing to do. Although he had been assured he would be reassigned, Mr. White experienced a level of stress too high to be managed by compartmentalization. Nevertheless, Mr. White tried to protect his wife by understating his anxiety.

> I haven't wanted Dolores to worry needlessly so I haven't painted a *totally* dismal picture. I'd say she is aware of the fact that people are leaving. I have no indication that Dolores is thinking about it. She's never indicated to me that she does. She's aware of the fact that X, Y, Z have left. But I haven't told her point blank that I spend a lot of time thinking about this. I haven't really gotten down to basics with her.

Two months later Mr. White acknowledged that he had not been able to hide his stress:

> My wife knew. I'd come home and she could just see me walking up the driveway and she could tell. I tried to shake it off walking from the bus home, a seven-minute walk. I tried to psych myself up, throw everything behind me. But I'd walk in and she would see right through me.

Mr. White's inability to hide his stress from his wife may have been of benefit to her in that it prepared her for what followed. Mr. White was reassigned to a new and important position, as had been promised, but after a few months a younger man was brought in to whom Mr. White was required to report. Mr. White remained in his job a few more months and then took early retirement.

Interviews with men's wives suggest that they usually knew when their husbands were experiencing stress. They might not know the reason for the stress, but they would recognize its symptoms.[3] One woman, married to a middle-level executive, said that she could estimate by dinnertime, if not before, how severe her husband's stress was. If the day had gone badly he would be snappish when he got home and taut at the dinner table. It was more difficult to guess what had led to the stress, but she would sometimes overhear a telephone conversation or be the recipient of a brief comment that would provide a clue. Still, she resented having to work out what was bothering her husband from overheard telephone talk and cryptic comments. She understood that she was being asked to provide blind support, but she felt she was being treated as a subordinate rather than a partner.

Often, instead of being grateful for being saved from worry by their husbands' reticence, men's wives were annoyed. They disliked being protected from worry when what that really meant was that they knew something was going on but did not know what and were helpless to influence it.

Mr. Cox sold and serviced typewriters. Unexpectedly his sales of new equipment were hurt by competition from computers. At the same time his repair work suffered because of the appearance of inexpensive electronic typewriters. He tried to protect his family from his business worries, but failed. His wife resented his effort. In a joint interview Mr. Cox said:

> I thought my business was so secure that I actually went out and borrowed money for expansion. And then all of a sudden it fell off. And I got very concerned about that. So I'm saying to Norma, "Don't spend any extra money this week," or "Try and cut down this month." My feeling is that she can help me more by dealing with those things than she can by crawling into all the details of my business. Which I judge she would like to know more about, and I basically don't feel that it is necessary for her to.

> I don't find that working out my problems with somebody else is my most successful way. I can't explain a damned thing to myself, let alone explain it to somebody else. And somebody else will pick up on something that I don't want to spend time on and I get very frustrated. I might not discuss the situation with Norma until I'm really looking for a double

check on what my final resolution is. If we are talking ten stages in resolving the problem, I'm almost at the ninth stage.

Norma gets angry as hell over this. She doesn't feel I'm sharing my life with her. I like to think I'm doing her a favor, that she really wouldn't want to have this to wrestle with.

Mrs. Cox listened quietly to her husband and then said:

He is so proud, telling people that he works things out himself and he doesn't worry his family. If he's got a difficulty he sits and ponders and he works it out and then when he has it all worked out, then he shares it with us. Well, that really isn't the case. Because what happens is, [if] he has a problem, whatever it is, whether it is a business slowdown or a difficult supplier or whatever, he just is a *bear*. He is a bear to live with until he has it worked out.

I can be supportive by shutting up and playing music or by not playing music or by staying home or leaving home or whatever. But it is very difficult when something is going on in his head, where he is trying to work something out, but if that process is interrupted, then he can be very infuriated. But if we say, "What is the problem?" he will say, "What do you mean, what is the problem? The hose was left out." Well, that isn't the problem. It would be nice if he could say, "I'm so fried over this supplier because he is not cooperating." "All right, would you like to talk about it?" "No." "Well, fine, but if you do, fine, I'll listen."[4]

Even when men are aware that they are completely preoccupied by a work issue and unable to attend to anything else, they may feel themselves to be behaving properly, and so feel a bit more in control, if they haven't had to admit their concern to their wives. There is a cost to men in admitting to their wives that something at work is proving more than they can manage.[5]

In dual-career marriages wives sometimes appear unaware when their husbands are under stress, although their apparent insensitivity may as often be a refusal to involve themselves as a failure to observe. In these marriages wives too are coping with work stress and may in addition carry the bulk of responsibility for child care and home maintenance. They may have all they can manage already, without attending to their husbands' problems. But this means that along with too little time for everything, another troublesome problem in dual-career marriages may be each partner's inability to respond to the other's work-produced stress.

Mr. Layton and his wife both have demanding positions. Mr. Layton is in charge of an investment group in an insurance firm; his wife is a vice president of a large home sales firm. The Laytons do not have children. Mr. Layton said:

> We went through a period that I was bringing home work. I used to come home and complain. And I just had to shut it off. Holly didn't want to hear it. And I don't blame her. She said, "Hey, I had a pretty bad day too." And she did. She was under a lot of pressure. Holly is working just as hard as I am, I'm sure.
>
> I have learned to keep Holly on the upbeat. It is different, coming home at eight o'clock and saying, "Damn it, I've had it," and you sit and rage and rave. But if you come home at eight o'clock and say, "I had a good day! Do you know who I was involved with today?" immediately, she is on the upbeat. I try and bring home only those things that are positive.
>
> She has rough days too. There are some nights when she will sit there and talk about her day and I'm thinking, "Oh, my God, she thinks this is important." I don't mean to put it that way. But she does the same thing. Rightly so. And so I try to keep it on the upbeat.

As Mr. Layton's comment suggests, men in dual-career marriages may not only regret their wives' inability to be consistently responsive to them but also their own inability to be fully available to their wives. Nevertheless, preoccupation with the threats and challenges of one's own work situation can make it impossible to give full attention to the threats and challenges of the partner's.

Emotional distance can be a second reason for wives—and husbands as well—to make little effort to be supportive of their partners. Mr. Ellis, an accountant, and his wife, a part-time human service professional, maintained a marriage of edgy separateness. Mr. Ellis said:

When I'm stressed she's sympathetic, I guess. There's been physical pain or mental pain, and sometimes it gets talked about. And sometimes, I suppose, it's ignored, not talked about. Forgotten. I don't know if she even knows.

She is under stress a lot because she has arthritis. She has some amount of discomfort, a certain amount of limitation. How much pain I don't know.

Stress affects everybody differently. It may be very serious to me and she may not recognize it. Or I may not recognize it in her. It's the type of thing: "What's bothering you?" "Oh, nothing."

Some men who successfully keep their stress states to themselves do so with their wives' collusion. But men feel more comfortable when they believe their wives would like to hear their troubles and it is their own choice not to share them.

Often men want their wives' support but do not want to ask for it. Asking for help, for many men, is admitting to inadequacy. The trick, for men's wives, is to recognize their husbands' need without requiring their husbands to feel needful. Should the wives themselves be preoccupied, distant, or angry, their husbands' unvoiced appeal is easily ignored.[6]

THE KIND OF SUPPORT MEN SEEK

Just as membership in a community of work is necessary to men's well-being, so is family membership. Simply having a home and family waiting for them after work tells men that outside the workplace as well as within it they have a place, an identity, and meaning to others. Men's wives are supportive merely by being there. The shopping, cooking, and cleaning that tend to be the wives' responsibilities, in addition to freeing the men's time for work, assure the men that there are others who are invested in them and to whom they, in turn, are responsible.

In consequence, men can feel supported by their wives and families even without interacting with them very much. Mr. Leverett, vice president of an electronics firm, regularly worked late in the evening and sometimes around the clock, a schedule that had led several times to marital quarrels. Nevertheless, Mr. Leverett's wife provided him with a home, and this alone helped sustain his morale.

Depending on how late I get home, home may just be a place to come to and go to bed after everybody else has gone to bed and is asleep. But the family is supportive. I'm home and I'm tired and everybody understands it and so, while they are not happy or delighted about my not having been there for dinner, I don't get beat up about it either.

The family would like more time. I count on their understanding the problems that I'm struggling with. My wife says, "When are you going to get unburied?" It's a problem for her, the lack of the husband and father. There are questions, particularly if it's on a weekend. "Where were you?" or "What were we going to do over the weekend that got scrubbed?" There are hard feelings. I guess if there weren't, I would be disappointed in that I'd feel nobody cares whether I'm around or not.

Support of this sort is provided to all men who are married and have families. To be sure, it is in some cases provided with friction, and grudgingly. And yet, even in unhappy marriages, men can find confirmation in having a home and in meeting the responsibilities of a husband and father.

Despite their policy of leaving the problems of work at work, men do sometimes seek their wives' counsel. They may want to talk through a new venture and feel that only their wives are available to them, or that only their wives can be trusted. Or they may stumble into sharing their concerns; in the course of telling their wives innocuous gossip they allude to matters of genuine concern and then, in response to their wives' encouragement, admit their uncertainties.

Men are especially likely to seek their wives' counsel when they are troubled by issues of human relations. Relations with others are, as was pointed out in an earlier chapter, a primary source of work stress. But relational issues may seem to men to be outside their sphere of competence. Because they are not matters men feel they should be expected to handle expertly, men may be less diffident about bringing them to their wives. They also believe that their wives are more concerned than they with maintaining and managing relationships, both inside the home and out. People and their lives are more their wives' domain.

I share stuff which I can sense she can be helpful on: more in the people area than the technology area. I am more of an engineer and she's more of a human type person. She is more interpersonally sensitive, where I'm more analytic. And so she tries to give me her views and help me in that side of the operation.

Occasionally we'll have people conflicts at work, and I can share with her what's going on and she can share with me, "Gee, you could do this and make the person feel better, as opposed to if you do that, it is probably going to aggravate them." Little things. Although I try to be sensitive to people, in fact in many areas I'm blind to what other people might feel.

Dr. Bentwood, engineer

Dr. Braden, a nuclear engineer, had been married for more than twenty years to a woman who was a pharmaceutical chemist. Although she too was technically trained, Dr. Braden asked her advice almost exclusively about interpersonal issues.

When we were first married I thought it would be impossible to describe my work because my work was engineering and Grace was not an engineer. And I forced myself to describe something that had happened and how I felt about it, putting the engineering aspects of it into laymen's terms. And I was amazed to find that I could do it and I could always do it. That helped me, because I could talk about things with somebody I really trusted, my wife. And she's bright. She's a Ph.D. pharmaceutical chemist.

Once in a while somebody will get under your skin at work. I would tell my wife what was going on and she would understand. She is pretty supportive in that way. I would describe the problem and say, "This fellow said this." And she would say, "Well, he's really telling you that he just doesn't accept you as a person, let alone your opinion." And I would think about that and say, "Gee, you might be right." And that would help me to deal with that individual in the future.

Men's belief that their wives are their superiors in dealing with others should not be taken at face value. Many of the men who maintain this belief are successful managers and administrators. To do their jobs they must be able to appraise others and anticipate their performance in various circumstances. But it may be that the men focus their attention almost solely on personality characteristics that they believe affect ability to contribute in a work setting: competence, loyalty, and trustworthiness as a subordinate, peer, or supervisor. And they are alert to characteristics that affect ability to respond to challenge: persistence and ability to function under pressure. Indeed, when men talk with each other they will sometimes offer assessments, perhaps guardedly, perhaps not, of men with whom they have worked, especially their competence, but also their style and their traits. What they are less good at is how to respond to hurt feelings, how to deal with someone whose home life is troubled, how to understand emotions unrelated to getting things done. The men's wives may be not so much more sensitive as less blinkered.

Men will also consult—or at least inform—their wives should they be considering resignation or planning a confrontation at work that might lead to loss of job. They do so because, first, they believe their wives have a right to know. But they may also want to be sure that their wives understand the situation well enough, and are committed to them strongly enough, so that they need not fear recriminations should things go badly.

Mr. Metzger, who was under ordinary circumstances adamant about not talking with his wife about his work, said:

> It's not to say I've *never* talked to Doris about my work. I have, on occasion. It probably happened, in eleven years, on two or three occasions where I got in a severe argument with my boss where I felt my pride was attacked. I would talk it over with Doris, and she always gave me the same advice, that we would get by, no matter what I make. I appreciated that type of advice. Even though it may not have been the right decision, it was very supportive.
>
> I know that careerwise I can do anything I want and Doris will support it. And that is extremely important to me. I don't think I would be able to exist in the household otherwise.

It was not actually his wife's counsel Mr. Metzger wanted when he was considering quitting his job. Rather, he wanted to be sure that he would retain his wife's respect whatever he did. He wanted her vote of confidence.

Occasionally men genuinely want counsel. A few men appear to be beneficiaries of two-person careers to which their wives contribute significantly as silent and unnoted partners. Kirsty McLeod believes that the success of many British prime ministers was due as much to their wives' contributions as to their own efforts.[7] This sort of arrangement seems much less frequent among men like those of this book. It does, however, occur now and again. Mr. Linnell, a middle-level executive in an architectural firm sometimes had his wife's help in planning his career.

> My wife is a hell of a strategist. She can contribute some good ideas to me. And when she is interested she is a good sounding board about how things are going and what I am doing about it. How much she is interested varies. I think it depends on what she's got on her mind. And also on how close she is feeling to me at any given time.

Some men find that they want their wives' counsel only for such significant issues as shifting jobs. Mr. Ryder, at that time a scientific administrator, had been offered an attractive job in a field new to him. It would be a good time for him to make a move: his children were grown and no longer needed his attention. He wanted a chance to do more than his current job permitted. But he worried about the risks of going with the new company. His current position was thoroughly safe, if unchallenging, and he was reluctant to relinquish its security. He and his wife gave a good deal of time to talking about the decision.

> We talked about it all the time. One of our favorite things is, we have a block here that is, from my house around the block and back, almost a mile. And we usually take a walk after dinner, and we talk about different things. This is something that we hashed over many times.

When we last saw Mr. Ryder he had taken the new job. He said that he was working harder than he had at his previous job but enjoying the work more. He did worry, at times, about his competence in the new field. Still, the job was developing in the way he and his wife had expected. And having talked over all the risks of the new job with his wife, Mr. Ryder felt less vulnerable now to disappointing her should it not work out.

SEVERE STRESS AND NEED FOR
HELP

Everything to this point describes the way men function under reasonably normal circumstances. Many men have times, perhaps only one or two in their adult lives, when things go very badly for them. Then they fear not only failing in some limited way but entirely losing their place in the world of their work. Their level of stress is severe. At such times men may need to talk with their wives about their situations. Asking his wife for help may, perhaps, damage a man's self-esteem, but when stress is severe enough this becomes a secondary matter.

One man who was constantly in conflict with a supervisor he thought was trying to make him quit said that he talked regularly to his wife to ensure that he wouldn't physically attack the supervisor. After he moved to another job, he returned to his earlier policy of keeping his work life to himself.

Another man, unemployed for a time, said that his wife's support had been indispensable. She had been unflagging in her belief that he would find a place for himself. He added that he would always be grateful to his wife. This statement of gratitude both acknowledged his wife's help and suggested that under ordinary circumstances he did not require it.

Mr. Stavros, an engineer and businessman, had been extraordinarily successful in bringing his firm to a yearly billing of hundreds of millions of dollars. In the belief that his company's financial situation was secure, he began to give his attention to the development of a radically new product. The new directors of the company made errors, the business climate changed, and the company became financially troubled. Mr. Stavros resumed control of the company. But for a time he seemed to have lost the knack of making things work.

I was working to finish a project and there was a swing in the economy and the down risk became enormous. And things that I did were wrong. It created one of the worst stress situations I have faced in the last twenty years.

It manifested itself in my not being able to sleep. I usually can sleep very easily. And I can sleep at odd hours. If I have fifteen minutes, I can fall asleep. I also sleep more than average for my age group: I sleep eight hours; the average is seven. And I need that. Sleep is for me a tremendous release of tension.

When I get to the point where I go to bed and I start thinking, and it is two o'clock and then three o'clock, I know I'm in trouble. That happened twice to me in the last four months. There were two periods that lasted for about five or six days when I couldn't sleep. My wife was very helpful, very supportive.

In the last twenty years every time I couldn't sleep at night, I'd tiptoe out of the room at three o'clock in the morning and try to have a warm drink. And my wife would get up and we'd start discussing other things. Tennis. She knows how to change the subject. She doesn't ask me what's wrong with me, because she knows. And so we change the topic of conversation. She's done that every time that I'm having a psychological problem.

Mr. Stavros and his wife seem to have had an unstated understanding. When his stress level became so high that he could not sleep, Mr. Stavros would leave his bed quietly enough so that his wife could choose to resist being awakened. His wife would then rouse herself and join him in the kitchen. But that was her choice; he had not asked her to keep him company. Then, by not trying to discuss whatever was keeping Mr. Stavros awake, she reassured him of her trust as well as her affection.

Men who are depressed by their situations, or barely fending off depression, may want something different from their wives. They may want their wives to help them sustain their morale, to reassure them that though the immediate situation appears hopeless, they will yet be successful, and in the meantime their wives are their allies.

Mr. Moss, an account executive in an industrial consulting organization, at one point displayed a mixed picture of stress symptoms and depression.

I was depressed. I don't know whether it was a midlife crisis or what. I just felt as though I didn't have much command over my life. I didn't sleep well. I got very anxious.

My wife was really available and supportive. I never forget that. That's when I *really* needed her. When I'm feeling fine and capable and basically able to run my life, I wouldn't want to be without her, but I don't *need* her. At that time I really needed her. And she was available. And that really is worth a lot.

I'd wake up at two o'clock in the morning. I couldn't sleep. Andrea had said to me, "If you want to talk to me, you can wake me up. It's all right, you can wake me up." And I did. And she was responsive. And I know how much she likes to sleep. And I know she doesn't like her sleep disturbed under ordinary circumstances. And all of those things were not issues.

Ordinarily men's sexual strivings diminish when the men are under stress. But attachment needs and the desire for comfort and touch are pathways to sexual feelings.

As a matter of fact, it was during that time that our last child was conceived. He wasn't planned. But it was really because we were closer and she was much more available and so on.

One decision Mr. Moss made at that time was to begin taking night classes in the law. A few years later he had obtained his law degree but had not yet taken the bar examination. By then he had become worried about the security of his job. He felt that younger people in the firm ignored him. (The incident is described in an earlier chapter.) He suspected that the agency head wanted him out. His workload had become extremely heavy, but his requests for additional staff had been denied. His wife's reaction was helpful.

I have been complaining about the fact that I am over-whelmed. I come home and I say, "I really don't know if I can keep this job. I just can't stand it. It is just too much." And instead of saying, "Well, don't worry, dear," or "It's only temporary," Andrea says, "Well, maybe you really should give that thought. Take another job." That's a totally new ap-proach. Because I'm not really ready to quit my job. But she's honest. This is not a ploy. She really means it. She says, "Well, if the job is that terrible . . . " That is her attitude about life.

What happens to me then is I feel supported. Because I have that option. And then I say, "Oh, no, I can't do that." I mean, this is absolutely one of the best jobs that anybody could have and still live in this area and be in my field. And it's an interesting job basically. So I end up saying to her, "Look, I may not be able to keep the job, but I certainly will never quit it." And so that takes care of that.

Eventually Mr. Moss was told he would be released from the firm at the end of the contract on which he was working. Rather than search for another position in the same field he decided to turn to a career in the law. But he worried that he would not earn nearly as much money. Again his wife was supportive:

The possibility that I shouldn't be earning adequately bothers me a great deal. We do have a couple of dependent children. It is not only putting away money for our own retirement, which we have been trying to do, but also giving our children as much as possible and trying to get some money for *their* education.

If I go into the legal profession I will probably not earn as much. And all of the benefits are gone. If there is a snowstorm you don't get paid. If you have a sore throat you don't get paid. And there is no vacation, no sick leave, no holidays and no retirement. And no Blue Cross. None of that. I keep telling my wife that. And she says, "Don't worry about it. You'll be all right."

She is quite supportive along these lines. I don't have the additional burden of having her worry about what is going to happen. She says, "Look, we can get along on less, and I'm still working, and you'll do as much as you can. And you'll build up, maybe."

By her responses Mr. Moss's wife gave Mr. Moss the reassurance he needed: She approved of him as a partner despite his problems in his work. She still respected him, and so he could continue to respect himself.

TWO CASES

Two executives had quite similar problems with their bosses. One of them reviewed his situation with his wife and was heartened by her response. The other did not tell his wife what had happened, because when he had done so in the past her response had been dismaying.

The account of Mr. Reynolds's fight with his boss was given in an earlier chapter. Mr. Reynolds was head of the design department of a large manufacturing firm. After a quarrel, his boss had attempted to get him fired, but he had been protected by the chief of operations. He said that at the time of the quarrel he had been under enormous stress: "Beat up . . . my gastric juices started to work . . . "

> I talked a lot to my wife during that time. And what she said was, "I know you and I know how valuable you are, how good you are. And I also know that we can make it no matter what we do." And that just really made me feel good. There was less at stake then after she said that.

Mr. Reynolds's wife's reaction in no way changed his situation on the job. But more was at stake for Mr. Reynolds initially than simply holding the job and retaining his integrity. In addition, he was responsible for protecting his family from distress. When his wife said that she would continue to trust him as a husband no matter what he did, he was relieved of the concern that in her eyes he was failing in his responsibility to his family by endangering his job.

The second executive, Mr. Davis, was head of quality control in a firm almost as large as Mr. Reynolds's. He too came under attack from a superior. In contrast to Mr. Reynolds, he said nothing about the attack because he was convinced his wife would not come through for him.

> My boss has a staff meeting Monday mornings at eight o'clock and that is when we get together and he tells us about things that have been going on. There may be six or eight people at the meeting, maybe something like that. And this particular staff meeting we had a discussion of quality control. And he said that quality control costs were just completely getting out of hand. Costs were about fifty percent over original estimates.
>
> We knew this problem had been boiling up. It was just a question of time before it got to the point where people would want to know what happened. So it was mostly making sure that our story was clear. Manufacturing always has the feeling that we are protecting our ass by identifying problems.

But we've been doing this job for quite some time, and we do have a track record.

The minute I understood what was being said I said, "Look, the reason quality control is so expensive is because you've introduced changes. Let's see if we can't redesign to improve reliability."

Mr. Davis said that he had not told his wife what had happened. He was sure that if he had, her reaction would have been unhelpful.

Sue's reaction is to rail at how can my boss be so goddamned stupid. She'll want to get in and try to problem-solve.

So I don't, quite often, tell her that much about work. Because what happens is, I'll tell her about a particular situation and she will jump in and want to solve it without really knowing enough about the problem to solve it. And I'll find myself in a position of having to comment on it in some way. Her expectations from me would be, "Sue, that is a good idea; we can do it." And I can't find the right way to say, "Sue, I don't think it is going to work because there is another factor that I haven't told you about." And what will generally happen is that she'll be angry because she is feeling that I'm being negative to her solutions. And so I just find myself not telling her that much about work.

Mr. Davis respected his wife's intelligence and acknowledged that she knew enough about his work to make constructive suggestions. But his need from her was not for advice but rather, before anything else, for solicitude.

There is a part of me that would like to have tea and sympathy and more mothering and whatever. And I don't feel that I get much of that.

When Mr. Davis's wife offered him help in solving his problems, not only did she not respond to his need for solicitude but she implied that he might not be capable of managing without help.

Sometimes husbands and wives are aware that helping each other by problem-solving can be no help at all. Mrs. Cox, wife of the owner of the typewriter store, contrasted how she and her husband had behaved toward each other in the early days of their marriage with the way they behaved toward each other now:

> I think back when we were both working, we both had such different jobs. I would tell him some things that were happening. But he wasn't then turning around and telling me what to do about it. He was listening. And I certainly couldn't tell him what to do because I didn't understand his work. But now we tend to tell each other how to handle it. "Rather than such and such, why don't you try such and such?" So now there is sort of a wall there.

Dismissive problem-solving of this sort can be practiced by either sex, with the same consequences for the partner. But dismissive problem-solving seems to be practiced more often by husbands than by wives. Husbands are more likely than wives to feel responsible for the management of problems in the spouse's life. Also, husbands are more apt than wives to find that just listening, without doing anything, makes them feel passive, helpless in the face of threat.

The result is that the man who is asked by his wife to listen to an interpersonal problem is likely to analyze the problem quickly, list the options, suggest advantages of one option or another, and urge his wife to choose a course of action. The man now feels he has done well; he has dealt with the problem. His wife is likely to feel less pleased: While the man's analysis may be entirely correct, the validity of her concern has not been acknowledged, and her own efforts to deal with the problem have not been respected. She has not been fully listened to.

CHAPTER
SIX
_____

Marriage

MARRIAGE AND RESPONSIBILITY

When men who have been married fifteen or twenty years are asked how marriage has changed their lives, their first thought is apt to be of lost freedom. No longer can they go anywhere and do anything. Not for them, now, are James Bond adventures of risk and exciting new women. Marriage has fettered them with bills and chores and responsibilities. But this first thought is quickly rejected. By marrying they have given up empty fantasies, but in exchange they have gained the solid reality of a home, a wife, and children.

When asked how his life would be different if he hadn't married, Mr. Brewer, for example, offered first the usual male fantasy of freedom and then acknowledged that the reality of unmarried life would be much chillier:

> If I weren't married I'd probably have one hell of a time. I'd probably spend my summers in Newport and my winters on the Caribbean.

> But being real truthful with you, if I had never married, much as I wouldn't want to admit it, I'd probably be lonesome with life. Because I know quite a few guys that got divorced and what it really comes down to, a lot of them go home at night to a cold home.

Mr. Metzger, the production manager, said:

I have my fantasies, I'm not denying it. I would be a big ladies' man and a jet setter. Maybe I'd live on the Riviera.

We all have those kinds of fantasies. But that's all they are, fantasies. I do have dreams occasionally where I picture myself an unmarried bachelor. There would certainly be less worry. Less worry, but less joy.

Mr. Patrick, a sales manager in his mid-fifties, put the same rueful repudiation of fantasy in slightly different terms: Maybe, if he were younger, it would be fun to be single.

The idea of going out with different girls and so forth would be fun, but I think that it would not be as much fun or as comfortable as being married. I think that being single would put a big strain on me. I don't like to be alone. I am quite sure I would not prefer to be single. Especially not now, not at this age. If you had asked me fifteen years ago, maybe ten years ago, I might have answered that differently. Not now.

But men who *are* younger, in their thirties, also disclaim attraction to the freedom—including the sexual freedom—they ascribe to the world of singles. They too say that it might be all right if they were younger, but not now. They agree with men in their forties and fifties: That kind of freedom is really irresponsibility and, though it might be all right for men who are immature, is not for them.

The responsibilities of marriage that limit freedom provide, by the same token, structure and stability. With marriage and, even more, fatherhood, men become family men, heads of families, with a stake in their neighborhoods and a place in their communities. Marriage gives purpose to their daily activities and meaning to their lives.

I don't know what it would be like if I hadn't found Myra. From what I see or hear about what's going on out in the singles world out there, I don't think I'd enjoy it today. Maybe if I were fifteen years younger I might enjoy it. But today, I don't know.

Without Myra I'd have someplace to live, I'd still have a job, but what I would do with my life I don't know.

> *Mr. Orcutt, middle-level manager in his late thirties*

Loss of freedom can itself sometimes be of value to men. The responsibilities of marriage can provide justification for their overlooking affronts at work that might otherwise require response. Awareness of their commitments to a home and family can make it possible for them to tolerate minor slights and conflicts on the job without having to ask themselves why they put up with them.

> If I hadn't married I might have moved before this. I don't think I would have put up with a lot of the things that I have gone through. I have been ready to go in with my resignation on more than one occasion. And then Holly would throw out buzz words like "mortgage," "food," that sort of thing. That has an impact on my decision. If I were young and single I definitely would have made a move.
>
> *Mr. Layton, middle-level executive*

The responsibilities of marriage do limit men's freedom. But these same responsibilities provide men with stability, with a home, with a sense of maturity and a sense of purpose. The *state* of being married, quite apart from the marital relationship and all it provides, is valuable enough to men to ensure that few who are married would willingly return to being single.

MARRIAGE, REGULATION AND MARITAL CONCERNS

More than any of their other relationships, men's marriages structure their lives. Within their marriages, men and their wives establish times to go to sleep and to awaken, to have meals and to join with friends. They establish a rhythm of work and relaxation, of sociability and solitude. With each other they establish a community of thought and speech and feeling.

Marriage can be seen as a relationship of mutual regulation, in which the partners keep each other on an even keel. Although men whose marriages are going well will feel "in tune with" their wives or "on the same wavelength," much of the mutual regulation of marriage takes place out of the partners' awareness.[1] That the marriage is essential to the well-being of each is likely to be noted only at times of separation, as when work or family responsibilities require that one of them go out of town. And even then the men and their wives may not be sure why, when they are apart, life seems slightly askew.

Men join with their wives in appraisals of people and things. They may begin in disagreement, but often enough shared perceptions emerge. Men also establish with their wives a view of themselves which, because it is shared, is less easily affected by events outside the home. Insofar as men can rely on their wives to support their belief in their own competence and essential worth, they can withstand, for a time, limited success on the job and the consequent skepticism of colleagues. They can, for a time, fend off self-doubt.

As has been shown, much of the way in which men bring their work home is motivated by a desire to protect their wives' belief in their essential competence. It is to this end that men tell their wives about their successes at work but are otherwise uncommunicative, and for this reason that they minimize their tensions and anxieties while making dramatic display of their fatigue. Men need their wives to see them as competent because their wives' view of them is so important to their view of themselves.

Marriage's mutual regulation of feeling and percept occurs constantly, whatever the issue at hand, whether it is washing dishes together or discussing a teenager's behavior. It is expressed in tone of voice, in looking or not looking, in touch and bodily posture, as well as in what is said and how it is said. It is a never ceasing subtext of marital events, occurring irrespective of the manifest content of interaction.

MARRIAGE AND THE COURSE
OF MEN'S LIVES

Men who marry young are likely to bring to their marriages hopes as yet only half-formed. Their ambitions are vague, and it is only in the marital partnership that their hopes become plans. Men who marry at a later age may do so with the enterprise that is their lives already charted, and assume that their wives have signed on as first mates. These men are headed for careers as engineers or businessmen, or are already physicians or architects, and before their marriages their wives' roles and responsibilities may already be specified in the men's minds; the men could, if pressed, write a job description. But marriages are interactive, and husbands must also accommodate to the life enterprises that are their wives'. The marital partnership, even when men intend that it will help them proceed along the course they have plotted, is likely to decide, at the least, the pace of progress; it may well modify the course itself.

Mr. Gilman, a man in his late forties, is a land use planner and economist. He has taught at first-rate universities and now heads a successful firm. He is a forceful although pleasant man who has always known what he wanted to do. Nevertheless his marriage has not only facilitated the development of his life; it has also shaped it.

After college, where he had enrolled in ROTC, Mr. Gilman entered the Air Force. He was assigned to Europe. His college girl-friend, an art history major, decided to do postgraduate work at a European school not far from Mr. Gilman's base. They spent all their free time together anyway, so it seemed a good idea to get married. After his discharge from the military Mr. Gilman remained in Europe so his wife could continue her studies. He registered for graduate work at a school whose program in economics was internationally recognized. He didn't like it.

> I spent two weeks at the place where I had applied to study and I said to my wife, "If I spend a year in this place I'm going to go bonkers." It was a superb economics department, but it was too far away from what I wanted, which is dealing with the problems of planning. So I walked into a college that had a major planning emphasis and I said to the head of the school, "If you're looking for a teacher, I've got a deal you can't possibly refuse. You can't pay me, because of the currency restrictions"—at the time you couldn't pay somebody from outside the country without all kinds of qualifications— "but if you need a teacher, I'm available."

Mr. Gilman got the job. A year later, when he and his wife returned to the United States, his having taught in Europe helped win him a graduate fellowship. But it was his wife's employment that really made it possible for him to go to graduate school. (Wives who work while their husbands complete graduate or professional training some-times say that they themselves are in the Ph.T. Program—Putting Hubby Through.)

> Then when we came back to the United States I was return-ing to graduate school and my wife was offered a job teaching in a good suburban school. Which was quite a plum, because

you didn't normally get a teaching job there unless you were a very, very good teacher.

Mr. Gilman's life seemed to be launched on an orderly and predictable course when it was unexpectedly redirected by one of the not entirely controllable contingencies of married life: a pregnancy.

About a year later we discovered she was pregnant. And so the teaching position which was going to keep us living, not on Easy Street, but I had the GI Bill and we would have her salary, suddenly we had the GI Bill and not her salary. So I figured I better get a job.

I was able to get a very interesting job with a land planning group. I walked in and they hired me because they knew who I was and what I could do. And, literally the next day, I was the job captain on a very significant project.

The marital partnership is, obviously, not only helpful—more or less, depending on the particular marriage—but also fateful. Though his wife and the children he has with her may never appear at a man's place of work, they may have helped decide what work the man will do, where, and when. And the man's responsibilities to his wife and children will help decide how much of his energy he can give to his work and how much risk he can take with his career. With marriage a man's life becomes a joint enterprise, no longer subject to his sole control.

THE ACTIVITIES OF MARRIAGE

The actual activities that bring husbands and wives together can have any of three different premises. Husbands and wives regularly must work together to manage the business of the home. Sometimes husbands and wives do things together because they enjoy each other's company. And sometimes they want to be near each other because each needs to know the other is accessible to feel that all's right with the world.

Before children are born, and after they leave home, marriages function much of the time as companionships, with husbands and wives enjoying being together, as they might enjoy being with any of their friends. Once there are children, marriage is primarily a partnership, like a business partnership, but concerned with the totality of life rather than only with earning an income. And, perhaps especially at times of stress, but at other times as well, marriages function as attachments, providing each partner with reassurance of emotional linkage to a trusted other and, with it, reassurance of security. As an attachment figure, a man's wife is someone to whom he is so deeply linked that her presence makes him invulnerable to loneliness; his linkage to her permits him to feel emotionally complete.[2]

At any one time it is likely that only one set of assumptions will underlie marital interaction, resulting in one set of concerns and one way of talking and feeling. The married pair will be working together, enjoying a conversation, or just being in the same space. But there always is spillover into other aspects of the marriage. Working together, while it is concerned with getting things done, is also an opportunity for companionship and for reassurance of attachment. Tension in one area is apt to diffuse: A dispute over who does the dishes can make for a silent drive to a party and a sense, during the party, of having been abandoned. Good feelings also diffuse: Working together well may help spouses enjoy each other after the work is done and also help foster the trust required for security.

MARRIAGE AS PARTNERSHIP

Most marital interaction deals with issues of partnership, large and small: when to have children; whether to use the money in the bank for a vacation; who will take the car in for servicing. Couples raising children together may have few discussions not concerned with partnership issues.

The understandings that inform the partnership aspect of marriage are similar to those that would be found between business partners. True, a man's life is a larger and vaguer enterprise than a business. But the woman to whom the man is married contributes to his life's stability of purpose, works for its success, and so deserves a share of its rewards, just as would a business partner.

Critical to the marital partnership is the decision of who does what—what will be the contributions of the man and of his wife to the joint enterprise that is the marital partnership?

The question of who does which of the chores required to keep a house orderly, the children fed, and the bills paid has lately been an area of skirmishing in that longest of wars, the War Between the Sexes.[3]

It was not, however, considered an especially troubling question by the men with whom we spoke. Virtually all of them believed that they and their wives together had established a division of marital labor that worked well enough; it was usually clear what each was to do; there rarely were arguments over tasks left undone. Most indicated that they and their wives were each grateful to the other for doing so much. A few, to be sure, harbored resentments because their wives weren't the housekeepers they thought they should be or because their wives too infrequently consulted them about the children. And at some earlier point in their marriages, several of the men seemed to have engaged in sometimes tense negotiations with their wives about how much the men were expected to help. But in most men's marriages what seemed to exist now was a division of labor that operated smoothly and with apparent acceptance by the men and their wives.

The division of labor in childless marriages differed from that in marriages with children. Couples without children tended to maintain a division of labor somewhere between the "everybody does everything" of roommates or cohabitants and the sexual allocation of responsibility of a traditional married pair. The men might be more responsible for the heavy tasks, the wives for domestic arrangements, but there was a great deal of sharing. Especially for marriages in which the wives' earnings were comparable to the husbands', who did what seemed to be as much a matter of personal preference as of conformity to traditional expectations.

But couples whose division of household labor had been roughly symmetric before the arrival of children witnessed an abrupt change once children were on the scene. The wives who had been working withdrew from the labor force so that they could look after the children. Most dropped out entirely, although a few kept some sort of part-time association, such as doing editing at home. The husbands, meanwhile, redoubled their efforts at work, since now they had a family to support.

Yet even after the arrival of children husbands did more than "men's work" around the house, and women more than "women's work." Husbands sometimes cooked, often helped with cleaning, and looked after the children. Wives did yard work and, when the children were nursery school age, returned to paid employment.

Despite this flexibility, husbands and wives seemed to decide who would do what on the basis of underlying principles. They might not themselves be able to say exactly what the principles were, but they seemed nevertheless to share belief in the principles and generally to agree on their application.

The Underlying Principles of the Marital
Division of Labor

All couples began their married lives with the recognition that some tasks were traditionally "men's work" and others traditionally "women's work," an implication of principles that might be referred to as *the traditional principles* of the marital division of labor. Most couples used these principles to establish a basic pattern for their lives together. They might then modify the pattern, but often enough they acted on the principles without thinking much about the matter. Couples who were ideologically opposed to the traditional principles were likely nevertheless to act on them after they had children.

Whether or not they believe that their household is organized along traditional lines, men know which tasks should be theirs, according to the traditional allocations, and which should be their wives'. They may have trouble, however, in developing an adequate formulation. Asked to say what makes something men's work and what makes something women's, they are likely to offer the rule that "Men are the breadwinners, and their wives take care of the house and the children." But they would agree that yardwork is men's work even though it is a part of home maintenance, as are household repairs and fixing the gutters. And they would agree that taking the children to a ballgame is something men should do, more than women, even though it involves child care. The traditional principles are not captured fully by "Men are breadwinners, women are homemakers and mothers."

More nearly fundamental, for the traditional view of the marital division of labor, is that men provide the household with a structure within which to live and with the social place that comes with it. Men are responsible for supplying the household with money, as an expression of their responsibility for the standard of living of the household and the respect it commands in the community. They are also responsible for the integrity of the household, which is expressed as keeping the physical structure of the household in repair and protecting its occupants. And they have first responsibility for launching their children into adulthoods in which the children have a respectable place in the society.

In this traditional division of labor, men are responsible for much of the household's relationships with the wider society. Their wives, then, are responsible for the internal functioning of the home; for child care and home maintenance; for relationships within the home; for the actual workings of the family.[4]

The traditional principles were ordinarily augmented by an additional principle, *the principle of helping out*. No matter who is supposed to do what, the other should be willing to help out if needed. If the man is not otherwise engaged and his wife needs help putting the children to bed, the man ought to pitch in. The responsibility, however, would remain his wife's.

The principle of helping out is entirely consistent with the traditional principles in that it does not lead to questioning the traditional allocation of responsibilities. Quite different is another principle often invoked in debates over the marital division of labor, *the principle of equity*. This is the principle that the work of the marriage should be divided fairly between the husband and wife.

The principle of equity can produce results different from those of the traditional principles of the division of labor augmented by the principle of helping out. In application of the principle of equity, fairness is all. If neither the man nor his wife enjoys cleaning the house, then the husband should clean the house one week, the wife the next, or they should clean the house together, each doing half the work. Or the wife might be compensated elsewhere; perhaps the man should do some other task that neither enjoys, like laundry.

It is also not fair for one partner to use a labor-saving approach that is not available to the other partner. If the man and his wife decide that they will share the cooking, it is not fair for the man to do his share by ringing up the neighborhood pizza parlor. Nor is it fair for one partner to perform child care by playing with the children when the other partner performs child care by preparing their food. Nor is it fair for one partner to claim press of work when the other partner works just as hard.[5]

Sometimes a man will perform a chore that is based in none of these principles. A husband will fix breakfast for his wife on a Sunday morning, although both agree that cooking is the wife's responsibility and there is no need for the husband to help or reason for him to believe that fixing her breakfast is only fair. Under such circumstances, his breakfast preparation is a gift to his wife, an expression of affection.[6]

The Principles in Practice

In their division of marital labor, the men of this study largely followed traditional principles augmented by the principle of helping out, even though they were also committed to the principle of equity. This was possible because the men felt that the arrangement they had established with their wives was fair.

With two exceptions, both in childless couples, one a man whose wife earned as much as he did, the other a man whose wife earned more, the men of our sample understood themselves to be the marital partner in charge of assuring the family's income. That does not mean that they expected to be the sole earners of that income, but rather that they considered themselves to be the main earners, the partners who were ultimately responsible. The men might need their wives to help out if the household was to attain an aimed-at standard of living, but that did not diminish their responsibility for the domain. If a family's income should be too little for its bills, the fault would be the man's alone, not his wife's or his and his wife's together. He might perhaps argue that the bills were unjustified; that his wife, as the partner responsible for the family's spending, had overspent. But if he accepted that the family's income was inadequate, the failure would be entirely his.

Most men believed it was also they who were responsible for the maintenance of the home and its grounds. In keeping with this, they were the ones to do whatever upkeep required building-trade skills, such as painting and carpentry, or to conduct the negotiations with the tradesmen who possessed such skills. However, maintenance of grounds, especially planting and gardening, could be assimilated to internal home care and become the woman's job, especially if the aim were decorative rather than functional. So could arranging for painting and carpentry. Indeed, men who felt they knew too little to hold their own with tradesmen, and so felt inadequate in an area that they believed to be theirs, could be relieved to have their wives take over. They could rationalize that it was easier for their wives to act as contractors because their wives were home during the day; and, in any event, their wives were only helping out.

Men believe without question that they are the ones to whom the family should look for protection. It is they who should caution a daughter's boyfriend to drive carefully, should stand between an angry neighbor and one of their children who has infringed on that neighbor's territory, and, if no one else can do it, should be the one to send away a persistent door-to-door salesman. Couples so strongly committed to achieving equity that they try to ensure that the husband and wife perform the same tasks nevertheless consider it the husband's responsibility to check out a noise in the night.

Men felt strongly that it should be they who sponsored their sons into the world of achievement: sports and, eventually, work. They also thought they should contribute to their daughter's movement into adulthood, but were less certain how this was to be done, especially after the daughters became adolescent. Sometimes they acted to support their older daughters' functioning at school or in work just as they might their sons', but at other times they seemed to feel that all they could offer was protection.

Men believed that their wives were responsible for the quality of life inside their homes. This included all the activities necessary to the logistic support of the members of the household: keeping the household in provisions, producing meals and clean clothes, and when necessary driving the children to their various activities. It also included attending to the emotional climate of the household. The children's feelings of security, the ease with which people talked with each other, the household's sense of comfort—all these they saw as within their wives' domain. They looked to their wives for information about the emotional well-being of family members and, sometimes, for coaching in their own relationships with their children.

Men believed that as an extension of the wives' responsibility for relationships within the home, their wives should manage the family's relationships with couples who were friends and with the family's kin, including the man's mother and sisters. The men, of course, did their own social arranging when it involved partners in sport or in leisure activities.

Men believed that they, rather than their wives, should interpret the events of business and politics for the family.[7] Managing the family's boundary with the political and economic world was in their domain of responsibility.

These principles of allocation of marital responsibilities are likely to appear so natural to men—and to their wives—that they become the basis for the marital division of labor without discussion or thought.

> Subconsciously, I rely on my wife to run the house, keep things organized. And so far as our social schedule, she probably takes care of that in the sense of what we're going to be doing on Friday night or Wednesday or Sunday. And I suppose she relies on me to bring the bread home and put it on the table.

> *Mr. Powers, businessman*

Mr. Abbott, a high-level technician, has been married almost thirty years. His wife is in charge of patient information at a local hospital. Their two children are now grown. Mr. Abbot said:

We've never officially worked it out, but I think that there are things that are categorized as the man type jobs such as painting the house, making repairs. She does a very good job with the house, keeps the house very clean. Shopping is her job, obviously. She doesn't mind. I let her pay most of the bills. She handles the budget in that sense. I take care of what I call the investing, whether it be savings or buying real estate or whatever. She won't interfere with that. We discuss major purchases. But I would have to say that she would probably leave that to me.

I don't have a great deal of difficulty in explaining myself if I want to invest in some silly stock. I tell her it's really going to become great in a short while. She'll believe me and we'll go ahead and do it. Some of my ventures haven't been that good, either. Some have been quite good.

In recent years there has been a good deal of criticism of men for insisting on a traditional division of labor within the home even when their wives work full time outside of the home. Men have been accused of using the power of their income (or of a supposed greater ability to make a life for themselves were the marriage to end) to require their wives to perform a disproportionate number of those tasks involved in running a home that are menial, repetitious, and degrading.[8] However, this is not at all the way men feel about the traditional division of labor. Nor does it seem accurate to say that men smugly refuse to acknowledge that they have a good thing. Rather, men seem deeply invested in doing well at what they believe to be their responsibilities. Far from wanting to shirk their responsibility for income production, they will accept menial, repetitious, degrading, and dangerous work, if no better work is available. When they fail to meet what they believe to have been one of their responsibilities—providing an adequate income, protecting a child—their self-blame can be bottomless even if the fault was not theirs.

There is another reason men object, if only through passive resistance, to sharing tasks traditional principles would say are their wives'. So long as they—and their wives—believe the tasks to be shared are in their wives' domains of responsibility, the men are answerable to their wives. Suppose a couple should decide that the husband will supervise the children's baths. The husband is asked by the children what toys they can take into the tub. Because the husband is functioning in his wife's domain—care of the children and their possessions—his response would be subject to overrule by her. If she said, "The boy shouldn't need to take toys into the tub any more," that would be it. Men accept that in their wives' domains of responsibility, their wives are the lead partner—not quite the boss, but certainly the partner with greater authority.[9] It's hard for a man, when doing the dishes, not to feel subordinate to his wife.

> I tend to go along with the wife's beliefs and desires in terms of what the kids should have and what would be good for them and whether they can get along without something or not, that kind of thing. If I don't think that things are extremely wrong, and I don't find too many that are, or if I don't really feel all that strongly about them one way or the other, it's more comfortable for me to go along with it.

Mr. Draper, executive and business owner

One element of the traditional view of the family is that the man is the family's "head." Yet the meaning of this status is by no means immediately apparent. One meaning it does not have is that he is the family's boss.

For several years, when teaching courses on the family or leading workshops on family issues, I have asked people to role-play a family meeting. I cast a family of mother, father, twelve-year-old daughter, and ten-year-old son. I say that the family must work out how to arrange the family vacation. I tell the father that he is an avid fisherman and wants to vacation near a trout stream, and I tell the mother that she does not want to spend her vacation cleaning fish. I go on to tell the mother that she would prefer a beach setting where the children would have other children with whom to play, perhaps a cottage along a safe shore. And then I ask the family to resolve the dilemma.

Almost always when I have done this, the woman playing the mother has taken the lead. She has asked the husband for his ideas, has elicited reactions from the children, has made her own suggestions and has piloted the way to compromise. She might first gain her husband's agreement to a plan that would provide something for everyone, would then turn to the children, inform them, listen to their objections, and gain their acquiescence by diplomacy, bribery, and firmness. Sometimes the man held out stubbornly for the trout stream, but always the woman won him around. In one instance the man suggested going off by himself, but when the woman said that she wouldn't want him to do that, he immediately dropped the idea.

To this point the woman would be the marital partner who was really running things in the family, though she would be doing so diplomatically, with deference to her husband. But now, with a decision agreed to, something noteworthy would occur. The man would turn to me and nod, to indicate that the family had come to a resolution. Though the woman had piloted the resolution, the man would assume responsibility for presenting it to me.

It happened once that the man and woman turned to me together to say they had completed the exercise. I then sat stone-faced, refusing to respond. By doing this I manufactured an emergency: an instructor who seemed to have gone into a catatonic trance. Now, even though earlier it had not been the man alone who represented the family, it was the man who took charge and said again, a bit louder, that the group had completed the exercise.

In family life, the man is not head of the family in the sense that he gets his way; often enough he ends by endorsing his wife's plans. He is family head in that he represents the family in its dealings with the world.

Men who adhere to traditional principles in the allocation of marital responsibilities almost uniformly also adhere to the principle of helping out, though with wide variation in the extent to which they are asked to help and actually do help.[10] The assumption that each partner will help the other underlies much of what appears to be role sharing. Should the woman be overwhelmed by tasks within the home, the man may help out by vacuuming, doing dishes, or taking the kids for a ride in the car. Should the man be unable through his own income to meet the household's bills, then the woman may, in turn, help out. Should the man be made anxious by confrontations, then the woman can represent the household in a neighborhood conflict. And should the woman hate to cook, the man may do the cooking.

In all instances of helping out, both men and women are aware of whose is the initial and formal responsibility. They understand that the one who helps out is doing something extra, and a partner may decline to help out if confronted by more urgent matters in his or her own domain. Men, especially, may give helping their wives lower priority than the demands of their work.

Along with working, she keeps the house up and does the shopping and keeps everything rolling inside, and I try to get everything outside. She takes care of the household end, I take care of the other stuff, the outside, the repairs, things like that. Paying the bills and things like that. She takes care of the food and the wash and whatever needs to be cleaned. Even though I try to help her out once in a while, I haven't been successful lately.

Mr. Brewer, owner of a catering business

As noted previously, one problem with helping out is that the helper is in a subordinate position. The domain is, after all, the spouse's. So when wives help their husbands in their husbands' work, the wives are apt to be treated as subordinates rather than partners. And when men help their wives at home, their wives are apt to give them direction.

Reliance on traditional principles plus helping out is always subject to criticism from the standpoint of equity. "Yes," a woman may say, "in our parents' families our mothers did the cooking and cleaning. But they didn't also work full time and bring in almost half the income. It isn't fair for me not only to work but also to have responsibility for the home and the children."

The principle of equity can make men uncomfortable because it implies that the men aren't meeting their obligations to their families through their work, their protectiveness, their captaining, and their helping out. Also, the men may anticipate becoming subordinates in their wives' domains of responsibility despite their wives' insistence that responsibility will be shared. The following scenario is one that some young couples report having followed.

The wife argues, relying on the principle of equity: "You ought to share the work of the home. I work as hard at my job as you do at yours."

The husband responds, rejecting the principle of equity, since he believes that he is already doing his share by meeting traditional expectations, and replacing it with the principle of helping out. "Tell me what to do and I'll do it."

The wife returns to the principle of equity since use of the principle of helping out leaves her with unshared responsibility: "You live here too. You can see as well as I what has to be done. Why should I have to tell you what to do?"

The husband now reminds his wife that others are likely to see the domain as hers by threatening her with inferior performance. "Well, I know your standards are different, but you'll have to put up with the way I do it."

The husband has a good chance of winning, because his wife is likely to agree that others will see her as the lead partner in home maintenance. In consequence it will be she who is embarrassed should a friend or relative visit and find the house scruffy.

DUAL-CAREER MARRIAGES

Mr. Foster is a former investment counselor who now, with partners, manages a program of mutual funds. His income is large. Mrs. Foster has done graduate work in business management. She holds a responsible executive position in an accounting firm that pays her well, though her income does not match her husband's. Mr. Foster told us that he admired his wife for her success and fully supported her in her commitment to work.

The Fosters had three children, all at home, the youngest just finishing primary school. Mr. Foster spent about as much time with the children as did his wife. When the children were smaller, Mrs. Foster had stayed at home with them. After about a year at home she had become deeply depressed, and her husband, searching for a remedy, had urged her to return to graduate school.

That time she was at home trying to deal with the kids, I think that was probably the hardest part of our marriage. She was just restless, very restless, and not feeling very accomplished. She was having a difficult time coping with being married and having kids and not having a career. At least that was my analysis.

I think that I would really say she was pretty disturbed. I remember now, the way she woke up crying a couple of times, like in bed, talking about her life. I used to get bored with it all. I'd say, "Just relax and go to sleep," that kind of thing. It was just sort of unarticulated anxiety on her part. It was a lot of self-doubt. She was not very confident, not as confident a person as she is now. And I remember it was very repetitive. It kept going around in circles. And she didn't quite know what was bugging her. But something sure as hell was bugging her. I was trying to be supportive. Trying to make it work.

What we did, she went back to school. It was a rallying point, an objective that was very definable. Everybody had a common goal to hold the thing together. And that was good. I was absolutely supportive of her going back to school. Absolutely! More than supportive, I pushed it. Because, why the hell shouldn't she? Why should she stay home? It's ridiculous.

Note how Mr. Foster applied the fundamental principles of the division of labor to his marriage. He thought of his wife as the partner primarily responsible for the children and became irritated when she could not adapt to staying at home. But he also thought of himself as responsible for making the family work. When he became aware that staying home was depressing his wife, he saw it as his place to act.

With his wife working, Mr. Foster began to share tasks in the home. He did some of the cooking (a bit less than his wife) and helped clean up after dinner. Most of the cooking and a good deal of child care was performed by a foreign student who acted as an au pair. While Mr. Foster's willingness to help at home was a critical element in freeing Mrs. Foster's time and energies for her job, having the foreign student may well have permitted the system to work.

Mr. Foster continued to define himself as the partner ultimately responsible for the family's support. As one expression of this, he made his bank account available to his wife, although his wife kept her bank account entirely to herself.

We've always had separate bank accounts, but I used to give Paula money before she went to work. Now Paula can sign on my account. I can't sign on hers.

Certainly Paula's working has made a very big difference in what we could do. But I'm the court of last resort. I mean, I'm the backstop.

Mr. Foster did not pay for everything. Mrs. Foster paid for items within the woman's domain: groceries and housekeeping services. Mr. Foster paid for the upkeep items, the items necessary to keep the house going. As Mr. Foster put it: "Paula runs much of the house and I run other things." Mr. Foster paid for evenings out—unless he was without cash, in which case he appealed to the principle of helping out:

Paula buys the groceries. There's a guy who comes in here once a week, and the groceries, that's a pretty good bill. And she pays for the housekeeping. And I pay for essentially everything else. I pay for the telephone and the lights and tuitions and insurance. She buys a lot of stuff for the house that she wants to buy. Large furniture, that gets in a gray area. If we go out to dinner, I pay, generally. If I have money.

Mrs. Foster was highly successful in her work and became an important member of her firm. Her contribution to the firm was not, in Mr. Foster's view, properly recognized. Mr. Foster became outraged on his wife's behalf.

After two years in the firm she believed she deserved a promotion and salary increase. They were refused. One reason given her was that she didn't need the status or the income since her husband was so successful.

This is a textbook case, what went on there. People who don't have daughters or wives, men who don't have daughters or wives who have gone through this, don't believe it goes on! This was so blatant it ought to be written up. I can't stand those people any more. I just absolutely see red! Just the hypocrisy! That's what it is, it's hypocrisy!

Mr. Foster's first thought, on hearing the story from his wife, was to provide her with understanding and support. But this was *his wife* who was being misused, and he wanted to do battle for her. Again, a traditional principle: the husband's responsibility to protect the members of his household. Mr. Foster, insofar as he did not protect his wife, was failing to behave properly, in a way he could himself respect.

In another dual-career family, when the wife reported harsh and unfair criticism from her boss, her husband felt almost impelled to call the boss and tell him off. The wife, alarmed, said, "Don't you dare! It means my career!" The husband reported the incident with full appreciation that his reaction had been misguided, but also with pride that he had been so strongly protective.

That the Fosters maintained a dual-career marriage does not mean that Mr. Foster changed his understandings of his responsibilities in his family. Rather, he adapted his understandings to his special situation. He saw himself as behaving well—indeed, unselfishly.

I think men who aren't accepting of their wives' working are probably pretty selfish. I know there are a lot of people like that. We spent Saturday night with a couple like that. He wants his wife *there*. Why the hell *should* she be *there?* At his beck and call. Women are people.

Mr. Foster viewed his acceptance of his wife's working as something he was doing for her. (That was why he saw himself as unselfish.) Men can also, of course, understand their wives' working as helping out. Especially if their wives are not overburdened at home, and expenses have mounted—as with children at college—men may urge their wives to work.

We no longer have any children at home. And we will need money, at least for a couple of years, to pay two tuition bills. So those two things kind of came together at the same time. And she is going to be working and getting some money to help us over the hump with the tuition bills. After the tuition bills stop or maybe after we have only one child in school, if she wants to work, fine, if she doesn't, it is really up to her.

Mr. Ryder, department head

At no point do men understand themselves to be no longer responsible for income production, neither when they believe that their wives are working to help out nor when they believe their wives are working for self-realization. Nor do they stop considering their wives responsible for the domains that would be theirs were they not working.

Men are ordinarily willing to help working wives by contributing to home maintenance and child care; even more, they are willing to accept that less will get done. They may, though, have moments when they regret having supported their wives' desire to work. Mr. Foster, for example, despite his insistence that he was willing to do dishes and to cook when the au pair was otherwise occupied, was irritated by evenings spent alone because his wife had to work. And though he said he didn't miss the social life that had been sacrificed to his wife's new priorities, he was thoroughly aware that it had been sacrificed.

Most of all, when men's wives work, men are likely to miss their wives' solicitude should the men be stressed or fatigued by *their* work. Working wives are likely to be less attentive to careworn husbands than wives who believe their husbands to be engaged in a lone struggle for the family's subsistence. In one dual-career couple the husband and wife had agreed that neither of them would begin their evening together by burdening the other with the problems of the day. But the husband seemed wistfully to wish his wife had more tolerance for his job complaints.[11]

MEN'S WIVES AS COMPANIONS

Companionship happens as married partners do things together, talk with each other, relax together, even work together. Enjoying each other's company can brighten and enliven a Saturday spent in chores to keep the house in order. Cleaning up after a party can be made bearable by being done together, each partner in harmony with the other, each with a sense of the other's movements. Companionship of this sort can give resonance to simply being together in the home.

Companionship is potentially present in any marital interchange. Companionship of a more deliberate sort, companionship that can be recognized as the point of an evening out together, varies more than any other aspect of marriage from couple to couple and within the same couple over time.[12] Before the advent of children, marriages have room for companionship they won't have again until the children leave. For couples who enjoy each other's company, the early years can be marvelous.

The advent of children severely depresses companionship. One man said that before he and his wife had children, they would go to a friend's home or to a movie at the drop of a hat. Now, with children, they have the hassle of finding a babysitter they can trust. Often they end up going nowhere. More important, the increased workload produced by children reduces the time and energy available for companionship. Besides, the children themselves distract the attention of the man and his wife from each other.

The Edwardses are a dual-career couple. He is an engineer, she a former museum director, now a computer consultant. Mrs. Edwards reported:

Sam and I had Cheryl after ten years of marriage. We had a grand time. We traveled throughout the world. We were probably spoiled in that we had *so* much freedom. And then after Cheryl was born, I stayed home for two years with her. After ten years of freedom, to be strapped down! We were very dedicated parents.

When children are born it changes your life-style dramatically. Or at least it did for us. We were very free in what we did, going out on a daily, nightly basis, on a weekend every week. When we had Cheryl it changed drastically. And I think it changes for every new parent. I don't care who tells you it doesn't, it does. They are lying through their teeth if they say it doesn't.

Mr. and Mrs. Edwards can be at home together in the evening, but though they share space, they are only fitfully company for each other. Mr. Edwards described a typical evening.

Many nights I'll come home and we'll have dinner about seven-thirty. We believe in having an evening meal together. We believe in sitting down to dinner together. Then after that, Cheryl will either take a bath or one of us—usually me, because Cornelia is doing the dishes—I'll take Cheryl and we'll either play Scrabble or checkers or I'll read to her. I lie down on the bed, I read three or four fairy tales, she's falling asleep and I also don't want to get up. And I find myself getting up at nine-thirty, ten. And then I maybe talk to Cornelia for twenty minutes. And many times I'll come into the bedroom and Cornelia will be in bed sleeping.

If you have a child of Cheryl's age and both of you are working, you don't spend very much time together.

One couple, parents of three boys ranging in age from nine to fourteen, set aside an hour after dinner when they could talk. They called the hour "parent time."

It doesn't happen every single evening, but we've started something. Right after supper the kids are told, "All right, time to go to do your homework. Go somewhere else." And the two of us sit and have our coffee. Not every night. Not if it's one of the nights when it's a quick bite to eat and then one kid to baseball practice and one to Boy Scouts, that type of thing. But when the opportunity presents itself—we've talked to the kids and heard their day's routine during the meal and it's time for them to start their homework—then, "All right, now you guys go take a shower and do your homework or do whatever." And Myra and I will try to just sit in the kitchen, look at the dirty dishes, and talk.

Occasionally we will get interrupted. We'll say, "Out. You finish the paper, then bring it back and we'll look at it. Don't come out here one problem at a time. Do the whole paper and then we'll look at it. This is *our* time, get out of here."

Mr. Orcutt, middle-level manager

Not until the children grow up and leave home are there again large blocks of time for uninterrupted companionship. Only after the children have left can men and their wives once again see each other as primarily companions rather than partners in household management.

My wife's mother has said, "Isn't it terrible now that all your kids are gone?" And my wife says, "No, it isn't. We enjoy it. We are happy that they are gone." We like to see them, obviously. But we don't mind that they don't live here. We just kind of get the chance again to enjoy each other. And we do. We enjoy just the two of us doing things.

Mr. White, executive

To be sure, the departure of the children may reveal to men that they and their wives no longer have much in common. The years had been occupied by talk about the children, worry over them, shared pride in their achievements, and shared concern over their failures. Now, the children gone, the men may wonder what they and their wives can find to talk about. A retired man said:

All of a sudden I find myself being an awful lot with my wife. I have more time on my hands. And not being the type that runs around, I am at home. I've been encountering more on the negative. It has uncovered certain weaknesses.

We are not quarreling any more than we used to. But it happens that we aren't able to do too many things together. She didn't share very much in my career. We don't have very much in common. It's putting a special strain on the marriage, it's so bad.

Other couples, in similar situations, may search for activities from which common interests can develop. Travel may perhaps provide such interests. Entering a business together may accomplish the same thing.

One man, anticipating retirement, bought an apartment house with his wife:

> Some property we bought was a very good joint project be-
> cause we had to furnish it and outfit it. We had to pick all the
> color schemes and the paint. So probably for three months we
> were buying furniture and dishes and everything and decorat-
> ing it. We got along very good on that project. I think it was
> good for her. It taught us a lot about decorating and buying
> furniture and what you expect. We'll probably do it again
> some place. Things are good when we are working on a proj-
> ect or something like that, doing things together.

Mr. Patrick, sales manager

Men's experience, then, with marital companionship is that early in their marriages their wives can be companions, but when children are born, they must accept that their wives are no longer available in quite the same way. Years later, when the youngest child leaves home, the opportunity for companionship reappears. If they, and their wives, are fortunate, they can again find it rewarding simply to be together.

ATTACHMENT

Robert Louis Stevenson, when away from the woman with whom he was in love, expressed a need for closeness with someone who would share his emotional life.

> Even while I was exulting in my solitude I became aware of a strange
> lack. I wished a companion to lie near me in the starlight, silent and not
> moving, but ever within touch. For there is a fellowship more quiet even
> than solitude, and which, rightly understood, is solitude made perfect.
> And to live out of doors with the woman a man loves is of all lives the most
> complete and free.[13]

"Attachment" is a way of referring to the emotional linkage established in marriage: the feeling, shared by husband and wife, that the other is emotionally available, and that each is augmented by the other—almost made whole by the other.

The process by which this bond of attachment is established is displayed by any young couple at a restaurant table who gaze into each other's eyes, listen to each other's speech with rapt attention, seek opportunities to touch. Most people recognize this and have themselves experienced it. The next day each member of the couple carries a sense of the other, perhaps the other's image, as background to everything each is doing. A telephone call is reassuring; yes, the relationship is real. Rejoining produces glad relief.

This almost uninterrupted focus of attention and energy on the other as a sustaining figure produces an emotional incorporation of a visual, auditory, and kinesthetic image of the other. It ensures that later, in time of emotional need, it will be the other who is sought and whose presence fosters feelings of security.

A couple for whom attachment has progressed beyond its initial stages can be recognized as quickly as can a couple just forming attachment. Now the couple may talk to each other companionably, but the talk lacks excitement and focus. Their attention, although it may be steady, is no longer rapt. And while they listen to each other, perhaps comfortably and in good humor, they can be distracted as well. Touch, should it occur, is no longer charged. This is attachment in place.

Once attachment is securely in place—once both partners are assured that the other's presence and commitment can be counted on—both partners can give their energies to other matters. Yes, the excitement is gone, but it has been replaced by feelings of security. So long as the other person is reliably accessible, there is no need to feel alone and anxious.

We know from studies of conjugal bereavement how much a part of the emotional system that sustains a person's feelings of security is the image of that person's husband or wife.[14] Against a background of sadness so intense that it has become pain, bereaved husbands and wives experience feelings of abandonment together with hopeless yearning for the partner's return. Widows and widowers, despite themselves, become organized to respond to the partner's image and so experience an immediate upsurge of excitement on seeing in the distance anyone who more or less dresses like the partner or drives the same automobile or has any other quality that could be a cue. There is a momentary conviction that this *is* the other person—followed by full realization of error and renewed awareness of loss.

Marital separation, because of the anger that has become intermeshed with attachment feelings, tends to produce intense ambivalence. Although the ambivalence of the separating can take many forms, perhaps most characteristic is one in which desire to be free of the relationship coexists with desire to reestablish it, and feelings of anger coexist with a sense of continued connection to the other and need for the other.

Because attachment, once established, is central to feelings of security, and because its interruption gives rise to almost intolerable discomfort, it is a most effective marital bond. It ensures that husbands and wives will not easily dissolve their partnerships, whatever may be the ups and downs of the relationships. Nor are figures who have once been incorporated into the attachment emotional system easily displaced by new figures. Men who have found new women with whom they want a continuing relationship are likely to discover that although it is not that difficult, emotionally, to take on the new, it is extremely difficult to put off the old. (More on this appears in Chapter Ten.)

So long as attachment is in place and uninterrupted, husbands and wives may not be aware of how important to them emotionally is their spouse's accessibility. Rather, their spouse's accessibility becomes an unnoted assumption of ongoing life, invisibly contributing to feelings of security, requiring no attention itself. Men may declare their love for their wives, but the love they are declaring is a settled love, a comfortable acceptance, and not the overwhelming investment of their courtship. They therefore do not suspect how much their emotional equilibrium depends on their wives' continuing presence. Only when a man's wife becomes inaccessible, because she is visiting her parents or is off on a business trip, does the man discover again his need for her presence. In her absence he may find himself, to his surprise, edgy, restless, and lonely.

Mr. Metzger, although he considered himself happily married, liked being able to get off by himself after dinner. He was aided in this by his wife's evening courses, which required her to study during evenings she was not attending classes. He was surprised to discover that when his wife and children went off on a vacation, he felt lonely.

> I believe in togetherness, but not total togetherness. In the evenings, of course we have dinner together, Doris goes off and does her homework, and I do my reading and fall asleep. But it's always been like this. I like to have some time to myself, by myself. I need it. Always did. Provided I know she's in the next room.

> A couple of times, once about eleven years ago, I sent Doris and all the children to visit her sister for Christmas vacation. And while we were planning it I was looking forward to it. And when it happened, I couldn't stand it. I did it again

about four years ago, for a little shorter period, and I didn't like that either.

I don't like an empty house. I like to be by myself, provided I know Doris is in the next room. And I don't like it when she goes out at night. Strange. I'm perfectly happy to be in one room by myself as long as I know she's in the next one.

A similar response to a wife's absence was reported by Mr. Powers, a specialist in the development of shopping centers and a man who prided himself on self-sufficiency. Mr. Powers described himself as having felt lonely only briefly after his wife left to attend a professional meeting. That may have been the case. Yet it is characteristic of Mr. Powers (as of other men) to minimize feelings of uncertainty or vulnerability, and he may well have minimized his feelings of loneliness.

I think when Barbara was in San Francisco and I was here by myself, after a while I started to feel lonely, [like] I'd like to talk to someone. It was just momentary.

It may not require actual physical inaccessibility to produce loneliness. It can be enough for the marital partner to be totally preoccupied with matters external to the marriage: work, an ill relative, another relationship.

Going back to the first of this year, there was a period when I was lonely. Her father played such a role in our lives that he was infringing on our privacy. I realized that her attention was going there. I was the other man.

Men need their wives' accessibility—emotional as well as physical—to feel entirely secure. If they are confident of themselves at work and elsewhere, the need may not be great. But if they are at all anxious, if they have any sense of vulnerability, then they will want the reassurance of their wives' presence.

Love, in marriage, is attachment in place plus everything else. The conjunction of marital bonds, in a partnership that is going well, provides men with a feeling that their wives truly share their lives. The feeling may be strongest at a time of high emotionality or special need. One man felt something like this as he attended his wife when his third child was born. Other men have felt it when their wives came through for them when they were doing badly at work. Mr. Foster spoke warmly of his wife's taking over the home chores when he was made immobile by a bad back; she had demonstrated then that he could depend on her. He was grateful to her and felt closer to her.

Based on attachment in place, rather than in formation, a comfortable partnership and an easy companionship, love in an established marriage is a different emotional state from the love of first encounter. It is a more settled feeling, less passionate, perhaps best rendered as a sense of special linkage. We two.

Mr. Brewer was asked by the interviewer how it was that he and his wife managed to work together as well as they did. He said:

> Well, a lot through love. It's kind of a uniqueness that we have between each other.

And at this point Mr. Brewer, ordinarily fluent, fell silent.

CHAPTER
SEVEN

Marital Upset

As they do in any partnership, disagreements arise in men's marriages. When disagreements arise in business partnerships they can be surprisingly distressing. But business partnerships are only about managing work and making money. The marital partnership is about children and caring, about the emotional foundations of life and the partners' essential worth. The potential for hurt in a marital dispute is greater.

Disagreements in marriage arise over initial assumptions and current understandings, as when the husband does not want more children but the wife does. They are expressions of different levels of tolerance for risk, as when the husband insists on remaining in a line of work where every project is a gamble. They can develop over who does what in the division of household labor and who gets what in the expenditure of family income. Each partner can complain about misuse at the hands of the other; for example, one wife complained that her husband went to a lodge meeting every Friday evening, leaving her with the children, while the husband complained that his wife was forever nagging him about his drinking. And each partner may claim that the other refuses to listen to criticism or talk about change but instead withdraws or blows up.

None of the men in our study had marriages free of friction. The Fosters, the dual-career couple described in the preceding chapter, seemed to themselves and to others to be unusually happy. Nevertheless, Mr. Foster complained that his wife worked too many hours and should be home more. He also thought his wife tended to be bossy. When she became too bossy he stopped listening to her. And there had been a time, earlier in their marriage, when Mrs. Foster had felt overwhelmed by home responsibilities and her depression had made for mutual distress.

At the other end of the range, some men described marriages in which tension was often high. These were marriages in which there were frequent quarrels and almost constant bickering, or where distance and silence expressed a resentful hopelessness. A very few of these men thought almost daily of divorce.

Most frequent as a source of marital friction was the way the children were being raised. About forty percent of the men with children described disagreements centering on the children, most often over how to deal with the children's misbehavior, but sometimes over the man's failures as a father (as seen by his wife) or the woman's failures as a mother (as seen by the man).

Relationships with children give rise to disputes partly because both husband and wife are enormously invested in the children and their upbringing. And although husbands generally defer to their wives' practices, they let their wives know if they disapprove. One man regularly quarreled with his wife about her permissiveness.

> My children can come home from school and sit in front of the TV for six hours and then go into school and have a bad day and then repeat it. My wife is more the permissive one, and I'm more for get the work done. She wins out. That's why they are such slobs. They are mental slobs and physical slobs. They have never had any discipline in their lives. This is so significantly bad that everything else pales by comparison.

But there are any number of ways in which being parents together can give rise to tension. A man's wife may want him to do more with the children than he feels able to do, given the demands of his work, or she may want him to do less, perhaps because she feels he is infringing on her domain:

> My relationship with my daughter is getting closer. Actually, we've been getting closer steadily since she was two or three years old. There's tension with the spouse, almost because she, I think, wants to maintain her priority, her supremacy.

> *Mr. Williams, owner of small business, father of six-year-old daughter*

A marital partner's accessibility was another source of friction. About twenty-five percent of the men in the sample reported tension over one partner's availability to the other. Most often it was physical absence that was the problem. The men's wives objected to the men working late and so missing the evening meal and to their being away on business over a weekend or, even worse, over a holiday. Men complained, though much less frequently, about their wives' paid or unpaid employment. The men who made these complaints felt that their wives gave too much time to activities outside the home, though they may have themselves initially encouraged their wives in those activities.

Marital friction also developed around issues of communication, generally because the wife felt that her husband did not talk to her enough. Still other issues that produced discord included relationships with parents, siblings, and friends, the way the wife kept the home, the husband's drinking, and his inadequate considerateness and helpfulness. But any issue that affected both the husband and wife could produce a marital skirmish, including setting the thermostat and stocking the refrigerator, managing the clothes (both clean and dirty), choosing television shows, and, of course, getting and spending money.

Men sometimes complained about their wives' complaints. They felt misused if they arrived home after a hard day only to be told that they should have been home earlier, that the children were out of hand because they were so little available, that house repairs awaited their attention, that they regularly started a job and left it unfinished, that they did too little, that they weren't cooperative, that they were getting away with murder. One man pleaded with his wife, "Let me relax a little; don't right away climb all over me." Another man said:

> I don't like being criticized when it's not anything I did. And the thing I hate the worst is to walk in the house after work and have my wife start in saying that because I haven't been home the kids have been terrible and have been misbehaving and haven't listened to her. When I'm tired and I'm just walking in the door I don't want to hear that.

In several instances men reported tensions stemming from their wives' psychological state, or their own. One man was occasionally irritated by his wife's depression, though he was sympathetic most of the time. Another man was institutionalized by his wife for two weeks' observation when his conversation stopped making sense. At the time he had objected; later, when we talked with him, he thought hospitaliz-ation had been unnecessary but seemed otherwise unruffled by its having occurred.

For a good many couples there were longstanding sources of tension. One man criticized his wife for being too relaxed a house-keeper; his wife thought him pathologically neat. When he decided the laundry needed doing he would ostentatiously begin it himself. To his wife the sight of him at the laundry hamper was infuriating.

Two men were alcoholic, to the great distress of their wives. In several couples there were disagreements over how to deal with a troubled child. Several men felt their wives were sexually withholding. One man's wife had refused him intercourse for years. He had stopped complaining, but he felt wronged. In one couple it was the man who wasn't enough interested in sex.[1]

Different couples devise different strategies for managing or mit-igating the inescapable tensions of marriage. Many voice their anger. There might follow an equally angry response, then a shouting match and almost certainly, in the end, hurt feelings. Some try to make their points through humor, at least as long as their composure lasts. Some try to talk out discomforts. In some cases the husbands or wives try to get their way by manipulating their partner's perceptions of a situation, as in *I Love Lucy*. Many husbands and wives rely on the silent treatment to let the other know they feel injured; they withdraw to a bedroom or go for a walk, and when they return are silent and emotionally distant.

Any of these approaches can work, though they give rise to different marital relationships. The couples in our sample who seemed most content with their marriages were those who reported that, as a policy, they talked out their disagreements. Indeed, inability to ex-press feelings is one of the complaints that in some instances leads to argument.

Despite the frequency of marital disagreements, only a minority of men reported that marital disagreements or quarrels had given rise to the symptoms of stress during the preceding year. Even in marriages in which there was a good deal of disagreement and in which resolution was more often brought about by the passage of time than by active discussion, men linked stress to trouble on the job more often than to marital friction.

If marital disputes do not give rise to stress symptoms, it is not because the issues matter less than those at work. Indeed, they would seem, at least potentially, to matter more. A serious dispute could easily include an attack on the man's behavior, capabilities, or character. And the attack would come from someone who knew him well and on whom he depended for reassurance of his essential worth. Sometimes the dispute would contain an implied or overt threat of abandonment: "If things don't get better I'm not staying in this marriage!" A marital dispute, one man said, contrasting it with a dispute at work, gets you deep down, where you really live.

One reason marital tensions do not ordinarily produce stress symptoms may be that men avoid attending to them. If there is no pressing need to deal with an item of marital disagreement, men are likely to choose not to deal with it. If their wives keep the house cold to save on heating bills, they'll turn up the thermostat without saying anything, or they'll make a joking reference to needing to bundle up inside the house. If their wives still want to keep the house cold, they'll put on a sweater, or a couple of sweaters, or get a space heater for their study.

Should a man detect that his wife is annoyed with him, he may ask what the problem is but will not persist in probing. Or he may not ask, but instead turn his attention to other things in the hope that whatever is wrong will correct itself. If, despite his benign indifference, the man's wife remains out of sorts, the man might feel forced to insist, "Okay, what's the matter?" hoping that he will be able to weather the confrontation with good humor and morale intact. He may be ready to talk out the problem or to jolly his wife into a better humor or, if it seems advisable, to become angry. Whatever works. Men tend to be pragmatic in their approach to marital problems.

Men do become thoroughly mobilized if there is threat to the marriage. If a man should be told by his wife that she is thinking of divorce, and becomes convinced that she is serious, he will give her every bit of his attention. Here is a problem he absolutely must deal with. He may resent the energy dealing with it requires, the distress it inflicts, and the time it takes, but he is likely to see keeping the family going as among his chief responsibilities.

If there is an issue less serious than this, but still serious enough to matter—a dispute about childraising, for example—and the man cannot resolve the issue by talking with his wife, arguing with her, making concessions, or becoming angry, then the man is likely to give up. At work, with a similar problem, he might continue to search for a solution and so remain mobilized and subject to stress. In his marriage, he is likely to accept defeat more quickly. He may withdraw physically; he may go to another room or turn on the television or attempt to disappear into a newspaper. His attitude is that he cannot change his wife and so must adapt to the unsatisfactory situation.

This might explain why marital disputes give rise to stress less often than do job problems. If men choose resignation as a response to trouble in their marriages—unlike their response to trouble in their jobs—unresolved marital disputes are less likely to lead to mobilization and stress.[2]

Three examples of this process follow, the first in connection with a trivial matter, the second and third in connection with something more serious. The first was reported by Mr. Ryder, a department head in an optical engineering firm. His wife did not have paid employment at the time of the story.

> When I would come down in the morning and there wouldn't be orange juice in the refrigerator I would really get upset with my wife about it. I would say, "You don't have any orange juice in the refrigerator this morning. You are not doing your job."
>
> The way I feel about it, we have a compact: I do my job and she does her job. I go out and work, and I work hard. And she has the whole day, and she is supposed to make sure there is orange juice in the refrigerator. That is her job. I'm not asking her to get up and get my breakfast. I do it myself. But I would like to have the proper things in the refrigerator.

Despite Mr. Ryder's nagging, his wife continued to forget to prepare orange juice for him. Always she would agree to do it and always she would forget. Mr. Ryder never inquired into the reasons for his wife's failure, although there would seem to have been a message in it—perhaps that she disagreed about its being her responsibility. In any event, Mr. Ryder said:

> There is this attitude in me, that makes me get upset when something like this happens, that there is a division of labor and I'm keeping my part of the bargain and she should keep hers. I guess she doesn't recognize that that is her part of the bargain. Or she forgets. It is not important to her. And that is where you really have the divergence of views.

Ultimately, Mr. Ryder's options became two: continue his nagging or accept that his wife was not going to prepare orange juice. Mr.

Ryder chose the second. As much as he could, he put the matter out of his mind.

> So what I have been doing lately is, before I go to bed, I check the refrigerator to see if there is any orange juice in there. And if there isn't I just put it in. Because I realize it isn't worth getting upset about.

Mr. Ryder here describes compartmentalizing his feeling of being short-changed by his wife's refusal to prepare his orange juice. He was not successful, actually, in banishing it from his mind; when he was asked about dissatisfactions in his marriage, the orange juice issue immediately appeared. But he no longer nags his wife about it.

The second instance is one in which the man has come to terms with having lost in a marital dispute. The report was made by Mr. Harley, a successful independent businessman who felt his marriage was a happy one:

> I have enjoyed raising the kids immensely. I'd like to have a dozen of them. Yeah, I would.

> Alice decided we wouldn't have any more. She really does have a bee in her bonnet to go out and beat the world. And she did more so then than now. And she said, "This is all over. I'm having no more kids." And she went out and surgically had it done so she wasn't going to have any more kids.

> We discussed it. It was not a decision that she made alone. But she was convinced that she didn't want to have any more children. And I respect that. I mean, it doesn't matter. Three is a lot of kids.

> It was no big problem. Mainly because I know what education costs. Although since my business has gone well I feel I would have, if I had known I was going to be able to educate more, I would have felt stronger about having more. I might have argued for another quick one then.

Mr. Harley's comment seems to have elements of both genuine acceptance and compartmentalization of distress. Mr. Harley can accept that his wife had a right to freedom from childraising. Still, he had wanted another child and, as it turned out, could have managed financially without sacrifice. But there is nothing now to be done about it.

He seems to feel some sorrow still, but not very much; anyway, what point is there in dwelling on it?

A third instance: Mr. Wilson, an energetic and successful professional running his own firm, had for fifteen years been refused a sexual relationship by his wife.

> My wife had a severe depression after the first child and an even more serious one after the second. She was six months in a mental hospital.

> This is hard to believe and some of it preys on me. I haven't had sex with a woman for fifteen years. We haven't had sexual relations for fifteen years. I don't really know how to relate that to other people's experience, but I sort of, I really, suffer from it. It is something that one doesn't go through a day without thinking about it. Sex is a basic drive, and I certainly feel it inside. And as you get to be fifty years old, you are very much aware of it.

> After you bring it up, you talk about it, and nothing happens, you realize that it is not a subject to pursue or hold out any hopes for. Or even think about trying to resolve. And so it becomes like an irritant. And you try to build a wall around it. You just contain it.

Mr. Wilson is aware of his sexual frustration and attendant feelings of despair. So far as he can, he has walled off his sense of deprivation and hurt. It is no longer an issue about which he is prepared to fight. He has given up hope of changing his wife. He will live with the frustration as best he can. He is not mobilized. He experiences no stress.

REFUSING TO FORGET AND REFUSING TO REMEMBER

Men and their wives appear, often, to differ in the way they deal with what they feel to be marital misuse. Assuming they are not about to walk away from the marriage, men's concern is to keep the marriage functioning. If there is nothing they can do about an issue, they will try to shrug it off, to compartmentalize whatever distress and discomfort they feel, and to put it out of their minds. Wives, on the other hand, seem more often to want to remember the misuse, as though putting it out of their minds would leave them vulnerable to its repetition.

To say that there is a man's style of dealing with misuse and a woman's style does not mean that this is the way all men and all women behave all of the time. Rather it means that there is something more than just a tendency for men to behave in one way, women in another, and that there is a plausible explanation for the difference.

In couples in which we interviewed the wife as well as the husband, we were told by some wives of husbands' behaviors that they could not forgive and that now prevented their fully trusting their husbands. In one case the husband, just after the birth of a second child, shifted from a safe and stodgy occupation to one in which there was high risk, some likelihood of eventual high gain, but little income for months and possibly years. His wife had earlier argued against his making the move and was furious when he told her he had made it anyway. Although the husband was correct in his belief that the new line of work would eventually prove profitable—five years after beginning in the new field he was on his way to becoming rich—his wife continued to remember her dismay and continued to be resentful. He had been right, yes, but he had betrayed her trust.

In another instance, the husband, a binge drinker, insisted on going out with male friends even though his wife pleaded with him to stay home. The wife was then caring for a recently born third child. The husband said that he worked hard for the family during the week and this particular evening was his time to come first. He may well have meant that at other times his wife and family came first. Whatever he meant, his wife believed she was being told that her needs did not matter. She repeated his words to us in our interview and said that until she heard those words, she had thought that each of them would put the other first. She said that at that moment she pledged to herself that she would never again put her husband first. She also said that because of that statement—and her husband's continued drinking—she was considering leaving the marriage when her youngest reached high school age. Her husband, though he knew his wife was at times angry with him, thought the marriage on the whole to be good. He minimized her continuing resentment. Still, he was aware that she remembered events he was able to forget:

> My wife gets hurt very easy. She's the type, if you have a
> fight, you can't yell something at her in anger, because it

stays there. She doesn't say, "Oh, gee, it was just said in anger." It stays there.

Here is another wife's story of a still-remembered hurt. It occurred when she was pregnant. The husband's failure was slight, and yet it convinced his wife that he was not entirely trustworthy.

When he was starting out in his business, once a week I would take Billie who was two or two and a half, and we would pile in the car and we would spend four hours driving around to make deliveries. And I was pregnant at the time. So there I was with a toddler and pregnant. I didn't resent it. What else did I have to do? I wasn't a homeowner and I wasn't into community activities. I was very happy to do these things. But then when I asked if he could help me with a stuck window he reacted, "Does it have to be done now?" And I burst into tears. I thought, "Doggone it, this baby could be born any time! I'm not going to have a chance to wash windows afterwards. And here is this window that is stuck. And physically I can't do it. If you could just push it, that is all I'm asking."

Here is what the husband now says:

The male-female thing is that the man can never remember the next day what it was that the issue was the day before and the woman can remember from five years ago you said such and such. And she says, "I've been wearing that as a cross ever since you said it. And it has affected our lives." And I say, "Well, Christ, I had no idea that it was that important." And she says, "Well, it was."

It is significant that, in many of the stories told to us, men let their wives down when the wives were pregnant or home with a new baby, often a second or third child with an earlier child still in diapers—a time when the wives were most dependent on the men's willingness to be attentive and helpful without asking for anything themselves. But these were times when the men, like their wives, had assumed new responsibilities. For the men, a new baby meant new financial demands and more to do at home at the same time that it meant less right to ask for the wife's attention. The men might have felt entitled to a bit of self-indulgence. And they might just possibly have felt free to be inconsiderate in view of how difficult it would be for their wives to retaliate, given their wives' situation.

But for the wives, being treated badly when they were most needful of support seems to have felt like trust betrayed. They had let themselves become dependent through pregnancy and childbirth and the partner they had trusted to care for them had let them down. They remembered, perhaps, in order to protect themselves from having it happen again. They may even have pledged to themselves, at a time when there was little else they could do, that they would not let it happen to them again. Thereafter they would have owed it to themselves to remember.

Men's style of compartmentalizing marital dissatisfaction fits with their approach to their marriages. The relationship is enormously important to them; indeed, fundamental to their lives. They are totally committed to keeping it going. If there's nothing that can be done about a matter by fighting about it, then the best way to keep both the marriage and yourself going is to put it out of your mind, to learn to live with it.

The cost of the woman's way of dealing with feelings of misuse is that her resentment is immediately available to her, ready to be put to use whenever there is anger or mistrust. For the man, the cost is that issues about which he cares a good deal are never discussed and so never resolved. Compartmentalization, indeed, means that men not only do not discuss what is bothering them, they do not recognize that they are bothered. But in consequence men may feel disappointed in their marriages or angry with their wives without knowing why.[3]

Ultimately both the woman's way and the man's way of dealing with unresolved marital disputes burden a marital partnership. Each keeps alive the hurts of the past: the woman's way by protecting the hurt, the man's by unwillingness to be aware of it.

NEGATIVE FEEDBACK AND BICKERING

Negative feedback is one of the processes through which marital partners regulate each other's emotional state and behavior. Just as positive feedback—agreement with a position, reassurance that a behavior is justified—can strengthen resolve, so negative feedback, by invalidating a position, can keep emotions and behaviors within bounds.

The value of positive feedback is obvious. Imagine a husband working on a talk he must give the next day, and saying to his wife, "I think the line of argument I've developed is convincing." If his wife then says, "Absolutely, you've got it dead right," the man's confidence in his talk is strengthened. The value of negative feedback is less obvious, but may actually be greater. Suppose an older adolescent child borrowed the family car without permission, and the man was angry enough to contemplate a month's grounding; his wife might then point out that the man hadn't been around to provide permission and that the child was a careful driver. This sort of negative feedback would help keep perceptions realistic and judgment sound.

One man relied on his wife to modify his reaction when he was ready to come down hard on an older boy.

> Occasions when I might be going a little bit overboard in one direction, I may blurt out something like, "All right, the bike goes in the garage! You were told not to ride it in the street and now it stays there for a week!" Then some time later Myra will say, "Do you think a week is right?" And we'll decide maybe two days or four days or whatever. We'll say to the kid, "We've talked about this," and one of us will say, "Maybe a week is a little bit too much punishment. For this time it is two days. But if it happens again, it will be a week."

Mr. Orcutt, middle-level executive

Men rely on their wives (as their wives rely on them) to help them evaluate their children, their jobs, themselves, and, indeed, whatever comes up for evaluation, from the quality of a book or movie to the quality of their lives. It is not that their wives tell them what to think; it is that their wives listen and respond. Studies of single parents suggest that without someone to provide feedback, single parents distrust their own decisions, become uncertain about how best to meet their responsibilities, and have difficulty in maintaining a consistent approach.[4]

But should a husband and wife be angry with each other, perhaps want to criticize or to hurt the other, negative feedback can become a vehicle for attack. In the illustration given above, the wife might have said not the respectful, "Do you think a week is right?" but rather the indicting, "You're too hard on the boy, and you've always been too hard on him."

Once marital partners anticipate a barbed response to any state-ment, each will be self-protective when talking to the other. One defense is preemptive attack. The husband might say to his wife about their son, "He doesn't listen to anyone because of the way you indulge him." To which the wife might respond: "And I suppose you want to raise him to be as screwed up as you." Communication becomes squabbling and bickering.

Yet note how little the distance is between the negative feedback that is all but necessary and the squabbling and bickering that are injurious. Each is disconfirming. The latter has simply added to what is disconfirmed. Now it is not the other's opinion alone that is discon-firmed, but in addition the other's way of doing things, the other's character, the other's self. One man's wife told us:

> We tend to disagree on little, goofy things. If I say the sky's blue, he'll say it's purple. That kind of stuff. Or if there's two solutions to a problem, I'll always come from this direction, he'll always come from that direction.

> We got a load of stone for the wall along the driveway. Well, rather than picking it up and putting it in a wheelbarrow and bringing it down in the wheelbarrow and taking it out of the wheelbarrow, my solution was just to take shovelfuls down. I figured the exercise was good and it was easier and I didn't have to lift it twice. When Hal got home that night and saw how I was doing it, he said, "Oh, *no!*" It's that kind of stuff.

There was a good deal of conflict in this marriage about issues of major importance to both husband and wife. One of the conflicts was over having additional children: The wife wanted another child and the husband did not. It is possible that the husband chose to disconfirm his wife's competence in minor matters as a way of weakening her position in more serious matters.

Bickering, once it becomes established, can be difficult to change, because each partner anticipates an attempt to hurt and be-cause each partner may have scores to settle. But men can adapt to it, as to anything else; they can learn to tune it out or simply to live with it. And men whose marriages are prone to bickering may yet value the relationship for providing them with the security of a home, a partner in child care, and so forth.

BLOWUPS

A marital blowup is an assault, ordinarily verbal, by a partner who has totally lost control and says the words that are there in his or her mind loudly, forcefully, violently. Sometimes to give emphasis to the words there are also actions in which anger is displaced, such as smashing a dish or hitting the wall, or, more rarely, in which anger is expressed in violence against the other partner.

There seem to be two motivations for blowing up within a marriage: to compel attention and to intimidate. The former seems more often to underlie women's blowups, although certainly it sometimes underlies men's as well, and the latter seems more often to underlie men's blowups, although it can underlie women's as well.

Blowups to Compel Attention

Mr. Frederick was a very successful consulting engineer. He had made enough money so that he could give himself a sabbatical in which to write a book about his field.

> I'd been working on a very difficult, very weird passage that I'd written. And then I got off to write a paper and then make a trip to the West Coast, a big break of time, and I got back and I couldn't even understand what I had written, much less how to pick it up. And it stuck that way for two months. And just this past week I finally started something that I was happy about. And my wife came down in the morning—she gets up after I do, I go to sleep earlier and wake up earlier—and all I said was, "Please don't interrupt me, I've finally got something going." Or something to that effect. Those were my first and last words to her in the morning.

We learned from Mr. Frederick's wife that this incident followed a week in which Mr. Frederick had become increasingly remote. At one point Mr. Frederick's wife, perhaps to elicit a response, had told Mr. Frederick to move his technical magazines out of the front room, where they interfered with cleaning. Mr. Frederick said that he was still reading them. That ended the overt interchange, although we might imagine that Mr. Frederick had been unsettled by the suggestion that he move his things into his own space and that his wife was resentful because he had been uncooperative.

The statement, "Please don't interrupt me," was packed with content. By it Mr. Frederick let his wife know that he was engaged in an important task, one that demanded unwavering concentration. He also communicated that anything his wife might bother him about would be trivial in comparison with his work. And there was the suggestion in what he said that his wife had interrupted him in the past, distracting him from his work, and although he had tolerated the interruption then, this particular morning the work was too important for that.

Mr. Frederick worked effectively through the morning. He rose from his desk elated. His wife had fixed her own lunch, without waiting for him. That might have suggested trouble.

I thought, Gee, maybe it's really going to work! Good! Wonderful. So I took a break for lunch and so forth. She had already gotten her lunch without disturbing me. She was working on the greenhouse pipes, which was a project she wanted to do for some time. And I hadn't realized that somehow, from what she brought to the day, she'd been stewing and building up somehow.

I asked her, "What are you, mad at me for something?"

The question "What are you, mad at me for something?" or a question like it seems to be a way in which men often begin an effort to deal with a wife's irritability. Its import is both "Why are you behaving so peculiarly?" and "Whatever I did, I don't even know what it was, so I couldn't have done it intentionally and you shouldn't hold it against me."

And then out comes this, this, *indictment!* Which I recognize, "Oh, yeah, here we go again!"

She did this whole blowup thing as she used to do quite a lot when she had all the stresses from the kids, complaining about how I hadn't been supportive, absent for so long, this old stuff.

The question "What are you, mad at me for something?" permitted Mr. Frederick's wife to voice her anger. Once she began, there was so much rage that she could not stop. Mr. Frederick may have thought he would be able to jolly his wife out of whatever was bothering her. The violence of her response took him by surprise.

> So we had a bit of a row, a shouting match type of thing. And it really got me upset because this was a day that I should have some form of feeling of elation at having finally broken out, having gotten past this thing. And you feel like you've been blindsided by something that is so unjust. It's the injustice of it that bothers me. I mean, you can stand the hurt, you can take the pain, all those things would be okay, but it's just *unfair!*

A man's first response to this sort of blowup is likely to be an attempt to stay in control. The man may remind himself that his wife had been like this before and nothing terrible had happened then. But the magnitude of her rage can be so great, and her attack so unrelenting, that the man comes to believe that she means what she says, that she means it when she says she is through being his maid and through putting up with his rotten moods, disgusted by him, sick and tired of living with him, through, through, through. This the man cannot shrug off. Nor can he resolve it. He may try being angry in return, but that makes it worse. He gives up.

Once genuinely convinced that their marriages are over, men are likely to sink into dismayed depression. One man, after his wife blew up in this way, retired to his hobby room, where he blankly wondered whether he could get his wife to leave the home rather than having to leave himself. Another man went to bed, unable to face anything more. Mr. Frederick went back to his typewriter and sat there, paralyzed.

> I was really hurt by it. It shattered all the rest of my afternoon. I couldn't even think, much less go back to doing the book. I couldn't even do *anything*. I was stunned.

Another man, trying to explain why his wife's blowup had been so shattering, said that it inflicts pain deep inside, reaching your inner self. The experience is one of abandonment, an abandonment that occurs because the man's wife, who knows him so well, has judged him to be despicable. And it is unjust, undeserved. What did the man do to make it happen? Nothing! And there was no warning, no opportunity for defense. It was just: Boom, there it was. And what did he say to cause it? Nothing!

Later, when the man and woman come together again, the woman is likely to display a sudden sunniness of temperament. From her point of view the air has been cleared. She has reassured herself that she is important to her husband. She has forced him to treat her with respect. Her feelings have been acknowledged. She has gained his attention.[5]

Women seem to blow up in this way after an interval of seething about their husband's inaccessibility. But afterward, they seem sometimes to display near-amnesia for the event. (This is in contrast to their sharp-edged recall of their husbands' failures.) Mr. Frederick's wife, when asked about the blowup two weeks later, had almost forgotten that it had happened and had entirely forgotten what had led to it. She was uncertain, at first, that she had actually been angry. With encouragement, she could recall a few of her feelings.

[INTERVIEWER   When you quarrel about the use of time, could you walk me through one of those?]

MRS. FREDERICK   It is never the same, I guess. I don't really remember.

INTERVIEWER   Those things you try to forget.

MRS. FREDERICK   Yes, exactly. I guess I feel he doesn't pay enough attention to what I do or what I say. He's not interested in trivia, so I try not to give him trivia. But occasionally I feel I have to unload trivia. And I guess I get unhappy when he doesn't want to listen to it. I guess it is when I feel he doesn't pay enough attention.

INTERVIEWER   When you feel like he's not paying attention, what might you say to him? Or do you say anything?

MRS. FREDERICK   I don't remember. (Pause.) I guess I get upset. And the fact that he's not paying attention—I guess not paying attention is the right word—makes whatever—if I burn a pan on the stove—it bothers me more than if he's mentally here.

We became aware of this type of blowup only toward the end of our interviewing and so did not ask our earlier respondents about it. But when we did ask about it, interviewing both husbands and wives, it seemed to us that about half the couples reported having had this type of blowup. And in workshops I have given on marriage, when I have asked those in attendance whether a blowup of this type had ever occurred in their marriages, between half and three-fourths have said that it has.[6]

Blowups to Intimidate

The other form of blowup reported to us was a blowup to intimidate. Blowups to intimidate are those in which one of the partners— most often the man—becomes verbally assaultive, and sometimes assaultive physically as well, in an effort to compel the other partner to behave in a certain way. This may follow an incident in the man's work or elsewhere in the man's life that makes him feel helpless to make things go the way he wants them to. His wife now acts in a way that intensifies his sense of inadequacy; for example, she criticizes him and refuses to stop when he tells her to. He may feel that blowing up is the only way he can stop himself from sliding into total impotence, the only way he can retain his standing as a man. He shouts, threatens, bangs on furniture. Just possibly, he hits.

Here is an account of an actual blowup to intimidate. The man whose report is presented had suffered some reversals in his business. He was worried about meeting his bills. His wife wanted him to sell the business and take a salaried job. The husband was sure he could bring the business back. In the meantime he wanted his wife to stop nagging him. The one thing she *could* do to help was to hold off writing checks.

> I said to my wife, "Gee, I really don't want any checks written for a couple of days. I want things to kind of cool down." And I go down and I look at the checkbook. Three checks missing. Nothing noted. I don't have the goddamnedest idea what they were for. And it turns out they were for everything that she needed to somehow manage to squeak through the three days without money. And that was just enough money to cause us to overdraw at the account.
>
> And I blow up. I have my emotional outburst. "In the areas in which I am managing, I'm trying to manage and I ask you to help me out, help me out! If I tell you not to do something and there is a tacit agreement that you won't do something, for God's sake don't do it!"

And I've raised my voice to the point where I couldn't be shouted down if there was a crowd outside. And I'm a guy that puts fists through tables. And it turns out, this is the thing that she dislikes and fears the most in our relationship.

The blowup here did intimidate the man's wife. She was careful afterward to tell her husband when she took checks from the checkbook.

Here is an account of a blowup in which the man's self-control was good enough, or moving to physical violence sufficiently alien to him, for the incident to stop with shouting:

I think the last shouting match we got into was probably about my dieting. I really very strongly resent her telling me not to eat. Because it seems like I've been on a diet all my life.

I'm very well aware that I need to lose more weight and that it's a problem. But I feel I've accomplished quite a bit. And I resent her saying, "You can't have that," because I'm a grownup person and it's my decision to make.

That's just the way I talk to her about it. "Why don't you just stay out of this?" I tell her, "It's your fault that I eat in the first place. Every time you talk to me you make me so nervous that I want to go out and eat something." And she says, "You fat people are all alike. You look for excuses." And that gets into a nice little shouting match.

Although the husband permitted the incident to end in shouting, his motive in beginning the quarrel was to intimidate his wife into silence. Not all men are able to accept having their wives shout back at them, as this man did. Some men, on some occasions, feel that they require the reassurance that comes from compelling their wives' respect. It is as though something inside them snaps and they have only one aim: to demonstrate that what they say has to be acknowledged. One man, now divorced, said:

I used to get frustrated because Julie never liked to do the housework. I'd wind up doing the housework. She didn't like to do a wash either. She would wait until she got this marvelous burst of energy to do the laundry.

She would decide to do the towels. She'd do every towel in the house. She would take the clean ones she had just put out, she'd put them in the washing machine. It would be late at night and she'd throw them in the dryer, put the dryer on. You put the dryer on, they're done, you fold them and you put them back on the shelf. She didn't. Seven o'clock in the morning, I'd go take a shower, reach for a towel, no towel. Where are the towels? The towels are downstairs in the dryer. Every towel in the house!

These are things that you can say they are humorous, but if you have enough of them and they build up and they build up, all of a sudden someone says, "Hello," and you go off the deep end. And once I kicked a two-inch hole in the door. That was an outburst. And I slammed a banister hard one time.

The man may not have stopped here. In any event, his wife obtained a restraining order.

In blowups to intimidate, violence is almost always a threat. And such blowups do sometimes escalate to violence. But even then, the blowup is likely to have a point: to compel obedience, to silence criticism, to repair self-esteem.[7] It is explicable, if not defensible.

I once talked with a student who was also a police officer about the "domestic" cases to which he had been assigned. He said that in several instances where the police had been called by the neighbors because a man was beating his wife, when he and the other police arrived the man was sitting quietly, a slight smile on his face. Once he asked the man why he seemed so satisfied with himself. The man said: "I showed her who was boss."[8]

MEN AND "UNSATISFACTORY" MARRIAGES

Because men attach such importance to the functioning of marriage as a stable and reliable base for their lives, in the sense of both an emotional base and a partnership they trust to care for their homes and

children, they may tolerate marriages that their wives would character-
ize as unsatisfactory.

As is noted above, even a marriage marked by bickering or distance provides men with logistic support and with a place in the
communities of friends and family. It helps to establish among men's
kin and friends that the men are responsible figures, family men,
among those who are taking responsibility for homes and children and
neighborhoods. Because the marriage provides a partner who will
assume primary responsibility for the care of their children, the men
can live with their children without all the problems of single parents.
There is much in marriage, quite apart from the quality of the relationship with their wives, that is sustaining for men.

Given all these reasons for keeping the marriage intact, men are
likely to try to maintain themselves in a troubled marriage by staying in
charge, as best they can, by judicious compartmentalization, and by
accepting as one of the facts of their lives that theirs is not the best
marriage in the world. The men may experience occasional irritation,
anger, and fleeting depression. But they are likely to put up with their
discomforts. And until there is genuine threat that their marriage will
end, they are likely to escape stress.

I have been told by a matrimonial lawyer (which means a lawyer
specializing in the ending of matrimony) that he and his colleagues had
observed that women leave marriages for other lives, but men leave
marriages for other women. Women, he thought, are more likely to
want to escape a troubled marriage; men are more likely to want only to
change the marital partner.

CHAPTER
EIGHT

Fatherhood

BECOMING A FATHER

Until the recent past, the rite of passage through which men became fathers emphasized men's distance from the mother–child pair. A man's wife shared her developing pregnancy with an obstetrician as much as she did with him. At the time of birth, the closest the man was permitted to the delivery room was an outer lobby where he could await a nurse's announcement of the sex of his child.

The inclusion of fathers in classes for expectant parents offered men a first opportunity to function as supportive figures for their wives during the pregnancy. Inviting fathers into birthing rooms completed the change in the rite of passage to fatherhood. The new rite of passage teaches men that they are members of a threesome—still a bit marginal, but present by right and responsibility. As fathers they are to participate in the family rather than provide distant moral support.

The impact on men of witnessing the birth of their children seems to be dramatic, with extraordinary power to convey to them that there is a small being for whom they have become responsible. Still, there can be uncertainties for men about what they are to do. Perhaps to guard against these, some fathers report having assumed the role of photographer, controlling the future memory of the event and yet outside it. The emotional impact of witnessing their child's birth is nevertheless great.

I was in the delivery room. To the point where I took pictures. And there never will be anything, I think, to equal that moment. It was happening there, right before your eyes.

It's a feeling that you can never get back again. Because you have the person you are closest to, your wife, there, and it's a combination of wanting that event, that particular event, and wanting to be over the pregnancy, to be over the other event, which is having to go through labor. And it's really something that you can't touch. You never again can have anywhere near that emotional feeling.

And it doesn't matter how anything else has gone, if you feel lousy or work has been terrible or anything else. That wipes out anything and everything. You really could care less about anything else. It really is the culmination of everything.

Mr. Sherman, partner in a small business

Men do want to be useful in connection with their children's births. In telling the story of the births, men may be pleased if they can focus on a crisis or set of crises they were required to meet. A wife's unexpected labor offers such an opportunity. Mr. Mundy, a landscape architect, told the following story.

My wife had gotten her typical burst of energy the day before. I came home to find her scrubbing the bathroom floor and I said to myself, "Holy smokes, I've got to make sure the bag is packed!" Because that is how she telegraphs that she is about to give birth.

It was four or five in the morning when she went into labor. About six-thirty I called my mother and told her to come get our younger son. I got my older son ready to go out to kindergarten and I called a neighbor to pick him up after school.

While I was getting him ready, my wife was trying to get herself ready and was having some difficulty controlling the contractions. And I was running around, shipping one child off to my parents and getting the other one off to school.

Having now dealt with the challenges of getting his children to their destinations, Mr. Mundy turned to getting his wife to the hospital.

We got into the car about nine in the morning. We had been talking to our health center and they said, "Come into the center and we'll go from there." We drove half a mile and my wife said, "My water just broke. What do you think we ought to do?"

So I pulled into a hardware store and walked in and shouted, "My God, my wife's out in the car, she's in labor! Let me use the phone!" And the guy behind the counter said, "Well, I don't know, let me ask the boss." And the boss said, "Here's the phone."

I called the Plan and I said, "Look, we probably ought to go right to the hospital." And they said, "Okay, we'll redirect the obstetrician."

My wife is in the back seat panting and puffing and I'm driving down the parkway. At a set of lights my wife is lying with her knees up, trying to control herself. And a truck driver in a truck next to us looks down, does a triple take. My wife said she wasn't worried. He would never recognize her anyhow.

We pulled into the emergency entrance of the hospital and my wife got out of the back seat with some difficulty, walked in, grabbed the counter and let out a low moan. And I said, "Woman in labor." They got her into a wheelchair and I went out to park the car because you can't leave it in the driveway.

Mr. Mundy's wife might have been the one delivering the child, but it was he who had delivered his wife. Now he provided his wife with the moral support of his continued presence.

I got up to the labor room, there was this great cluster of people, including a young and nervous medical student who botched drawing blood and managed to get her to bleed all over the place from the inside of her arm.

And then the chief resident came in, wearing a flannel shirt. And he said, "We have to give you an internal to find out how things are going." And he put on his rubber glove and put his hand in and he said, "You are going to have the baby right here. Because here is the baby's head." And my wife said, "I'm not ready." And the nurse and I looked and said, "Yup, there's the head!" And she gave birth right there.

The baby was healthy and pink. Binny bled all over the place before they got the placenta detached. I wasn't doing too badly except when the blood started to run off the gurney onto the floor. Which wasn't a lot, but it was something. I said, "Well, I'm going to go out and make a few phone calls." And the nurse asked me if I was always this pale.

In his account of the birth Mr. Mundy had been his wife's partner from beginning to end; indeed, until their arrival at the hospital he had been the more responsible partner. He told the story with self-deprecating humor, but also with pleasure.

Everybody just cleared out and we had the baby to ourselves. As I recall, I pushed my wife and somebody else pushed the baby and we went up to the maternity ward. It was a very nice experience. It was nice for my wife, it was nice for me. It was nice to be in a situation where the baby was not kind of yanked away immediately, as they were to some degree when we had our other kids.

It was probably, of the three births, the most gratifying. Because my wife was in the best mood afterwards and the baby was real bright, quite healthy. I sat in a rocking chair and held the baby and talked to my wife. I felt very fatherly at that point.

Men who have adopted children can find the same basis for feelings of achievement in the production of the child by seeing their experience as a struggle, first to have a child of their own, then to adopt. The arrival of the adopted child after months or, more likely, years of search and application can then be as gratifying as the birth of a natural child.

THE MEANING OF FATHERHOOD

Fatherhood helps men make sense of their lives. It helps them understand why they work as hard as they do. As one man said, "It gives you a reason for effort."

Fatherhood gives additional meaning to marriage. Without children, marriage can be thought of as no more than legal cohabitation, an especially convenient form of dating. With children, it becomes a partnership responsible for the care of dependents. Divorce becomes, if not inconceivable, at least less conceivable. Children may not improve a marriage, but they provide new and powerful reasons for it to continue.[1]

People say that when you get married you get a new sense of responsibility. I don't think that's true, necessarily. I think it changes a little. But if you are married without children, other than it being a personal commitment, it is no big deal. Even if you wanted to split up the marriage, there is no big deal. Once you have children, there is a much greater responsibility.

Mr. Brock, owner of a small business

Children also burden a marriage. There are more decisions to be agreed to, more work to be done. And, with children to occupy their wives' time and attention, men lose their wives' immediate accessibility. In marriages that have been close, this can be a deprivation. But in compensation, men have something new to talk to their wives about, to enjoy with their wives, to worry about jointly. In marriages in which there had been little in common, in which the men had sought companionship in the male activities of sports or gambling and their wives had remained close to mothers or girl friends, children can provide substance.

Fatherhood also adds new linkages to parents and siblings. Men's parents are now grandparents to their children and their siblings are their children's uncles and aunts. Men find themselves head of a new sort of family linked to the families of parents and siblings in a single inclusive entity: the larger family of family reunions, of Thanksgiving and Christmas. The men and their wives, even if not themselves deeply invested in this larger family, are likely to view it as valuable for their children. And so they have new reasons for calling parents and siblings, for remaining aware of the birthdays of nieces and nephews, for buying presents and making visits.

Fatherhood also changes men's friendships, as they and their wives are drawn into linkages with other couples whose children are their children's ages, with whom they can exchange information about nursery schools and pediatricians. It changes men's views of what is a desirable neighborhood, making them want one that will be safe and spacious, with good schools and the right kind of playmates. The suburbs become attractive.

Fatherhood, even more than marriage, turns men into "family men," more stable, anchored by new responsibilities to their homes, with additional reason to be serious about their work. They present themselves differently, are seen differently, feel differently about themselves.

Men's journeys through life are marked by ever increasing responsibility. When the men were themselves children, their responsibilities were to parents for obedience and development and to friends for fidelity to the small boy's code of manly honor. As young men they assumed the additional responsibility of establishing a place in a community of work. Having achieved a good job, or good job prospects, they could marry and become responsible for a home and a marriage. As fathers, they assume responsibilities for the protection of the home now understood as a nest as well as a base for their own lives, for the family's financial support, for the emotional support of their wives, for whatever help their wives may need in raising the children, and for the open-ended responsibility of being a good father to the children.

Responsibility and freedom are inversely related; with increased responsibility comes reduced freedom. Fatherhood makes men less free to move to another job and another place, less free to take risks with their income, less free to call their time their own. Men may have mixed feelings about accepting these limitations on freedom. They may want more time to explore life, to adventure, to test and develop themselves. It can be wonderful news to learn that your wife is pregnant, but many men at least momentarily feel, with dismay, I'm not quite ready.

One man whose children, whom he loved, had come along a bit too soon for him, blamed his wife. That is not an unusual male reaction: It is, after all, the wife's body that is producing the child.

It put a strain on our relationship when I found out that she was pregnant. Because I sort of left the responsibility of birth control to her. I thought she could handle it. And she didn't. There was an accident. So I think that was really, probably, the worst fight we had, when I found that out. Because I assumed that she knew what she was doing. I was very upset. Of course, she was upset, too. And we sort of blamed each other.

Mr. Albright, department manager

Once Mr. Albright's child was born, he became a devoted father.

PARENTHOOD AND THE DIVISION OF LABOR

When first married, husbands and wives may lead roughly symmetric lives. The birth of a child sends them in different directions.

The Edwardses, a dual-career couple, are parents of a three-year-old. Before the child's birth, Mr. Edwards was an engineer, and Mrs. Edwards had been appointed associate director of an art museum. When their child was born, Mrs. Edwards left her job to be with the child, while Mr. Edwards not only retained his job but believed his work to be even more important. It was now on the basis of his work that his family—his wife and child as well as himself—would have a place in their community. Mrs. Edwards said:

After Cheryl was born I stayed home with her. I left a profession in museum work. I had been very, very successful in it. And I missed it a lot. It's a lot to give up, to have a child. But I'll tell you, it's worth it.

Mr. Edwards said:

It gives you a lot of responsibility that you really didn't have before. One, the financial responsibility. If we were just the two of us living together and one of us decided to leave our job, which I have done in the past, or said, "Let's go move to another city," or something like that, we would just do it. But you can't do that when you have a child. The financial burden is terrible. Especially if you are upper-middle income, if you are in our situation, you have certain aspirations for yourself and your family.

For both the Edwardses, the responsibilities of parenthood meant a loss of freedom. Mrs. Edwards, by becoming a mother, lost the freedom to work; Mr. Edwards, by becoming a father, lost the freedom to *leave* his work.

Before children are born, husbands and wives can shrug off the traditional sexual division of labor and run their marriage as a partnership of intimate roommates. They can contribute equal amounts of their employment income to the upkeep of the home and share equally the cooking and cleaning and furnishing and repair. With children, they are virtually forced to accept a sexual division of labor. The mother then becomes the more nurturant parent, the father the parent responsible for financial support.

Nor does this happen because of anything as mutable as "socialization" or "culture." It is, rather, a consequence of the unbudgeable nature of the mother–child relationship. The mother is emotionally linked to a baby that recently emerged from her, with whose bodily rhythms hers are attuned. The father, in response, is likely to see mother and baby as a unit. A father may feel left out, or he may feel gratified that his wife is devoted to his child, or both. Whatever his reaction, he is likely to feel that his primary contribution to his family will be through his effectiveness in his work outside the home.

None of this is to say that mothers of new infants do not need their husbands' help to reduce their fatigue and interrupt what could otherwise be isolation. But although husbands can make themselves enormously helpful by sharing childcare and by contributing to the work of the home, they are likely to feel that their first responsibility is to provide for the home's financial support and social place.

MEN AS PARENTS AND MEN AS FATHERS

Some of the things parents do with children are associated more with fathers' relationships, some more with mothers' relationships. Some are simply parental, the sort of thing that can be done equally well by fathers and mothers—though probably not in the same way.

Fathers tend to be specialists in the world outside the home. Men feel they are acting most as fathers when they can interpret the world for their children, train the children to deal with it, protect the children from its dangers, and sponsor the children—the boys especially—into a place in the world. Fathers give a teaching or coaching emphasis to their play with children. Their play is likely to tend toward puzzles, word games, model construction, and, of course, sports.[2]

Mothers also want children to achieve in the wider world, but concern with this is less of a persisting theme in their interaction with the children. Whereas fathers tend to specialize in training and encouragement for their children's eventual lives on their own, mothers seem to specialize in care for the children as they are now. In consequence, children are likely to want the father's, as well as the mother's, applause for competitive success, but they are more likely to turn to their mothers for comfort and care.

Mothers, as an extension of their responsibility for life within the home, are likely to be seen as more aware of the way children should behave within homes, although, at least for boys, not in the streets or at the playground. Fathers tend to defer to mothers as the parent who sets standards of behavior within the home.

Sometimes fathers are away from home when their sons have to be registered for soccer or taken to the ball field. They may then rely on their wives to take charge. They are likely to register this in their minds as a failing, requiring rationalization: It didn't really matter; my work is too heavy; I'll make it up later. If the child eventually does poorly, the father will have a basis for remorse.

But if fathers specialize in sponsoring children into the wider society and mothers in responsiveness to children's present needs, there is still a wide sphere of parental behavior that is simply parental, neither in the paternal mode nor in the maternal mode: keeping an eye on the children to make sure they are safe, transporting them from place to place, cooking for them, helping them straighten up their rooms. Many of these chores fall to the mother because they occur within the home, but if they occurred on a camping trip the father might well assume responsibility. Where physical setting decides which is the appropriate parent to take charge, there is nothing intrinsically maternal or paternal in the chore. And both parents are likely to want the children to behave themselves—to clean up after themselves or stop squabbling or work quietly on their studies.

Still, men tend to perform genderless parental activities differently from their wives. They are less nurturant: more playful sometimes, more matter-of-fact at other times. Their play, too, tends to be different, with more awareness of eventual role-taking and social participation. Rolling a ball back and forth is more nearly a father's idea of play with an infant than a mother's.

Parents who report that in their homes the father and mother are no different in their care of the children are, in most instances, not looking closely. A man who claims, with absolute sincerity, that he shares equally with his wife in childraising is likely in actuality to do somewhat different tasks and, insofar as he does the same tasks, to do them differently.

The Kendalls believed they shared responsibility for the care of their single child, a daughter not quite a year old. Both had demanding jobs, he as head of a firm of financial professionals, she as a department head in State government. Although Mr. Kendall was strongly committed to shared child care, he and his wife felt differently about looking after the child. His wife enjoyed simply being with the child; he did not.

> Annie is really a lot of work. I would not want to spend a tremendous amount of time with her. Lisa is just much more tolerant of that than I am. Annie is just going constantly. And a one-year-old has no fear of anything. They have to be watched constantly. That's very tiring. I can't imagine how people do this on a full-time basis. I would go nuts. Because it seems to me you're on edge all the time trying to control this child.

Mr. Kendall was aware that he spent less time with his child than did his wife:

> I sort of feel guilty about how much time I spend with Annie versus how much time Lisa spends. It is not the case that just because Lisa is the woman she always gets the responsibility of Annie. I think it's like thirty percent of the time it's me. Lisa said that she has no problem with that.

Mr. Kendall, to some extent, compensated for doing less than his wife in surveillance duty by performing activities more in the paternal mode. He shared child care by going out for things. The Kendalls lived in a high-rise inner-city apartment house. While talking about who did what, Mrs. Kendall said to her husband:

> If it's eleven-thirty or a quarter to twelve and I've just run out of formula, then even if you are all undressed and in bed and I've got my clothes on, more likely than not you'll be right into your clothes and out the door before I can object.

Mr. Kendall replied:

> I would just as soon that you not go out at midnight around here. I don't regard it as a difficult thing to walk two blocks to the store.

As far as taking care of the kids generally, I feel that we should be doing that equally. If I think it gets to the point where she's doing unfairly more than I am, then I feel guilty about it. And I guess I think of myself as doing these little errand type things.

If we count a midnight run for formula as child care, then Mr. Kendall did his share. But he did his share by an activity traditionally male: an errand that would have been just a bit risky for his wife.

Men tend to come into their own as fathers when their children are four or five and develop the latency-age child's infatuation with the world outside the home.[3] Then it is possible for the father to induct his children into sports, teach them the use of tools, take them on hikes. Men who own boats now use them as arenas for acting the father.

I'm really sort of good with the ten-to-thirteen-year-old boys. We sail together. And on the boat there are a thousand things for someone to question. And they are fascinated with all the gadgets on the boat. It's a big toy, and there are all of these things to play with. We have a little navigating computer on board and they were particularly fascinated with it. They were just fascinated with these flashing digital lights. I just kid them and get them going.

Mr. Foster, manager of mutual funds

Through sports, men can teach their children, especially their sons, the skills and attitudes of adult life. They can encourage the characteristics of determination, resilience, ability to function under pressure, graciousness in victory and defeat. And so men register their sons for Little League, drive them to hockey practice, take them to the playground to play ball and shoot baskets, and, when they can, attend their games.

My younger son's a junior in high school and all of a sudden he came up with lacrosse. Which is a pretty tough game. He got a stick and a pair of gloves. And we lost a TV set because he was practicing cradling the ball in the living room and all of a sudden the ball came out of the stick.

Well, we kind of eased our way through. He would come home beaten half to death, whining and moaning about sore feet, sore elbows, sore fingers. I ask him how he feels and he says, "Terrific. I'll see you later." And he goes to bed.

He used lacrosse to grow beyond that little whining stage. It was really kind of starting to aggravate me because it was going beyond his sixth and seventh and eighth year. And he worked out of it himself. And that was very pleasing to me.

Mr. Eggert, middle-level executive

The manliness men try to teach their sons can include not only self-assertion but also the self-possession that the father in the following account implicitly endorsed:

My son was a nonparticipating member of the team on a particular day. And I mentioned something about it and he said maybe he's not that good a player compared to the other five. I said, "Yeah, but do you think maybe if you had a little more chance to try playing you might get better?" And he said, "Well, I can practice down the yard. I don't have to practice during the game." So I didn't pursue it.

Mr. Orcutt, middle-level manager

Men believe it to be among their more important responsibilities as fathers to encourage their sons in sports. One man, to defend his having done well enough for a son who was later in trouble at school, spoke of having driven his son to hockey practice at five in the morning. Other men reported traveling long distances to watch their children in high school or college—almost always their sons—play sports. They, and often their wives as well, enjoyed watching their children and participating with them through identification, but the men felt themselves to be good fathers by being there.

Men are likely to have a clearer idea of how to coach and sponsor their sons than their daughters.[4] Until their children reach puberty, it may not matter very much, for men's involvement with the children, whether the children are boys or girls. After puberty it generally does. Some fathers of adolescent daughters who are bright and capable support the daughters' school achievements, as they would those of adolescent sons. (High-achieving women often report this sort of encouragement from their fathers.) But many fathers of daughters lose confidence in their ability to support and direct the daughters' development when the daughters become adolescent.

> Rachel and I do a lot together. We ski together and we sail together. And she goes to a school where I went to school and I'm a member of the Parents' Advisory group. So that's a nice connection. But now that she is adolescent she doesn't talk quite so easily with me.
>
> My son is never really much of a problem. He and I have always talked an awful lot. I'm not quite sure why. I think it is maybe because I am a very masculine person myself. He's gotten a real framework on which to climb, the same framework I climbed on. And he's the kind of kid, you give him the rules of a game and he'll play that game for all he's worth.
>
> But with Rachel, it's much more difficult. How do you act coquettish? You have got to, if you are going to get a boyfriend. And I have a hard time advising her about that. We could probably have an intellectual conversation about it, but I don't really understand it. I don't feel it. So I probably communicate my lack of understanding to her.

Mr. Foster, manager of mutual funds

The diffidence between father and adolescent daughter may go both ways: The daughters may themselves withdraw from the fathers. The men may more or less recognize that sexuality has something to do with the withdrawal, but may prefer not to inquire further:

> The youngest girl, I'll come home and something is wrong with my shoulder and I'll be sitting there reading the paper and she will give me a backrub. Or, "Can I go down the store and get you something?" My older daughter used to be like that, but, now she is sixteen, I think she is at a point where she is a little bit leery of me. Maybe all of a sudden. Maybe I'm the dirty old man or something that lives in the house. I don't know. But she is sort of falling into this pattern where she doesn't kiss me goodnight any more. She is real nice, pleasant, and all that. It is a stage.

Mr. Yule, foreman, construction crew

There remain some things men can do for adolescent daughters. They can demand that they behave properly at home and elsewhere, can inspect the young men who come to take them away in cars, can insist that they be home at a reasonable hour.

Mr. Brewer's daughter and her boyfriend stayed out beyond curfew one evening.

> Boots is going with a fellow and they came in an hour and a half late. Well, I got excited about that. I told the young fellow I didn't think we needed him around here any more. And he had enough moxie in him, which I give a lot of stock to, he came back two days later and wanted to sit down and talk. I give the kid a lot of credit. That told me he has something behind him. The reason why they were late, they were at his boss's house and the electricity went off in the town. And I said, "I don't want to hear that. If you have a commitment, you meet it. No matter what happens." We talked and he knew where I stood.

Mr. Brewer was firm and authoritative on his standard of proper adult behavior, but the young person whom he instructed was his daughter's boyfriend and not his daughter. In relation to his daughter, all he could offer was protection and constraint.

Many men, perhaps most, are able to care for children in the maternal fashion if the need should arise.[5] This is evident from the reports of divorced fathers who have custody of their children. Men whose wives are away only for a week or two, on a business trip or visiting their families, may feel no special motivation for replacing them. The men will boil hot dogs for meals or send out for pizza. But men who have won custody in the courts are likely to be determined to be maternal parents as well as parents in other ways. They seem to be able to learn how.

Mr. Harris won the custody of his two children, a girl of ten and a boy of six. Before becoming a single father he had been close to his children in the way traditional fathers are close.

> I had always been very close to my children. We had done a lot of things together in the sense of working outside.

On becoming a single parent, Mr. Harris was required to do what his wife had done previously. Cooking, especially, concerned him—and, perhaps, the nurturance of which cooking can be an expression.

Initially my worst fear was that I wouldn't be able to cook for them, that I couldn't feed them. That was my biggest fear. I could do everything else. I knew I could get the laundry done. I could stumble through the ironing. But how could I feed them?

I used to make up a list of menus to take me through the next ten years. But I used to really be concerned about that, how could I ever cook for these kids?

It wasn't that bad, actually. I burned things and I made a lot of mistakes. But the kids were very understanding. They'd say, "That's all right, Dad. So it's burned. Just cut off the bottom."

Eventually, Mr. Harris was proud of how well he had mastered being a parent within the maternal mode. Although he continued to act the father when appropriate, he could act the mother as well. Asked when he felt most fulfilled as a father, he said:

Well, putting Bobby [now eight] in the bathtub the other night so I could get all the dirt out of all the wounds he'd got during the day and then putting a band-aid here and a band-aid there and one over here and a big bandage on his knee. I guess that's a time. And when they enjoy a meal, I feel good about that.

As a single father, Mr. Harris, like single mothers, was pressed for time. He could not devote himself to his work as fully as he once had.

You've got work and you are trying to write a memo or you are trying to write a letter to someone, the kids call. Bobby'll call you on the phone and say, "Dad, Marie is punching me," or Marie will come on and say, "Bobby is punching me." That's always a little bit of an irritation. But you just have to put up with those things. That's part of the game.

Before assuming custody of his children, Mr. Harris often remained in his office well past the five o'clock quitting time. If he had a project nearly completed, he would remain at his desk until he had it finished. Now, as a single parent, aware that there was no other adult in his home looking after his children, he left the office promptly at five. Doing well at work no longer was his primary responsibility to his family. Men who add to their other parental responsibilities those usually met by their wives can expect to do less at work.

Married fathers can also become heavily involved in child care should there be a need. Fathers whose wives are alcoholic or whose wives for any number of other reasons reject one of the children are likely to pick up the slack. A boy nearing adolescence may give evidence of difficulty in moving toward an independent adulthood, and the father may assume, almost as a mission, the task of helping the boy along.

The second son of Mr. Leary, an official in state government, appeared to Mr. Leary to be emotionally troubled. At age ten, the boy was solitary and uncommunicative and seemed unhappy. Mr. Leary abruptly reduced the time he gave to his work. His primary concern, far more important to him than his work, became to help his son find a place in the world outside the home.

> All Bobby wanted to do was read. He had no friends and no interests. And I told my wife that we had to find something. There was a recreation center in town that had all sorts of activities, from banjo playing to pottery. He read through the whole catalog and picked riflery. The next day my wife called me up and told me that they had told him he had to be twelve years old and he had broken out crying. He'd been upstairs crying ever since and I should come home. So I said, "Well, we finally found out what the boy wants. I don't know what the hell I'm going to do about it, but I'll find out."

> I started off by getting a permit to carry a firearm and then buying a rifle and getting a membership in a rifle club. And then I would go there off-hours and have him shoot on his stomach from fifteen feet midway down the range. Then a man came by and said, "You need to get that boy a sling." And I got him a little sling and I got him a jacket.

Mr. Leary devoted himself to supporting his son's interest in riflery. He bought his son equipment that matched the boy's capabilities.

> The first rifle I got him wasn't very accurate. I bought the cheapest model that would shoot. The barrel was too long and too heavy, so I had a gunsmith shorten it a bit, so he could hold it. But the barrel would waver, so my sister took a roll of

solder and put an extra pound of weight on the end of the barrel so it stabilized for a holding position. He shot that rifle until he outgrew it and we got a full-size one.

Mr. Leary continued to meet his responsibilities at work. He was in his office early in the morning, and left at a regular quitting time. But his weekends were spent with his son at rifle matches, and many of his evenings were given to planning the next trip.

By the time we got his third rifle, I guess by the time he was twelve, he was shooting in competitive outdoor matches. When he was thirteen he was classified as a sub-junior, but he could wipe a match in the sub-junior class. When he got to be fourteen, in the regular class, shooting against eighteen-year-olds, it was a little more difficult. When he was fourteen he won in a match for adults.

We would leave home every Sunday morning to go somewhere for the rifle match. It might be a hundred miles away, it could be five hundred miles away. We would go for overnight trips quite a bit when he was thirteen or fourteen. We would read the magazines and find out where the matches were, and he would decide which ones he would want to go in and we would go on the overnight trip together. We enjoyed that. That would probably be when we were at our best.

Mr. Leary extended to the situation of a needful child the usual paternal responsibility to witness and support a son's participation in sports. Later, Mr. Leary felt that he had been more or less successful in helping his son toward a satisfactory adulthood.

Bobby became quite good, and that gave him a measure of self-respect so that he would try other things. He went on to a good prep school and did crew and cross-country skiing and cross-country track, as well as doing the straight academic work. But we had an awful hard time getting that fellow out of his shell. I worked at it from the time he was ten until he was about sixteen.

Always, fathers are concerned with whether their children, especially their sons, will be able to manage when they are on their own.

They try to teach skills, attitudes, discipline, and character—whatever may be useful later on.

> Sometimes I think they feel maybe I get a little too upset over small things. Like taking the barrels in after they are emptied. I say, "When you come home from school, you bring the barrels in. I shouldn't find them here when I come home from work." "I didn't have time." "You *make* time."
>
> It's not that I'm making a big thing about taking the barrels in. I'm trying to teach them that they should accept some responsibilities. I try to tell them, "Someday you are going to be out in the working world. And your job will say you are going to do this. And if you don't do it you are not going to have your job very long." That is the direction I am trying to head them in.

Mr. Orcutt, middle-level manager

Men are often uncertain of how best to direct their children. Is it really worthwhile, all the emphasis on sports? Should they be more protective or less? Should they ever encourage a child to risk, say, climbing a tree, or should they let the child follow its own wishes, or should they make sure the child doesn't get hurt? Is is valuable to take a child with them to work? Would the child get bored and be turned off? Are there any general answers, or does everything depend on the particular child?

Among the more common dilemmas is the conflict between protecting the child and encouraging the child in exploration and independence.

> My son was maybe eight or nine years old the first time he started to climb a tree. And I felt like saying, "He can hurt himself up there. Maybe I should tell him not to climb that tree." But I didn't want to say that because I wanted him to have that sense that he could do something on his own.

Mr. Ryder, department head

It is odd that there is so much literature available to help parents—mothers especially—to nurture their children and support the children's movement from infancy to childhood, and so little to help

parents—fathers especially—encourage young people to develop independence, self-reliance, and effectiveness. A number of organizations,
including Little League and the Boy Scouts, offer themselves as vehi-
cles, but fathers need guidance in choosing among them and in working
with whatever they choose. In general, fathers need help in clarifying
for themselves what they are about in their relationships to their
children. Some of the answer may be in helping fathers to be better
parents, but much of it, I think, is in helping fathers to be better
fathers.

CRISIS MANAGEMENT

Men generally are their families' managers of crises involving
events outside the household. That is implied by the traditional division of labor in which men see themselves as responsible for the
household's protection, whatever that might mean.

Mr. Humphrey, owner of a shop selling posters and paintings,
happened to be the only parent at home when the news arrived that his
daughter had been arrested. He started out in charge of the crisis
simply because he was the parent who was there, but he retained
responsibility for its management because he was the father.

> I get home at eight. My wife had gone out with her sister,
> shopping. Where's Anne Marie? The other kids are at home.
> Quarter of ten, there's a knock on the front door. A police-
> man. "We've been trying to call your house for an hour and a
> half. Could you please come down to the station. We have
> your daughter there."
>
> I go upstairs and my other daughter is on the phone. They
> have fifteen minutes any one time and then they have to
> hang up. The first thing I did was take the phone out of her
> hands and hang it up. I wanted to tear it out of the wall. I
> said, "You have been on the phone for over an hour. The po-
> lice have been trying to get me. You stay off that phone."
>
> I went down to the police station and talked to the arresting
> officer. Anne Marie was driving through town on a back
> street, a friend of hers in front, two guys in the back with
> beer in their hands, a case in the trunk. They got stopped for

speeding. The arresting officer said, "She wasn't drinking. She didn't have a beer in her hands. But we got her for transporting and speeding."

Anne Marie came out. I could see she had been crying. I said, "Okay, come on, let's go." So we get in the car. I just said, "Anne Marie." She said, "I know, Dad. I know." I didn't say anything more.

By the time Mr. Humphrey returned home, his wife was there. Mr. Humphrey relied on his wife to scold his daughter. Had it been a son in trouble, Mr. Humphrey might have done the scolding himself.

We got in the house and my wife was waiting there. Anne Marie was going to her room. We said, "You get in here." And my wife gave, not a lecture, but probably five minutes of just basically going over the whole situation. That she's getting to the age where there are a lot of things that she might think she wants to do, a lot of temptations, but the consequences are going to be a lot tougher.

Now Mr. Humphrey arranged for his daughter to be safeguarded from truly serious consequences while yet experiencing some penalty.

I got a lawyer that I retain for the company to represent her. I knew it was no big deal. It was continued without a finding. If nothing happens over the next year it is not going to be on the record. But I felt it was important for her to realize that it wasn't a nothing incident. So she had to meet with the lawyer and pay the lawyer's bill.

In stepfather families, where the children's mother is the primary parent rather than first among equals, the stepfather may assume responsibility for a child in trouble with the law. It is when a child has this kind of trouble that a mother who is a single parent may feel most beleaguered.

Yet fathers busy with other matters or uncertain of their ability to manage a crisis can define the situation as not serious or as something their wives can handle well enough. They can say to themselves and their wives that they have confidence in their wives' ability to manage and that it is a better deployment of family resources for them to remain at work. And so they leave to their wives the task of rushing a child to an emergency ward or defending a child before an irate principal.

Should the family define a situation as serious, the father may be required to appear at a clinic or a principal's office. If a boy at boarding school is homesick, his mother may visit him, but if he is threatened with expulsion, then the father is likely to meet with the headmaster. Should a boy indeed be expelled, as for theft, the father will certainly become involved. The more serious the threat, as viewed by the family, the more likely that the father will take charge.

Fathers seem to view protecting a child from harm as "coming through" for the child. Failure to protect a child from, for instance, a punitive and perhaps sadistic headmaster would be felt by the father as having failed the child and could be a reason for continuing guilt and shame.

The kinds of crises in which fathers become involved include every possible way in which children may diminish their chances of successful adulthoods. A daughter who becomes pregnant out of wed-lock and so may have to drop out of school, a son who fails two courses and is suspended, a son who is discovered to be drug dependent, a daughter whose car is demolished in an accident—all these become occasions for fathers to involve themselves actively with adolescent or adult children.

A man whose college student daughter had become pregnant said:

> I had a feeling, well, here's one more crisis that has to be
> dealt with. Does this ever stop with children?

The father had a friend who could help. Men's friends, as is shown in the next chapter, are often allies on whom the men feel they can call for help, should ever the need arise.

> There they were, alone, two young people, very confused and
> traumatized by this thing. I had a friend on the faculty at the
> school, and I wanted them to go and spend some time in dis-
> cussion with him. I called him and asked him if he could
> counsel them, talk to them in the kind of depth you don't do
> by telephone, and be sure they were not going to do some
> dumb thing that would really be hurtful to them. So they
> spent some long sessions with my friend. He called back and,
> without going into details of their sessions, those of course

were privileged, said that he thought they were approaching the whole thing in a very mature way.

One aspect of responding to the crisis was maintaining the morale of the other members of the family.

It's always a strain when your kids do something dumb. And there's the strain associated with bucking up the spirits of the others who may not rebound so quickly. It was hard to get Mother to be cheerful for a while. And little sister didn't take the whole thing well.

This was an event that evoked a certain amount of heartache and a background feeling of disappointment and a feeling of continued crisis in which one had to support and wanted to support the people immediately involved.

Men reduce their investment in work during the interval of a child's crisis. One man took off a week to be with his daughter when she was hurt in an auto accident. Even when they continue to show up at work, the crisis preoccupies them. The father of the pregnant girl said:

It happened at a time when I had just started a new job. I remember thinking, of all the times when it could happen, that was just about the worst. You move to a new company, there are a lot of things to learn, to get under your belt, and your attention is diverted by this kind of major family crisis. It was kind of a negative emotional background against which to be coping with all the other things that you cope with in the work situation.

It was not a thing I could put out of my mind and forget for those hours of the day when I was at work. I don't mean that it rendered me ineffectual or unable to think of other things. I just mean that when the demands of work were not very intense this whole line of thought would come flooding back in. It occupied all of my private thoughts during all my waking hours for a number of weeks.

Men can find a kind of affirmation of self in managing family crises. But they are likely to be annoyed at the overload they produce.

PRIDE AND DISMAY

Because men invest themselves in their children's ability to achieve a place in the world, they experience pride when their children do well. The pride is the same feeling they have in their own achievements at work, but stronger, because children represent a deeper investment of self. Men can experience enormous pride in a child who is praised or honored.

My son, out of a class of about one hundred twenty five at his school, was chosen the valedictorian, and then he won an award for the student that was the best citizen and that contributed the most. I'm *proud*. I think it's terrific.

Mr. Foster, mutual fund manager

It doesn't matter how a child achieves distinction. The child who does well can help the father feel he has done well himself.

There have been a lot of occasions when Amanda has performed publicly in one way or another on the piano with acclaim from whatever audience she was playing for. She was the pianist at last year's high school performance. And she'll be doing that again this year. She was the accompanist for the junior high school musical and she was the only instrument supporting the whole show. Three performances. She let me participate as the page turner. I thought that was neat.

You go to those things and it is just the same as having a son on the football team. You hear the cheering, so to speak, and feel all of those things. Pride in her accomplishment. Satisfaction to see her having carved out a niche for herself.

Dr. Sorenson, department head

When children do badly as they enter adult life, men feel the dismay of personal failure. They may earlier have become aware that a child's development was problematic, when the child was adolescent or preadolescent. They may have consulted psychiatrists or social workers, provided tutors, sought out potentially therapeutic summer camps. They will, of course, have devoted time and thought and energy to the child. If, despite all this, the child continues to do badly, the men can become angry and bitter. One man, enormously successful in business, described the despair he experienced because of the disappointing life adopted by a daughter.

Valerie has been a very exasperating and, I've got to say, hopeless kid. I've never seen a kid like this. I know there are loads of them out there. I'm sure she has got a lot of company. Otherwise we probably wouldn't need all the psychiatrists.

I would be on a business trip and I'd call home to find out how things are. Valerie was supposed to be living at home and she hadn't been seen for hours. She was late. She would come in a bit tipsy at two in the morning.

At this point it is her mother and father who need the psychiatrists because of the tensions that come from trying to get along with this kind of experience. It affects you in everything you do. It is a thought that we just can't get out of our minds. We are driving some place alone, it is rolling over in our minds. We are trying to figure out, who else can she see? What else can we do? Where else can she go?

The man cringed inwardly when friends or family asked how the child was doing. The question broke through whatever compartmentalization he had erected and exposed him to the pain of failure and disappointment—and to shame for having done so badly.

A lot of my contacts are friends, relatives, advisers, friends of friends. A lot of these people know me and the family well enough so that they ask me questions about, "How is the family?" "How is Valerie?" And all they have to do is say, "How is Valerie?" and all of a sudden I get that feeling that, oh, shit, I have to go through this again. I'll put that big smile on my face and try to fake it. But things really are lousy.

This man's other child was doing well. He could reassure himself that Valerie's problems couldn't have been entirely his doing. But the disappointment over Valerie contaminated everything else.

I can smile with pride when somebody says, "What's Ralph done recently?" Because he is a sound kid. But when somebody brings up a subject that leads in to Valerie, we are afraid to answer the question even with a half-truth because they are perhaps going to pick up on it and keep going. That can affect my disposition and my attitude and my approach to things in a business situation. And it has.

Because men feel responsible for sponsoring their children into adulthood, they blame themselves if the child goes wrong. A man whose son never recovered from drug use said:

Maybe I have a guilt feeling. I'm certainly not close to him and never have been. Maybe that's something I created. It is certainly possible. It was very hard for me to relate to him, very hard for me to communicate. I think I tried. I obviously didn't try hard enough or wasn't capable of doing the right thing. I think that is probably fair.

I'm not laying the big guilt thing on myself. At least, I don't think I am. I have reinforcement that the other son is totally opposite, the fact that there doesn't seem to be a definite pattern.

He was the first child. Things were very tough. Very tough. I remember one week I had seven dollars and fifty cents to buy groceries with for the week, and five of that had to be baby food. Maybe I'm saying this to make myself feel better. But what I'm getting at is, I can't overlook the fact that his feelings are maybe about a situation that I could have done something about.

Always, men could have done more. Even when men feel that they did their best, they can blame themselves for not having done better. A man whose children were doing reasonably well, but not as well as he had hoped, said:

I think that if I had set higher expectations in a more authoritative way, had been more a disciplinarian, I have the feeling that in some ways my kids would have benefited from that. Particularly my oldest. And there are passing regrets about that. My oldest has been a good student, but not as good a student as he should have been. And I have often thought that I could have pushed him further, set more limits, helped in that maturing process, academically at least. There are passing regrets about that.

Even when everything is going well, when the children are developing well and the marriage is strong and the man has been fully participant in the household, some men nevertheless worry that they have not been good enough disciplinarians, guides, or models, that they have not been close enough to the children, or that they somehow have let the children down.

I did the usual things that a modern father does, as opposed to my father. But still and all I was not comfortable taking the kid for a day, that kind of thing. That is the thing I would have liked to have done, but I was too uptight to pull that off. When I say that I'd have liked to have done that, I would not have liked doing it at all, but intellectually I would have liked to have done it.

But what else could I have done? If there were only a choice, then there would be some fairness in it. But there isn't a choice. I'm not even close to providing what I consider to be a minimum standard of living now. So what could I do different? Maybe I'm doing the right thing. But I don't think I could have done it any other way.

But I still feel that I'm not around as much as I'd like to be, I'm not as big a part of her life as I would like to be. And I'm not able to have the impact on her that I'd like to have. I really feel that if I could have applied some of the mental energy that I spend at work to her I probably could have done a lot of things for her in the last six years and have made her future life a lot richer. I'm sorry that didn't happen.

Mr. Williams, owner of small business

It is quite common for men to worry that they may have failed their children. Of the fifty-nine men in our study who were married and had children old enough for the men to feel regret or guilt for not having been more of a father, twenty-one, more than a third, expressed such feelings. This strikes me as a very large proportion to harbor feelings so dismaying. And our methods, since they required clear evidence for categorization of a man as feeling regret or guilt, would be likely to produce an underestimate.

MARITAL SEPARATION

Women who have gone through separation and divorce sometimes generalize about callous fathers on the basis of ex-husbands who have been late with support checks and irregular in visits. If, now and again, the ex-husbands have been whimsically generous toward their children, it has been a moment's impulse, without awareness of the children's needs.

Sometimes the ex-husbands have fathered second families to which they are now attentive. Or they have become stepfathers to other men's children. In either event they seem to their former wives to have replaced the children of their first marriage with new children, as though one set of children is as good as another.

Other women whose marriages have ended have been confronted by ex-husbands determined to gain custody of their children. The women wonder why. Before the separation, their ex-husbands had seemed almost without interest in the children. The ex-husbands had then come home late from work and when at home had claimed to be too tired to play with the children, or too preoccupied by work still to be done. They had been irritable when the children tried to get their attention. Sundays they retreated behind newspapers or the television set. Where was all the caring for the children then?

Yet both the men who visit their children only sporadically and the men who fight for custody are likely to have been deeply invested in their children at the time their marriages ended.

When the men were married they demonstrated their love for their children as fathers typically do. They worked for the children, took joy in their existence, and were pleased that the children could look to their mothers for nurturance and to them for applause for achievement. They thought of themselves as available should they be needed, and were grateful when there was no need. But with the ending of the marriage this way of being a father becomes impossible. The men see their children growing apart from them. When a visit ends they know the pain they feel, and they see the pain their children display. They wonder how best to manage their relationships with the children so there is benefit and pleasure rather than pain. Once they would have consulted their wives, but their wives are no longer trustworthy. The fathers are alone with their perplexity.

What women who have become skeptical of men's commitments to their children do not recognize is the pain, grief, and confusion that are likely to precede a man's failing his children. The man may well have been confronted by a situation that seemed to him hopeless. If a father is the man of the house, how can you be a father if you no longer belong there? If a father is a protective presence, how can you be a father if you no longer know what is going on? If a father is someone whose standards the children can internalize, how can you be a father if the children no longer believe in you? How can you support your children into adulthood if you see them only every other weekend? How can you provide them with direction if you have been stripped of parental rights?

Noncustodial fathers routinely experience pain when they visit their former homes. They anxiously scan their children's faces to see if the children have been hurt by the breakup. Whatever troubles the children may report, from bad grades to fighting with siblings, the fathers take as evidence that they failed their children by ending the marriage. They hate the feeling of distance on first meeting the children, their ignorance of the events of the children's lives, their sense of being strangers. They hate their new relationship to the children: the parental visitor. The day after they have seen their children, they may be hung over with grief and remorse.

Many of them, including those most reliable about child support and visits, now and again wonder whether they are right to continue to visit, whether it might not be best for everyone if they just disappeared. And then their former wives tell them that the children were upset after their most recent visit, or came down with a cold, or that they have heard reports from the children that convince them that the fathers lack both common sense and morality.

Sometimes fathers decide, shortsightedly, that support payments are being wrongfully extorted from them. It's not their house any more, nor is it their family. Yes, the children are theirs, but the money doesn't go to the children, it goes to the former wife. And there is nothing they can do about it. They have been fixed by the court. Writing the support check is acquiescing to injustice. It is no more than self-defense to be slow to send it, or send it only after other bills are paid. From a similar perspective some fathers will not pay the children's college tuitions, although they would have paid without question had there been no divorce. They want to be done with their responsibilities to the marriage, and they fail to see that it is their children whom they hurt.

Some men who have become hopeless about making a difference to their children act to cut their losses. They stop visiting and perhaps stop sending support payments. They compartmentalize off their parental feelings and try to make a new life for themselves. As they might in response to a failure at work, they try to put it behind them, to avoid "Shoulda, woulda, coulda." Again, their children are hurt.[6]

Still, men who become single fathers, whether this came about because they won custody in the courts or because the children's mothers died or became ill or just wanted time for themselves, seem to be as good parents as women who have become single mothers, with the same mixture of devotion and sense of burden. Like women who are single parents, they commit themselves to raising their children as their first priority in life. They do this despite loneliness and the belief, which they share with women who are single parents, that life as a single parent is incomplete. But should they find someone, they are nevertheless likely to say that, whatever the cost, their children come first.

> No matter who it is I'm seeing, she can't compete with the kids. I've told my girlfriend that she's got to understand that. I've said, "You can't put me in a situation where I've got to choose between you or the kids. Because you are going to lose." I would do what the kids want or do what I think is better for them rather than what she wants.

> *Mr. Ward, mid-level executive, single parent of two children*

Men are different kinds of parents from women, but they are as deeply devoted to their children. If, after marital separation, it appears that men's devotion to their children has waned, the explanation is not that the men no longer care.

WITHDRAWAL AND COMPARTMENTALIZATION

A father of a young man who had become addicted to drugs said:

> We went through six months of not knowing where he was, of expecting to get a phone call that he was either in jail or had been killed. He was living in the gutter. And we had to come to terms with that. We just said, hey, we might lose him. And there is nothing we can do about it.

This response is extreme, and unusual. And yet, how much pain should a man tolerate before he seeks to block it so that he can go on with his life? Sometimes men whose children are doing badly may resign themselves to the situation as hopeless. Or men who have left their homes as part of a bitter separation have to accept that their children are lost to them. They are hurt, disconsolate, in pain. Then they ask whether they should give up on the possibility of a gratifying life or somehow come to terms with their loss and instead go on with their lives. If they choose the latter path they may withdraw, try to check their feelings, try not even to think about the children, and go on. This is, they believe, all that is left for them to do. A father of a psychiatrically disturbed son said:

> My boy had a psychotic break. We got him into a good hospital with a little string pulling. The people across the street had a good friend who was one of the head psychiatrists. They tried different drugs and they thought that they had something that worked. It turned out that it really hadn't. He was in the hospital for three weeks. Then he was in a second hospital on another episode. And then in another hospital. And then back to the first.
>
> At that time the Blue Cross benefit was fifty thousand dollars. And he had to leave the private hospital because he was about to run out of Blue Cross. On his second time there the damned staff person told him that they were going to have to kick him out because our insurance had transferred him to the public hospital.
>
> We were worried that he couldn't hack it in the general psychiatric service of a public hospital. But we would not sell the house in order to pay the private hospital, which would have been the alternative. If we lost the boy we would still have ourselves. We would be very sorry, but we would not sacrifice our lives.
>
> It probably affected me at work. I don't know. I was still writing articles, going on trips. You just turn it off and turn on whatever you have to get done. You don't let one interfere with the other.

Other studies suggest that there is a cost in work efficiency to this sort of massive compartmentalization. Yes, a man can put out of his mind a young adult child in relation to whom the man feels hopeless. But the cost is vigilant defense against reminders, against stray thoughts, against letting the topic enter conversation. The man is less free to think what he wants, say what he wants. He must check his impulses before expressing them—indeed, before permitting himself to be aware of them. He is more controlled than he otherwise would have to be, and his emotional life is to that extent flatter.

CHILDREN AND THE MEANING OF MEN'S LIVES

Children, for men, are a commitment, an investment, an obligation, a hope. They are men's chief contribution to the world and justification for their lives. The children are loved for themselves, yes, but they are also loved as carriers of their fathers' efforts and hopes and selves. Indeed, the two kinds of love cannot be disentangled.

It is easy to underestimate men's investment in their children. Men so often display that investment not by being present and nurturant but rather by working hard, somewhere else, to provide for the children. That the men believe their work is a way of caring for their children may be evident only through framed photographs on their desks, but in the backs of their minds they value their work at least in part because it makes it possible for them to support their children.

Fortunate are men whose marriages have persisted and who have successfully launched their children into adult life. Thoughts of their children can then provide them with reassurance that whatever else happens in their lives or has happened, in this critical respect they have done well.

The speaker in the following excerpt is Mr. Yule. Mr. Yule, a carpenter, is foreman of a work crew in an industrial park. He was one of the men interviewed who had seemed in a brief telephone discussion to meet our criteria for reasonable occupational success, but who were actually in occupations lower in social prestige.

I'd say the only success in my life is that I'm still breathing. No, my life is not a success. I'm just muddling along, the average working-class person. I'm not a doctor or a lawyer or something like that. I'm not better than my father was. I'm just making a living and getting my kids into school and getting rid of them. I don't see where I'm going to do much more.

Here the interviewer interrupted to ask about the man's accomplishments. Wasn't there something he could be proud of?

Five kids. I'm proud of that. I own my own home, I have a couple of cars, there's no sheriff knocking at my door. And the kids are all in school. I don't know what more I could ask for.

Even if a man has achieved nothing more than his neighbors, to be able to say that he has supported himself and raised his children is to have a basis for pride. What more does he need to defend himself before his internal appraiser, the evaluator he carries within himself, than this: "I do honest work and I do it well. I have my own place and my own transportation and I owe no man anything. And, most important, I have had children and have brought them up to be people who respect themselves and whom others respect."

Mr. Yule was able to say this. And, being able to, he could respect himself.

*CHAPTER
NINE*

Communities

SOCIAL LIFE

Work and the family are the sectors of men's lives that have priority in their thoughts and commitments and time. But men maintain other relationships that are also important to them: relationships with kin, friends, neighbors, and fellow members of voluntary associations. These are relationships that occur within networks of people who know each other, where the man too has a place, where he belongs.

Men's standing at work and their family situation help establish how they will be seen in these other communities of their lives and whether they will feel accepted and want acceptance. But standing and situation are only loosely determining: a physician and a warehouse clerk can become tennis partners and, from there, people who think of themselves as knowing each other pretty well. If a man is married and a father, he will have more in common with other men who are married fathers, but his neighbors may include an elderly widower with whom he becomes friendly. By and large, people form friendships with others in similar work and family situations, but not exclusively.

Kin, of course, include people in all stages of life and at more than one social level. Yet it does count whether a man has done well—better than his siblings, say—and his role in the family is likely to be decided, in part, by whether he is married and has children.

Friendships, kin ties, and relations with neighbors and with fellow members of voluntary organizations all enrich men's lives. They are sources of companionship and of help, and provide the kinds of linkages that help men feel part of a social world beyond the close confines of work and home. And yet, however important the relationships within it, this third sector is more nearly optional in men's lives than the sectors of work and family. In dual-career families with small children, when there is simply not enough time for everything, it is sociability with friends that is allowed to drop off and, after that, visits with kin.

Because relationships in this third sector of communities are more nearly optional than relationships in the sectors of work and family, men vary more among themselves in the ways they develop this sector than in any other aspect of their lives. Some men, outgoing, social, and with a talent for friendship, have an extensive circle of friends, including some from their boyhood, while other men see friendship as emotionally unimportant and often a bother, and prefer a life that is socially restricted. Some men feel close to their parents, siblings, nieces, and nephews, and take every opportunity to visit and talk, while for other men relationships with kin are responsibilities to be met only as necessary.

To see what is involved, for men, in social life, we might follow the entrance into a new community of Mr. Brewer, later owner of a small business, but at the time a middle-level executive in a national corporation. He, together with his wife and two teenage children, had been moved by his company to another region of the country. He was living in a rented house until he could find something permanent.

Mr. Brewer had told a sister to whom he felt close that he was being moved. Mr. Brewer's sister, though she lived at a distance, found it possible to be helpful.

My sister who lives in the Midwest called and said, "My next-door neighbor has an uncle that lives up there that is a realtor. Everything is lined up for you."

Mr. Brewer purchased a house from the realtor. Five days after he and his family moved in, one of their neighbors held a party to introduce them to others in the neighborhood. That was unusual, and helpful. Others, when newcomers, have strolled through the neighborhood, meeting people as they could. Or the wife in the newcomer couple has waited for neighbors to knock on her door to welcome her to the neighborhood. Where there was no such knock, it may not have been until one of the children of the newcomer couple brought home a friend from across the street that a linkage in the neighborhood was formed. Until the neighborhood grants acceptance, newcomers may be treated warily. But for the Brewers, the welcome came early.

As soon as we moved in, the lady next door had a cocktail party for us, had the other neighbors in. And her husband was past president of Rotary and Little League, you name it. And it all started from day one.

It was hard at first, just introducing yourself around, not being able to pick up the phone and call a merchant or call the bank, call this one or call that one. That was hard. But it didn't take me long. We just fell in line. And we just got to know everybody. I'm the type of guy, if I don't know somebody, I just introduce myself and we go on from there.

Mr. Brewer and his wife discovered that they had moved into a neighborhood in which they fitted. Mr. Brewer also had the time, energy, and skills required to enter the more or less organized social life of the neighborhood. Although he was a new person in the branch office to which he had been moved, and so was required to prove himself there, he was also able to give energy to achieving a place in his new community. Most men would do less.

You have to extend yourself, get involved, to be accepted. Once you are accepted, you get in Town Meetings and you get in Little League and you get in Rotary, the whole deal. But you have to extend yourself to get in just to know people.

Some of the people Mr. Brewer came to know he called friends. Yet he believed the new friendships to be thinner and less trustworthy than the friendships he had made earlier in his life. He could not count on his new friends as he could on his old friends. At any rate, he was skeptical of the new friends.

The majority of the people here grew up together and more or less have their own friends and we're kind of the new-comers. As we go around, it's not like it would be at home. It's like a transplant in that it just doesn't work here as it does where you come from, where you have established friends for over thirty-some years.

You make acquaintances, and then you make, you might say, friends. But it's not like friends that you have at home. The friends that we have here are a different type of friends, more of a social, business, type of a situation. When you get together it seems like everybody's on guard, protecting themselves. You go to dinner at somebody's house, or you have people in for dinner, it's more of acquaintances instead of friends.

The friends back home, the friends whom Mr. Brewer missed, were not men with whom Mr. Brewer shared intimate concerns. Perhaps, with one or two, he could have had he wanted to, but this was not what made a person a real friend. A real friend was someone you had known long enough to trust, on whom you knew you could rely.

We have quite a few friends where we used to live before we moved here. I grew up with them. We more or less started in seventh grade and went through high school and college with some and worked with others. And we've kind of kept a relationship all through the years. And now with their children and everything else.

Maybe you don't hear from them for three, four, five months, but all of a sudden the phone rings and they're there. Or they understand that we are coming into town and they've set a party up or a dinner or lunch or something. And they always manage to communicate during Christmas, either by card or phone or something like that. There're some friends that I haven't talked to in years but I could pick the phone up and communicate with them.

At home, we're noted for floods. If somebody got water, you just went in and cleared them out. You just showed up. You didn't worry about it.

The people who played a role in Mr. Brewer's settling in were his kin, all of whom were obligated to help, one of whom actually did; neighbors and fellow members of Rotary, who provided an organized setting for sociability; and friends. The friends included new ones, with whom there was opportunity for companionship and the beginnings of trust, and old ones, with whom companionship was more limited, because they lived far away, but with whom there was much more trust.[1]

KIN

Men's relationships with their near kin—their parents and their siblings—begin at birth or, in the case of younger siblings, at the time of the siblings' birth. As men move on in their development, from infancy through childhood to adulthood, men's images of their near kin change, along with their images of themselves.

Once men have homes of their own, other members of the families in which they grew up constitute a community for them: people who are linked to one another, among whom the men have a place. It is a community that maintains its linkages by telephone, occasional visits, and comings-together at family holidays. It is understood as a community in which the man's place cannot be lost. Nor can his obligations to it be honorably denied.

Always, men's relationships with kin take place within a context of history, so that the most ordinary interchanges have endless resonance. Sibling rivalries persist, though maturity dampens their expression. Men's relationships with their parents continue to be affected by their boyhood relationships with them, though the men have attained equal or superior standing as adults.

Some themes that appear frequently in men's reports of their relationships with their kin are these:

In men's relationships with their mothers, beneath a surface of responsible solicitude may be vestiges of desire for the mother's attention and care. But by being solicitous, even indulgent, toward their mothers, men demonstrate that they are no longer immature and in need; on the contrary, they are capable and responsible. They call or visit, display concern about their mothers' health and activities, and eventually decide their mothers' living situations. Far from needing their mothers to be attentive to them, it is they who are attentive to their mothers.

In their relationships with their fathers, men seem to be responsive not to an earlier nurturance (so that, perhaps, they now feel diminished by awareness of having required it) so much as responsive to having been sponsored, perhaps clumsily, into a successful adulthood. Often, a remnant of the experience is a still rankling feeling of only partial acceptance. Or men may display affection for a father who had been a guide, combined with resentment because he had been too distant, too authoritative, or too weak. They may regret not having been closer, not having talked more and listened more. They seem to want to remedy defects in the relationship now, but are unable to do so.

In some instances a man wants to gain his father's approval of a self different from the one the father had tried to foster. Or a man wants to demonstrate to his father a level of achievement that the father cannot deny. For just as a man is often acutely aware of his father's desire to be proud of him, he can be equally aware of his father's fear, perhaps stemming from the father's own self-doubt, that his son has not measured up. Mr. Draper, now the owner of a successful business, said:

> My father, who is now seventy-six years of age, creates an emotional problem for me, which I recognize and can't do a damned thing about. He doesn't really know that he's got me all wound up in knots, but he sure as hell has. I'm happy when I keep my distance from him.

> No question, I get all choked up when I'm talking to him. It doesn't matter if he's forty miles away and I'm on the telephone or he's six feet away. He puts a certain something out there, a standard, that I am afraid I don't come up to in his eyes. He has never said how well I've done something. Those kinds of words don't come from my father.

> He has achieved a great deal through hard work and considerable brilliance. And he is intolerant of others in the family who may not have achieved as much.

> My business, although I've had tremendous success in material terms, has not been the type of success that my father would give me a lot of recognition for. It kills my wife that he doesn't recognize me for having achieved a comfortable station in life.

Mr. Draper was also, in a muted way, resentful that his father had not supported him in the pursuit of a career that the father might have respected more: a profession or an academic career. But as his father ages, Mr. Draper becomes more concerned with indulging him:

> I respect him and enjoy participating in things where he is around, up to a point, because I recognize that's a son's duty. So I go out of my way to do things for him and with him to make him happy.

When men's marriages are still in their early years, their parents may help them with clothes for a baby or with babysitting or with the down payment on a home. As the marriages and the parents age, the direction of help reverses. For some men, keeping in touch with parents is then an opportunity to demonstrate devoted attention. For others, it is a chore. For many, it is both.

> We needed to spend our vacation every summer seeing my mother and my wife's mother. We had no choice. They couldn't travel. And so we went there. And that was the way we spent the summer vacation. Looking back on it, at times it was awful.

> *Mr. Craig, high-level administrator*

But men accept without question their obligations to their parents. Not so with their siblings. Although obligations to help are implicit in all kin relationships, in their relationships with their siblings men find a good many other factors modifying the obligation. The quality of the relationship matters: How close is the sibling? Obligations to the men's own families matter: Men are likely to feel that their obligations to their wives and children take precedence over their obligations to their siblings—and if the men themselves do not, their wives almost certainly will. In addition, the men's parents once cared for them, so there is indebtedness; with siblings, there is a sense of independent lives. Furthermore, parents may be aged and infirm, but siblings should be able to care for themselves. Yet, with all this, men can feel they have responsibilities for siblings in need, although the responsibilities are without the absolute force of those to parents.

> My youngest sister is somewhat backward. My parents get worked up. "What should we do with her?" "Will she ever marry?" "Will she get a decent job?"

> At some point it's going to be someone else's problem. Mine, probably. I hope she is going to have enough money to live on, but if for some reason she doesn't, that's clearly going to be a stressful situation for the family and, presumably, for me. It's going to be a drain on resources.

> You get back to the moral issue. It's your flesh and blood, so

to some extent it is your problem. But that can be very tricky. If there is plenty to go around, it doesn't matter. But if you've got enough for yourself and to educate your children the way you want to, and things are just about balanced, and then you've got another drain on your resources, it is your problem and it's not your problem.

Mr. DeVries, salesman

Men's relationships with their parents change greatly as men move from dependence on the parents through separation and independence to ultimate responsibility. Their relationships with their siblings are much more of a piece. Earlier understandings of rivalry and alliance continue to define the sibling relationship. If, as children, an older brother would have been an ally in a playground confrontation and a persecutor at home, the same combination of family loyalty and personal ambivalence is likely to continue into their adult relationships.

I've got two older brothers. Our relationship has tempered itself from trying to beat each other to a pulp on the football field and running through each other and who can score more and whatever into the adult world of "I can better you." It's a game the three of us play. We know we are playing it, trying to compare with each other. If one brother, he's an athletic director, he'll say, "Hey, we had an undefeated season this year," I'll say how good a year I had.

Mr. Norris, middle-level manager.

It is not that sibling relationships are impervious to new experience. Rather, the new experience tends to express and reinforce earlier definitions. Then the new instances of helpfulness or animosity are remembered along with old ones—entered, like everything else, in the history of the relationship. Mr. Brewer said:

There was a time when my brother could have gotten me a job and he didn't. He is in the head office of the telephone company at home and I had an opportunity to go in and he wouldn't go to bat for me. I don't know if it was jealousy or he felt that I was going to override him or to put a black mark against him. But that will always stay with me. That has hung around for a lot of years. One of these days I'll nail him and say, "Remember when . . . "

It is not uncommon for men to become estranged from siblings. The men simply stop calling. When they see the siblings at their parents' home on Christmas or at a wedding or funeral, they are correct and a bit distant.

My relationships with my sister and brother are very poor. I felt very strongly that they were never very supportive of my father and the business. They just really were stockholders. From a business point of view, they took advantage of it.

When my father became disabled they demanded more and more monies out of the business and more and more control of it. When we were taking it into a new venture I suggested that they put up so much money and come in as one-third, one-third partners. They never put up the money. But when I sold the project, they demanded a third.

I felt very strongly that they had not done anything. Everybody connected with the project and all the lawyers felt the same as I did. So it ended up in a legal battle. But rather than go to court I settled it as equitably as I could, under the circumstances. The return to them was in the hundreds of thousands of dollars from putting nothing—zero—into it.

That led to a good deal of hard feelings, extremely bad relationships. I've just made up my mind that they might be my brother and sister, but I'm not ever going to have any financial dealings with them ever again.

Mr. Powers, owner of middle-size business

Yet estrangement from kin is rarely complete and forever. If the parents are alive, family holidays bring kin together. So may family crises: a parent's illness or death. Should the man have children, there are the children's family ties to consider. The siblings are his children's aunts and uncles, their children his children's cousins.

We do see my brother's children, and they are very cordial. It is a very friendly relationship. And my daughter sees my sister's daughter. They are very close. And my sister's daughter is getting married, and my daughter is going to be her maid-of-honor. So there are still family relationships.

Mr. Powers

When men live near parents or near brothers or sisters with whom they get along, they are likely to be in touch frequently. With parents, a personal contact at least every other week, augmented by an occasional telephone call, seems about the norm; with siblings the frequency of contact depends on the quality of the relationship, on proximity, and, in some families, on the availability of a parent to act as a message center. If parents or siblings live near enough to each other, the men's children may learn to treat the parents' or siblings' homes almost as extensions of their own, and the men may see a good deal of their nieces or nephews.

Often men have attended schools or taken jobs distant from their parents' homes and then have settled where they moved. Then they are likely to reduce the frequency of their telephone contacts with parents and drastically to reduce the frequency of such contacts with siblings. They may actually see their parents and siblings only at Christmas or at the family gatherings precipitated by a marriage or a death.

Men are unlikely to invest themselves in the domestic issues of familial understandings and misunderstandings. As a result, they may not have a great deal to say in telephone calls to mothers and siblings. Sometimes men prevail on their wives to manage the chores of keeping in touch. For men, a good relationship with kin does not require frequent communication, although they might feel it irresponsible not to write or call their parents, or have their wives write or call, at least once a month.

Marriage makes men's relationships with kin more complex at the same time that it provides them with a partner for their management. Men will have to deal with their wives' relationships with their families as well as their own. If a man's wife dislikes his brother or sister or their spouses, the man will see less of the brother or sister. The same holds, though less strongly, in relation to a parent. When men's wives do not like being with their husbands' families, the men are caught in between. They love their wives, but they love their families too, or at least feel responsible to them.

She doesn't like to visit my family. They live in the South-west. Not only are my mother and father there but also a sister and a brother, both married. So it is a big reunion type thing. I like to visit them whenever I get an opportunity. I try to go out there once a year.

She does not enjoy going, but she'll go. Because she knows I want her to go very badly. It's hard for me to explain why she's not there. For a while she would not go at all. I don't know why she wouldn't go, because they all like her very much. She's a very outgoing person and they really do enjoy her.

We just went. It was a stressful time. She was not extremely pleasant all the time she was out there. My brother and sister would want to do something and she wouldn't want to do it. I didn't know who to keep happy there. It was difficult trying to keep my parents happy and her happy. It was kind of a stressful thing.

Mr. Patrick, sales manager

Because they rely on their wives to manage their relationships with kin, and because they are more likely than their wives to be geographically distant from kin, men may see a good deal of their wives' families. Men seem to accept this. Some men enjoy their wives' families more than their own. With their wives' families, there are no submerged icebergs of earlier feelings around which to maneuver.

Certainly the kin network, when it works well, can constitute a community sustaining to men's families. The men's children, especially, can find in the world peopled by their grandparents, uncles, aunts, and cousins a sense of assured, protected place. A community of kin that was exceptionally effective suggests what is possible:

We are blessed with this extended family that's really supportive. We help each other a lot. I remember going skiing once when we could just leave the kids with my brother and his wife. And now he and another brother are going through business difficulties and I've been father confessor and adviser to these guys. They need someone to talk to.

We took a two-week cruise this June and there were ten people on the boat. Eight Fosters of three generations. We've done that for twenty years. My youngest son got to go, and he was very much a part of the scene and the way we all operate on a boat. I think the more of that we can pass on to him, the better off he'll be, the better person he'll be. He can understand the continuity there. That's important.

You can't do things alone on a boat. You have to work together to accomplish the common goal. And you have to anticipate. It is a very intellectual kind of thing. Working on the foredeck, taking the jib down or the spinnaker, you have to really be thinking the whole thing through. A lot of teamwork is involved. And we all do this sort of automatically as a bunch of brothers. And to integrate your own child into that kind of a system is special. It worked out terrific for him. He got seasick. It was fine.

I never asked him how he felt about it. He probably today can't really articulate what it all means. No special deal is made out of this. It's just that's part of the way things work. When people try to make it special, it won't work particularly. You got to just do it. What I hope he learned is that there are people there standing behind him and that they care about him and that he can turn to them.

Mr. Foster, mutual fund manager

Kin can be a kind of tribe within a less caring larger society, providing a social setting within which men's own smaller families are sustained. Men who have this are fortunate.

FRIENDSHIPS

Men's friendships may be relationships virtually limited to a single activity, such as playing poker, or may include much of the friends' lives. The friendships may be exclusively masculine, centered on gambling or barroom sociability, or may be embedded in a relationship of couples, with the presence of wives almost required. They may vary in frequency of interchange, level of trust, and emotional importance. The one universal in men's friendships is that their justification is what they contribute to the friends' lives. There is no obligation to maintain a friendship.[2]

Friendships contribute to men's lives primarily as companionships in which common interests provide a basis for talk and recreation, and as alliances that provide help and the assurance of help. Friendships ordinarily include both these aspects.

> I think most of my friendships are oriented around relaxed recreational types of thing, either individual or as family things or traveling. Or having dinner parties, that sort of thing.
>
> There are always times when there are problems within families, where you can be extremely helpful. We look to each other in that sort of thing—if there is a death in the family or if a child is getting married. I've had a lot of friends, just like we all do, that have had times when they've had problems. And you respond to them. You do things for people.

Mr. Powers

Friendships may form first as alliances and later become companionships. Allies in political campaigns or neighborhood picnics naturally feel friendly. Or it may be the other way around. Companions, even in an activity that engages no more of them than does jogging, easily develop the mutual sympathy that is the beginning of alliance.

> One friend and I see each other quite often in the sense that we run together in the morning. We got chatting about business. I had a business venture that was not going very well. It was really getting to be a serious situation. And he had followed this project. And he said, "Look, you need some help." So we sat down and he said, "This is what we are going to do." He was very positive. It was mainly the infusion of a lot of money for a short period of time. He was of great assistance to me. Of tremendous assistance.

Mr. Powers

Relationships that do not contain both the liking and the shared concerns of companionship, and the sense of alliance that underlies a willingness to help tend to be called by a term other than "friendship," possibly on the order of "somebody I play tennis with."

Men are likely to become skeptical of a relationship in which there seems no desire to spend time together unless help is needed. Nor are men comfortable when they feel they are being used merely to fill otherwise empty time. One man said, of an unmarried friend who was in touch only when between girlfriends, that he wondered how real the friendship could be.

By the same token, men may become acutely uncomfortable if they find themselves unable to be loyal to someone they like and consider a friend.

> I had one friend who had been my friend for a couple of years. This was a time when he was married and I was single, and most of our discussions were about women and what to do about women and why I was getting into the mess I was getting into. When I met my wife and that period of my life ended, he got a divorce and we ended up talking about women from his perspective for a long time. And then my wife had a girl friend and we fixed the two of them up and it was the worst relationship I have ever seen. And what was really bad about it was that we were hearing things from them that were completely different. My friend would say, "She is on the verge of making a commitment," and I would hear through my wife that the woman was just not interested at all. It used to drive us nuts. It really drove a wedge into our relationship.

> *Mr. Cooper, head of convention display firm*

The help that friends can provide includes information and advice, transportation and other small favors, and, along with everything else, the assurance of willingness to help. Simply being aware of friends who care, who feel themselves allied, is sustaining. And there are times of emergency when having friends who are just the right ones to call makes all the difference between handling things well and not knowing where to start.

> When our eight-year-old fell out of a swing and it was half her teeth, the first thing I did—we were out in our country place—I called a friend who is a surgeon and I said, "Hey, I've got a problem here. What do you recommend?" And he said, "See an oral surgeon." And we went in and saw an oral surgeon that he had set up.

> *Mr. Marshall, professional who heads an organization*

Despite their insistence that friends be people they can trust to help if they were to be in need, men generally are reluctant to ask help of even very good friends. They don't want to be in the position of supplicant, and they don't want their friends to feel used. Should men receive help, although there is no necessity that they reciprocate, they feel better if they can.

> I fortunately or unfortunately have never had a situation where I had to call on a friend to help me with a problem of any kind. Well, one of the people that I have as a friend is now my personal lawyer. I guess I've called him in that capacity often. He almost never charges me. He's building a house now, so it is my turn to pay him back. Which I'm delighted to do.

Mr. Brock, owner of small business

Should a man have real need for a friend's help, he is most benefited if he does not have to ask for it. A man whose wife was about to undergo major surgery was offered use of a friend's summer home so that the couple could escape the distractions of their family; a man who had been the subject of an unfavorable newspaper story was invited by a friend to have dinner that evening. The men were helped by the friends' support, and doubly helped by not having had to ask.

Men's understanding of real friendship is that it is first of all an alliance. A real friend will come through when needed. Mr. Brewer, quoted earlier on the difference between his real friends back home and his newer friends in his present neighborhood, emphasized neither ability to confide nor involvement in current life but rather trustworthiness. And yet men's reluctance to ask for help may mean that they are not entirely certain which of their friends are real friends until a crisis, such as unemployment, gives the people they have thought of as friends or potential friends an opportunity to sort themselves out.[3]

Mr. Draper, at the time he had retired from one position and was looking for another, asked a very large number of men he thought to be friends for information and assistance. Some came through for him, but he would not have known in advance just which of them would.

> I figured I had enough connections with people I could trust—legal and financial business associates, family, friends—

that I'd at least explore what that realm had to offer. So I did my own networking. I alerted about a hundred people from a mailing list that I created that I faced a change in my employment circumstances and there were some areas that I would want to explore, and I wondered whether they might have a little time to help me. If I could bounce some ideas off of them so that it might steer me in the right direction, that would be helpful.

I would say that out of a hundred of those people I probably talked to forty or fifty on the telephone and about twenty of them really were open to allow me some time. Of those twenty I would say ten were just doing it gratuitously and ten are the friends that would do something for you if you asked them to, that you could count on their follow-through. They would talk to people for me, would pick up the telephone, would try to make an introduction, make an appointment, see what was possible.

Friends who come through will thereafter be remembered as real friends. Friends who did not will be remembered as having failed when they were tested. No amount of friendliness will ever undo that; they will not again be trusted, although the patina of friendliness may be maintained.

On Confiding in Friends

Mr. Daniels, thoroughly upset by a business error (the story is told in Chapter Four), was delighted to see an old friend. Asked by the old friend how his work was going, Mr. Daniels said it was going fine. In his avoidance of self-disclosure, even to one of his two closest friends, Mr. Daniels behaved as most other men would have.[4]

There are costs to men in confiding in friends. One cost to Mr. Daniels would have been the dissolution of compartmentalization. But there could be other costs as well. Men want their friends not only to like them but to accept them as allies. You're not of much value as an ally if you can't manage yourself. You might then be someone to be sympathized with; you would not be someone to be relied on. You might, indeed, be seen as a bit of a risk, a possible burden.

Mr. Daniels would not have had to stop to calculate these costs of confiding. Awareness of them would have been part of his way of relating to other males from the time he was a boy. They would have been among the things he learned about acceptable behavior in the course of growing up male.

And yet men do find it sometimes useful, sometimes almost necessary, to talk with friends about their concerns. The trick is to confide without appearing unreliable. And so men confide, partially and almost incidentally, in the context of evaluation or of consultation, making it evident that they remain in charge of themselves. They do not pointlessly emote or display their anxieties (they may mention them, but they make it evident that they have them under control), nor do they ask for understanding and sympathy. They may, however, seek another perspective.

> I use my friends as sounding boards, no question about it. There are a couple of guys I use more than others. One is a physician. The other one is an accountant. These guys know me well. One guy I've known for twenty years. And the other guy I've known for about seven or eight.
>
> I'd say those are the principal two. Then there are other friends that I use as sounding boards for other kinds of things. But with the accountant, I talk over financial matters, investments, that kind of thing. With both, I'd talk over a problem I may be having at home. My personality versus my wife's. They know both of us. Work. Dealing with management. Those kinds of issues. You get another perspective.

Mr. Viner, financial analyst

If not another perspective, then men might accept being provided with consultation on strategy. It makes sense to men to talk over with other men how to make something work—once they have accepted that it is worth it to them, all things considered, to talk about their concerns at all.[5] Here is one man's comment on how he responds to a friend's story of a work problem:

> This fall, he was beginning to feel more acutely the same kinds of tensions and frustrations about the situation in the group that I had felt, because he's getting abused by the same people in the same ways. He's contributed even more to the group than I. I'm glad to be able to give him a chance to

have somebody to talk to, and give him my reactions to how he can deal with it.

Mr. Linnell, account executive, architectural firm

A different kind of confiding and response can take place under the protection of alcohol. Alcohol fosters relaxation of defenses. But more than this, the use of alcohol signals a time out in which men need not take full responsibility for themselves. They are drinking, and their sober selves should not be blamed for their behavior.[6] One man, talking about a period just after he was divorced, said:

I had a drinking buddy. We used to sit up and we'd drink and we'd just get stoned together.

This was after the divorce. We used to sit and talk about the problems, about what was happening. Swap sob stories. He also had a wife in his past, and he was giving me all this advice.

He was somewhat of a heavy drinker, much worse than I was. He could consume about a quart of vodka a night. We used to get so drunk we'd go to sleep. And then we would get up the next morning and work. And do the same thing that night again.

But what if men want to explore with someone the way they feel about their lives but want neither to drink nor to adopt the conversational mode of a strategy session in which they talk about themselves in a focused way and with full control of their feelings? One answer is to confide in a friend who is also a woman.[7]

With a female friend men are likely to feel that they can admit weakness without risking rejection. There is, therefore, less need to couch confidences in the framework of problem-solving. It is possible to muse about current discomforts—to wonder, for example, why close relationships aren't satisfactory—without being required to devise a plan of action. Expression of feelings is less likely to be embarrassing. And there can be an awareness of sexual possibility that enhances mutual interest. One man, a department head in a pharmaceutical firm, said:

Over the years I have discussed a lot of very personal things with the woman who is our laboratory manager. She knows things about me my wife doesn't know and I know things about her that her husband doesn't know. I even thought of having an affair with her once. We discussed it, considered it, decided it would ruin our relationship, and didn't. But we have a very close relationship. It's nice to have.

Very occasionally men's need to talk about a troubling situation overcomes their caution and they do confide in a friend who is male. Afterward they may feel uncomfortable, as though they had behaved badly. They may then return to their former self-protectiveness and hope that the break in their composure will be forgotten.

Ill-judged confidences can be discouraged by kidding. Kidding is a friendly teasing as well as a toughening-up drill like that of newly adolescent boys punching each other in the shoulder. It establishes intimacy even as it penalizes display of weakness. A divorced man said:

Artie's also divorced. I'll tell you the kind of relationship I have with him. I went to a party one night and I met this woman and she gave me her name and her number. Her *first* name and her number. So I called her up a week or so later, and that wasn't her number at all. They had never heard of her. I told Artie about this. And he still teases me about it, still kids me about it.

The woman said her name was Patricia. One Saturday I was home and the phone rang and I picked it up and some guy said, "Is Patricia there?" And I thought it was Artie, being funny, and I sort of played along with it. But it was really this guy looking for Patricia. Different Patricia, I'm sure. But Artie brings it up, not every time I see him, but almost. "How's Patricia doing? You seen Patricia recently"?

It may be worth noting that the kidding reported here is within bounds. The one being kidded is tweaked but not assaulted. If done properly, kidding even suggests a certain respect: "I wouldn't kid you this way if I didn't think you could take it." Of course, done the wrong way, kidding is an effort to demean. And so, "When you say that, stranger, smile."

The Roster of Men's Friends

As was noted earlier, men differ from each other in their treatment of friendships more than in any other area of their lives. Some men have friends with whom they share their lives; other men can hardly understand how this is possible. Some men include dozens of other men, and some women, in their roster of friends: old friends from schooldays, new friends from sports or other activities, friends from their work and friends who are married to friends of their wives. Other men are not sure they have any friends at all. To an extent these differences are definitional: What is a friend? But there are real differences as well, indications of the very great latitude available to men to form friendships or forgo them.

Nor does the quality of men's lives seem to depend on a particular approach to friendship. Men whose lives are filled with friends do seem to have a wider range of interests. They are likely to be better able to deal with the challenges of everyday life, because they can call on their friends for help. But men who dislike what they would consider pointless sociability seem content with their lives, and they seem to manage well enough.

Men for whom friendship is important may have so many friends with whom they are in touch that it becomes difficult to understand how they can keep up with them all. Mr. Powers, whose jogging friendship was described earlier, has friends made in the course of his work, neighborhood friends, and friends from his church, in addition to a very close friendship dating from prep school and several other longstanding friendships that are not quite so close. He also included in his circle of friends people who had initially been friends of his wife:

> My wife is from the South, but she went to boarding school up here and we see quite a few of her friends who are in this area. I have met quite a few husbands or wives of friends of hers, that sort of thing. One gal was in school with her that we see quite a lot of, and I have seen quite a lot of her husband.

Mr. Powers viewed friendships as opportunities for the enrichment of life. Other men treat friendships as impositions; they have other things to do. Most men might be restless with no one to talk to other than colleagues and family members, but some are not. A man who obtained a Ph.D. despite a physical handicap said:

> I have a few old friends. Particularly friends that I made in college or graduate school. But I'm not doing very well in

maintaining relationships. We might get together once in a while. We don't meet very often.

In graduate school I didn't make very many friends for a number of reasons. For one thing I had to devote a great deal of my time to my academic studies or I wouldn't have been able to get through. And then I got married and my wife and I tend to have our own private lives. Then the children came along.

Most of the social contacts my wife and I have are with other people in my field. It's very difficult, because I work with them all week long and I tend to like to have a quiet life over the weekends. And I have my kids to think about. There are the soccer games that my daughter plays in, and my son has his sports.

I'm not the type that socializes or relates to a lot of people, and so I would say that friends are few and far between. Maybe once a year we might get together with friends. I'm not a great socializer.

Dr. Miller, head of government agency

A man who was accustomed to a limited social life returned to it after an interval of participation in an active friendship.

I am not a particularly social person. I went through some period of years when I was really very anxious about that, felt a sense of loss at not being comfortable in situations. I'm now quite reconciled to it. It doesn't affect me in the same way. I'm not really antisocial, but I don't seek out social events. I'm quite comfortable doing things either myself or within my family structure. And I don't feel a particularly strong need to bring other people into that.

There are some people that we got to know rather well a year or two ago who were extremely social. We started going places with them a lot, and we found after a while that we didn't like that. It wasn't that they weren't nice people, but they never go anywhere without other people. And sometimes it is not really what you had in mind.

Mr. Craig, high-level administrator

Men vary not only in the number of friendships they maintain and the time they give to them but in the kind of friendships they maintain. Men for whom masculine avocations such as auto racing or drinking are important develop friendships in relation to which wives and girlfriends are irrelevant. Men for whom home and family are all-absorbing are likely to establish relationships as members of couples. A problem they may have, though, is that their wives too must like the couples with whom they become friends.

> Cathy and I saw a couple once or twice when we lived down South, and we sort of had a good time. But they're a quiet couple and Cathy, particularly toward the guy, just thought he was dull and uninteresting and sort of a drip.
>
> They've had us to dinner at their place and now they must be wanting to get together. We ought to have them to dinner at our place sometime. I'm perfectly happy to do it. The couple are nice folks. But you just can't convince Cathy to do something like that. I just hate to not see somebody for a long, long time when you know that they want to get together. But talking it over with Cathy doesn't get anywhere. She says, "I want to see who I want to see." Period.

Mr. Linnell, account executive, architectural firm

When men's wives have demanding employment of their own, men's social lives may be truncated along with their wives'. Their wives may say that because they too work full time, they are too busy and too tired to entertain the men's friends or colleagues. They may object even to accompanying their husbands to social events. But unpartnered sociability tends to be single-sex. Men can meet the male halves of couples for lunch, but the social life of evening hours, in the world of the married, is organized around couples.

Men in some occupations form many of their friendships from among those they meet in the course of their work, while men in other occupations tend to keep working relationships separate from friendships. Men who own their own businesses, though it is awkward for them to form friendships among those who work for them, may be members of a colleague group of fellow businessmen. In contrast, men who work in organizations sometimes feel that social life with colleagues produces confused work relationships as well as extending the work situation into the hours of leisure.

Time Spent with Friends

It is characteristic of men's friendships that they need not be affirmed by frequent contact. Although men may see some friends frequently (especially friends with whom they share an activity such as jogging), they may see others only at long intervals.

A woman's best friend is very likely to be someone with whom she discusses intimate issues frequently; quite possibly, every day. A man's best friend is more likely to be someone he trusts totally to come through for him, no matter what, whether or not he sees the friend frequently. "He would take a punch for me," one man said of his best friend, whom he saw about once a week. Another man had two best friends, each someone he could count on totally. He saw neither of them as often as once a year. Of one, whom he saw perhaps every two or three years, he said, "Whenever he gets married, I come to the ceremony."

This is an aspect of men's friendships that can be puzzling to women.[8] How, women sometimes wonder, can a man say that someone is his best friend if they are in touch no more than once in two or three years? They don't know anything about each other. But "best friend," to a man, means someone who can be trusted absolutely, not someone in touch with the man's current intimate life. And so men can be out of touch with their best friends and yet genuinely feel them to be best friends.

Men sometimes extend this sense of a friend as someone who can be counted on, rather than someone who shares ongoing life, to family friends. These are, ordinarily, couples whose families have known the men's families for years and who are, in a way, going through life on parallel tracks.

Probably a couple of our closest friends don't even live here. This is a guy I met in the Army who was a friend of my cousin's. They get here probably once a year to stay overnight as they are passing through going some place. Maybe it is not every year. And we have gone to their home on several occasions. They have three kids, I guess about the same age as ours. Two of their kids got married last fall and we went to both weddings. They came here to our daughter's wedding. Now we get together, and he and I play cribbage, which we did in the Army. We talk business, sports, anything. We cover the family.

Mr. White, middle-level executive

Because keeping in touch is not critical to men's sense of friendship, men can reinvoke a friendship after years without contact.

> One person who I have not really seen since ten years ago, I called him the other day just out of the blue for a specific thing of business. And we both said, "My gosh, we haven't seen each other in so long!" We are going to get together next week.

Mr. Powers

If you haven't seen a friend in years, how can you know if the alliance is still in force? Try the friendship. Call him up.

> I'm having lunch this week with a guy I haven't seen in six months, but we are very close friends. I would consider him one of my closest friends, even though I don't see him from one six-month period to another. I consider him a close friend because of the fact that we worked together for two or three years, he's been our client for five different projects, and we worked together very closely for four or five years. And we became very good friends during that period of time. And the fact that the friendship doesn't receive the kind of attention that a new friendship might, or a friendship with somebody we see more often, that doesn't mean the friendship is disappearing, just that it's in a different state.

Mr. Gilman, head of planning firm

Because so much time is permitted to interrupt contacts, it can be reassuring to have reconfirmation. There is no real risk that men's friendships will disappear just because there hasn't been contact, but every once in a while men may want to make sure.

Dropping Friends

Men can give up friends or lose them, and it can feel bad and make them uncomfortable about themselves. But the level of stress experienced is manageable, the pain mild, and the grief short-lived. Loss of a friend, even a close friend, can be adapted to much more easily than loss of work or loss of a member of the family. The difference is not merely one of degree. It is so great as to be a different thing entirely.

The male friend that I had the falling out with, we were very close friends. We would see each other at least once a week. And we would talk on the phone every day.

He worked for his father, and his father used to put him down constantly. He would do this in front of people, just put him down. I said to him, "Why the hell don't you get out?" And he said, "I can't. I get this big salary. If I leave and start my own business, I'll be nothing. I'll lose too much money." And I said, "Yeah, but this is crazy. I mean, how much abuse can you take from this guy?"

Suddenly his father died and he becomes the president of the company and is very, very wealthy. He owns this big building and these restaurants. And he's a big deal. We'd go have dinner at his flagship restaurant, and the restaurant is very chic and expensive and my wife would love the restaurant. And, how some people like to put down waiters—well, when you own the goddamned place, you can really do a job on someone. His father would do that, and I just saw him acting the way his father acted.

I told him that I thought he was getting as cruel as his father could be. I said to him, "Listen, you've just got to realize that you're very emotionally tied up with your father, but it is important for you to remember that this guy might have been a nice guy to some degree, but was also a son of a bitch to other degrees. I have the sense that if you only remember the good side, there is a chance you're going to become your father."

Well, he just lit into me. He said maybe I had issues with my father, but he didn't have any issues with his father. He just completely blew up. And if you have to worry about someone blowing up in your face when you say something, that person is not a close friend.

He wouldn't return phone calls. And I just said, I've misjudged this guy. This guy's not a friend. Not a *close* friend. We didn't speak to each other for a year.

A year after this had happened, he made some overt gestures that he wanted to get back to being friends again. And we had lunch a couple of times. And it was just not the same. I just felt that this guy was not the friend I thought he was.

Mr. Beckford, bank officer

There are so few tests of the alliance aspect of friendships that if a friend once proves untrustworthy, he may not again be tried. He could remain someone to see, someone to do things with, but he would no longer be understood as a friend and no longer be relied on. He would no longer be understood as contributing to the security and richness of life.

COMMUNITY

A community is a collection of people who feel themselves linked and who share understandings of who belongs among them and who doesn't. Membership in a community provides a sense of mattering to others.

That whole friendship base has all been very supportive. If we go to a party, everyone always asks me how things are going, and this and that. It's a supportive thing.

Mr. Andrade, president, high-technology firm

Some men see themselves as moving through life in a convoy of friends, the friends together helping each member of the group deal with the challenges he confronts. If they are in the same stages of family life, they together can construct a social world supportive to their families. A respondent with small children said:

In some cases where my wife and their wives hit it off we have a network going, and particularly if there are kids who are our kid's age, we get together and do family things.

The following report is of a very unusual development, friends who organized themselves into a group to provide themselves and their families with a sense of community:

We have this group that gets together on Saturday afternoons. Four couples. It used to be with our kids. We have been getting together, except in the summertime, pretty much weekly. It is a very warm, very nice, group. We celebrate holidays, life-cycle events. We usually try to structure a meeting on Saturday afternoon around some religious topic. We will read from the Bible or we will discuss articles on religion or ethics. Sometimes we'll not do anything, we'll just sit around and talk about things. It has been a really positive relationship.

It started over ten years ago because I wanted to give our kids some sense of community, and the kids used to be involved. But as the kids got older, they stopped coming. And we don't force them to come.

Sometimes we'll all get together. For instance, it has been a tradition, when a kid is ready to go off to college, we'll have a big party. And the kids will come then. And the kids will come if we have some big celebration with food.

This has been going on for ten years, with these four couples. We have also been celebrating twenty-fifth wedding anniversaries. We have celebrated two so far. Ours is just coming up in another couple of years. Another younger couple haven't been married for that long. I mean sixteen years, something like that.

That has been an anchor. And it has really been very nice. It has been very important to me.

One of the secondary costs to men of marital separation is that they may have to leave their family-related communities as well. The community of work remains available to them, but the communities they participated in as husbands and fathers can become almost inaccessible. They may see the people involved and exchange greetings with them, but they will no longer be invited to gatherings as a matter of course. They no longer will belong in the same way.

Still, many men who are securely married are full members of no community except that of work. There is no community of friends or family available to them into which they can induct their children, which will support their children through the children's developmental years and beyond. Indeed, the model of membership in communities other than those of work may be so unfamiliar to these men that they are not sure exactly what it is that they miss.

CHAPTER
TEN

Time Out

Marriage is, of course, a sexual relationship, but apparently less so as it continues. The frequency of intercourse is reduced with length of marriage and, judging from the reports of respondents, so is sexual desire.[1] Several explanations for this are possible. The explanation given by respondents, often, is that after dealing with work, the children, and the worries of the day, they desire only to sleep. The following comment was made by Mr. Jackson, a self-employed businessman, married about ten years, with two children:

> Sex is not particularly good with us at the moment. One of the reasons, I think, is that I'm so darned busy. The children go to bed at eight-thirty or nine and I have a load of work that I have to do. If I don't do the work, I'm going to get behind. So I might go to bed at eleven or even twelve, or later sometimes, and by that time I'm so exhausted that I don't feel particularly like getting involved in that kind of thing.

But fatigue is not the only problem. The passion of early marriage has largely disappeared. Sex is no longer a compelling need but has instead become something else to do, a possible nighttime activity after watching television: nothing special. In the midst of sex, the man's thoughts may continue to be of the day's concerns. Mr. Jackson went on to say:

> I'm dealing with ongoing problems [in my business]. And when a problem happens, you can get depressed or you can

figure out how you are going to solve that problem. And just maybe you are thinking about the problem when your wife wants to make love. It's darned difficult. It is difficult to try and shut those things out of your mind. You suddenly think of some solutions at bad moments.

Mr. Jackson saw his wife as possibly more interested in sex than he. Most men see themselves as the more interested partner. But even then they admit that there isn't the desire there once was.

Mr. Stewart, a high-level executive, has been married for more than twenty years to a woman almost equally successful. They have no children.

I would say that there is a good deal of room for improvement in our sex life. If there's any aspect of our marriage that is not ideal, it is the sexual aspect of it. Frequency is the biggest problem. By most standards I would say that we do not have sex very frequently. Sometimes you read about couples that do it every day or every other day or something like that. I think that's pretty frequently. We don't do it anywhere near that much. We have sex, it could be, once every three weeks or four weeks or something like that. Which is a long time.

In the early relationship there was a tremendous amount of passion and sex. Now my wife seems to be able to go for long periods of time without any sex at all.

Mr. Stewart's initial explanation was that his wife was, by nature, without much interest in sex. Or it might be that she worked too hard.

Some people have stronger sex drives than others. In the case of Judy, I'm not sure whether she doesn't have a strong sex drive or whether it is that she is so preoccupied by what she's doing.

It's possible she just doesn't have that strong a sex drive, as strong as other people might have or other females might have. But I think that possibly she is preoccupied. Overworked. I think that could be the root of the problem. I think that she's tired a great deal. She doesn't get enough sleep, enough rest.

Then Mr. Stewart noted that he, too, wasn't particularly ardent.

> But I can't just smugly sit back and say Judy doesn't have as
> much of a sex drive as I do, because I should be initiating
> more than I do. I think that generally she would respond if I
> did.
>
> And I probably exacerbate it to some extent, because I tend
> to stay up later than I should. She's up an hour before I am
> and, as a result I end up staying up later at night. So we
> haven't coordinated our going to bed together as we should.
> If we did, that might possibly help.

There may be some possibility that aging significantly decreases
the sex drive of husbands and wives. However, respondents in their late
thirties reported diminished interest in marital sex while new relationships seemed often to lead to increase in sexual drive. There also may
be some possibility that diminished interest in marital sex stems from
lingering resentments over marital tensions and quarrels. But the decline of sexual passion as marriage continues seems so general that it
seems likely that something more is at work. Habituation appears quite
regularly to develop as marriage continues; getting used to the other
partner seems regularly to reduce the urgency of sexual desire. Couples
observe, sometimes, that desire is renewed by vacations when the
setting, if not the partner, is new.

   Occasionally men complain of the sameness of their sexual activity. Their wives, they say, permit only a limited, constrained sexual
life. The result is boredom. The complaint may be a way of seeing the
problem as habituation to a sexual practice rather than to the sexual
partner.

   Mr. Smith, a department manager, expressed some resentment
because whatever he was to experience sexually, if he was not to involve
himself in the clandestine, he would have to experience with his wife.
And she just was not interested in anything new. Mr. Smith felt
cheated by his wife's restricted range of sexual practices. Although he
tried to be a good sport about it, he felt that because of her refusal to
experiment, his wife was limiting what he would know, sexually, in his
life.

> I guess I thought when I first got married that I could change
> my wife in certain ways. I thought that was a component of
> love. One way I tried to mold her was that I tried to get her

to be more physical. Maybe take some initiative in affection or sex. Or things like that. That hasn't worked out very well. My wife refuses to be changed, to do things the way that I want them done.

We would talk about it and I'd say, "I feel this way, I would like this," and she would respond back how she feels. I think what is really happening is that I moved a little this way and she moved a little that way, getting closer together.

The conflict over sex, it's there, but it is just not the issue that it once was. It is not as important to me as it once was. We just agree to disagree. There is no right or wrong, just, people are different. And it is not, probably, a good thing that one should dominate over the other. I just learned to accept things. It has involved the realization that, well, my wife is her own person and she is entitled to do what feels right for her. And I am too.

But I guess I feel deprived. I agreed to a monogamous relationship, but somehow I'm not getting out of it what I think I should be getting out of it. My wife is my only sexual partner, and if I don't experience certain things with her, that is my only chance.

In a certain sense I feel anger, I guess. But I don't express the anger because I don't want to hurt my wife. My wife is very sensitive. And, I guess, I look at the anger in a way as being childish. Although I'm not so sure it is.

Perhaps as an expression of a syndrome of marital habituation, the great majority of men seem to have fleeting fantasies of sexual encounters with unknown women and less fleeting wishes for sexual encounters with the better-known women they meet in the course of their daily lives.[2] There is, as Jimmy Carter pointed out, a difference between lust in one's heart and lustful action. One man, nearing retirement, said that of course he had his fantasies. "Pick up any novel and look at the fantasies. Mine aren't much different. Except mine aren't kinky." But he had never acted on them. They were fantasies, that's all.

The fantasies may not be entirely repressed. Although men may be firmly attached to their wives, rely on their wives for their sense of security, and assume that they will live with them for the rest of their lives, it is often other women who are sexually exciting. It is other women with whom it is fun to flirt, with whom talk again has intensity and focus, and with whom touch, if it occurs, is charged.

There may be something especially attractive, sexually, about a woman just because she is unknown. The new woman is adventure and discovery, a challenge, and so an opportunity for the man to prove his worth. Sexual conquest can change her from someone uninvolved to a supporter and ally. She can even be thought to contain mysteries that are disappointingly absent in the man's wife.

Sexual acceptance by any valued woman can be deeply reassuring to men. Men can better deal with the threats of their work when strengthened by a sexually phrased expression of trust or alliance. A man who had been divorced for several years was worried about a talk he was scheduled to give to his organization. He called a woman he'd known for years. Their sexual relationship was long over, but they were still friends.

> I told her I was worried about the talk, that I was scared. She said, "Bobby, is there anything I can do?" I said that I wanted to come over. She said all right, come ahead. So I stayed with her that night. The next day I gave a good talk. I felt surer of myself.

Men who are unsure of themselves may want the boost to their morale that sexual acceptance can provide. Nor is it only among the unmarried for whom this produces the desire to search. A man in a troubled marriage who could not ask for his wife's sympathy when his business went bad looked for another woman to sustain his morale—as it happened, unsuccessfully.

> That was a situation that I didn't really want to handle alone. I ended up calling some young ladies that I had known from years before. They were all off on their things. I realized we couldn't just go back. And I'm a firm believer that you don't try to make time with people coming into your place of business.

But married men who are under no special stress and whose marriages are good enough may also harbor hopes of realizing their fantasies of other women. Of course, the man who is married is hampered in looking for another woman. He is socially ineligible, a handicap that may require delicate management. A still weightier constraint may be his commitments to his wife. Infidelity would hurt her if she were to learn of it and might somehow change their relationship even if she didn't. The man would have to lie, which would violate his standards for himself. He would constantly feel guilty. He might endanger his marriage and his home and his ability to be a good father to his children. And what of the new woman? What of his responsibilities to her?

And yet. If there were no risk at all. If his wife wouldn't know and so wouldn't be hurt. If he could somehow make it all right with the other woman, so that the relationship was gratifying to her and without injury, so she wound up feeling good about it. It could even be good for his marriage. He'd be more content, have fewer resentments. And if his marriage wasn't adequate sexually, didn't he have the right? He worked hard for his family. And you only live once.

Extramarital relationships can be understood as providing something more than does marriage alone, as constituting another source of gratification and of experience. The perhaps now dated characterization of extramarital relationships as "cheating" carries the connotation not only of misusing the spouse but also of taking something desirable (though taking it wrongly) for the self. Men who have been faithful all their married lives may wonder whether they have not missed something.

> I don't think either one of us has had any extramarital tendencies. That has been helpful to mutual respect. Although in this day I'm not so sure there isn't a case to be made for some permissiveness. I hear people talk about how it doesn't have to be detrimental to a marriage, in fact it can be strengthening to a marriage. Which is kind of interesting.

Owner, middle-size business

Men meet potential partners throughout the day, in the course of their rounds. The idea that something might happen certainly occurs to them. A department manager, happily married, said:

> If you meet a lot of people you may meet attractive women in other people's offices. It seems to me the grass is always greener. I think that that's certainly an issue.

Men meet potential sexual partners not only in the offices of colleagues and in their own offices, but at church and Cub Scouts and PTA meetings, at parties and dinners. They may have flirted with the wives of their friends, although, to be sure, fooling around with a friend's wife could end the friendship. They may also have flirted with the friends of their wives; especially if they are angry with their wives, that can seem more nearly all right. Sometimes men have longstanding friendships with women, which are tolerated by their wives on the understanding that the relationships are no more than friendships—but they need not remain so.

Only rough estimates exist of the proportion of men who have at least one extramarital sexual encounter during their married lives. To obtain more precise estimates would require better sampling and more effective ways of obtaining honest responses. A man interviewed at home is unlikely to talk about something he is trying to keep secret from other family members, even if they are not present. And he may prefer not to talk about this sort of thing—perhaps not to think about it—anywhere else, either.

Forty-plus years ago Alfred Kinsey estimated, on the basis of large samples of questionable statistical merit, that about fifty percent of American men would have at least one extramarital experience during their lifetimes. More recently Morton Hunt, relying on a better sample, estimated the incidence to date of extramarital experience among white middle-class men, many of whom had not yet completed their sexual histories, to be about forty percent, which suggests a lifetime incidence of around fifty percent.[3]

In any event, many married men have some sexual experience with a woman other than their wives, and most married men consider the possibility. Often enough, a conference or a business trip provides an occasion for looking around. Adding motivation to the search might be the loneliness men commonly experience when away from home. Justifying it can be the routinization of marital sex and its loss of excitement.

In every way I'd say my marriage is very good, except for one way. Sexually, it's not very good. That's probably the only thing missing. She's a very fine person.

I think you probably find people in my position have very strong sex drives. I don't know why. It just happens to be there. I mean people the type of personality I am. Marriage seldom does it. From time to time it's created a little disappointment. Probably led to a little more drinking than I would like to do. You drink and then you go to sleep.

Very infrequently I've gone elsewhere. Not frequently. Very infrequently. Usually it's not around here. It's a business trip or a social trip. You meet somebody. Usually it's a very nice person, not just a sexual object. And it's big dinners and this and that and shopping, that sort of thing. But it's not very often.

Head of large sales firm.

Once involved in an extramarital relationship, men find that its very separateness from the rest of their lives gives it a special value. It becomes a kind of time out from responsibility, an interval in which they can again be free from the burden of social expectations.

If the extramarital experience occurred out of town and the man believed that he had behaved properly toward the new woman and there were no residual commitments, then he could return home with only a bit of apprehension and, possibly, quickly dissipated guilt. In time the incident would be forgotten.

Some men find it preferable to engage prostitutes, to whom they would owe only money. By doing so they also avoid the tensions of courtship and the risks of failure and loneliness. For the experience to be gratifying it is necessary only that the men be able to tolerate an impatient partner or, with a partner who obscures the encounter's commercial basis, to suspend disbelief in her expressions of pleasure.[4]

Mr. Gilbert, head of an employment firm, was participating with a friend in a two-week training conference. They had worked five days, after which they had a weekend off. They spent the weekend at a resort where gambling was legal.

We were in the room and I was looking at the escort services in the back of the guest book. I said we ought to call. He said he was scared. I called [anyway] and I was told that they would call me back to confirm, and then when the girls came to the door I would have to show my driver's license to prove that I was who I said I was.

The girls were absolutely beautiful. And clean. It was wonderful. It made me feel like a boy. It was so wonderful that the next morning I said I felt like calling again. My friend said, "You horny bastard." I go ahead and call the escort service again. I mean, you're only there once, right?

The girl said that she would meet me on the second floor. When I got down there, she was waiting for me. She was wearing jeans and boots. And *she* was beautiful. And she came over to me and said she'd been thinking about me and she could hardly wait. We got in the elevator, and she started nuzzling me and kissing me. I almost jumped her right there.

She made me feel terrific. I knew it was all baloney, but it made me feel terrific anyway. You know, "You're so big," all that stuff. I was wearing a condom. She said I would have to, and I wanted to, too.

I'm glad I don't live any nearer because if I did I'd be calling all the time. They were beautiful.

My wife asked me what we'd done and I said we'd gambled.

This was an episode that was thoroughly satisfying to Mr. Gilbert's fantasies. There was the shared adventure, with Mr. Gilbert the leader. There was the thrill of calling an unknown, only marginally legal service and successfully meeting its challenges. There was the reward of forbiddingly beautiful women who were nevertheless pliant and admiring. The experience was so pleasurable that Mr. Gilbert may have genuinely feared addiction.

Mr. Gilbert dealt with his guilt by assuring himself that his time out hadn't hurt anyone. In the days immediately after his return he thought of the episode as successful mischief. In the spirit of that mischief, he called his friend to kid him.

My friend's girl was named Cindy. Well, a few days later I called him at his office and said, "Cindy just stopped in and wants to see you." For a minute I had him going.

We talked with Mr. Gilbert again about a year later. He shrugged off the experience that had earlier been so vivid for him. He was embarrassed that it had occurred and embarrassed that he had reported it.

A DESIRE FOR MORE LOVE, FOR
WARMTH AND CLOSENESS

Unlike one-night stands and brief affairs are relationships with new women in which men believe, at least for a time, they have found someone to share their emotional lives, with whom they experience closeness, warmth, acceptance, understanding, and love. The men's marriages may have become distant as a result of arguments and injuries or simply as a consequence of a division of labor in which their wives are deeply invested in the children, and they in their work. Mr. Crane, a department head, said:

> Before I fell in love with Janet, Gail and I had just let the marriage descend to a very minimal plateau. The relationship diminished year by year. We shared the kids and that was about it. She had her life and I had mine. I had my friends and I was close to them. Over the years my friends became the people I would tell things to.
>
> You know, if you have stressful work, you have to have someone really close to you. You really do. I didn't have that at all. I don't think I ever talked to Gail about the job. I must have, but I don't know how much in depth I did. It's funny. With Janet it is so different.

With Mr. Crane's permission, we talked with his wife. They had, by this time, separated. In describing their marriage Mrs. Crane presented the wife's view of many of the marital behaviors described earlier in this book. To begin with, her husband shared little about his work, except for events of major significance.

> How much did I know about what he did? Day-to-day, not much. I knew about problems, but I didn't know. He would answer the phone and then he'd talk to five people and then, like, I wouldn't know what was the major point for him. I didn't get details. Mostly he talked about successes and failures and not the routine stuff.

Her husband helped out when Mrs. Crane asked him to. But she would have to say clearly what she needed done. Looking back, she wondered how much attention he really paid her.

He was helpful if I was sick. He was very good to me if I really needed him. He would come through. And he would do the dishes at night if I was tired. Give me that sort of help. But I don't know, honestly, whether he really was there emotionally. It is hard for me to say now, in retrospect. I would have to spell things out to him. I would have to clearly enunciate what I needed. I'd have to really know I needed it and really demand it.

It was when the children were born that their relationship had changed. Mrs. Crane thought her husband might have resented no longer being able to count on her being responsive to his needs.

You know, what I think changed the marriage a lot is having children. That changed our relationship. I had less of me to give to him. I had to be able to spread my focus in more ways than one.

We had a very traditional marriage. His focus was work and my focus was him and the kids. And once it became the kids, then there was less for him. He preferred, I am sure, to have it all on him.

With the advent of childraising, the marital relationship became one in which Mr. Crane had his domain, Mrs. Crane had hers. Working together to keep the home going and to raise the children became more important than talking about shared concerns.

I think also that it was the same time when I stopped working. Then we maybe talked less about work. I probably became less aware of the day-to-day business of his work because I was so preoccupied with children. He would help me do practical, helpful things with the kids—diaper a baby—so that probably was enough for me.

As often happens when men become fathers, Mr. Crane's work became even more important to him when his children were born. Along with all its other meanings, his work became a way of providing for his family. This, Mrs. Crane did not entirely understand.

His work became more of an investment. And I will say about him and work, that no matter how much emotional stress we have all been under in the last year, work remained his top priority. My top priority is my family. He might say family too, but I don't think it is true. I really don't. I think that when push comes to shove, work usually wins.

I used to tell him many times, if you earned half as much money and were home more, I would be happy. But it was necessary for him to do it. I really do feel that is the one area in his life he functions well in. And functions so that he knows that he is functioning well. Work is the one area in his life that he feels good about, the one thing in his life that he really gets his self-esteem from. More than from his new girl-friend or from me or from the kids.

Mr. Crane's new girlfriend, with whom he believed he had fallen in love, was a younger colleague with whom he played bridge. She understood his work and shared his involvement with it. Mr. Crane thought that his falling in love had simply happened, a matter of chemistry between himself and the woman, with his marital dissatisfactions in no way contributing.

Janet and I had been bridge partners for a while. And we were playing in a tournament. And we wound up going to dinner with two other couples for some reason. I can distinctly remember, during the meal, just enjoying each other's company. And I was talking to her about something trivial and I remember just looking at her and sort of thinking to myself, just admitting it to myself, "Well, I don't know when it happened, but I am really in love with her."

Then two weeks later we had a big party at work and we were dancing. It was a slow dance and just seemed the most natural thing to do. We danced and we sat down and we said, "Well . . . " And we both knew.

We talked with Mr. Crane about a year after he had told his wife that he was in love with another woman. He then contrasted his current relationship with his marriage. His relationship with Janet provided him with the sense of being understood, of being able to share his emotional life, that he now saw his marriage as having denied him. Janet understood the issues in a tense negotiation, could struggle with Mr. Crane to fashion a successful project, and could share with him the sense of affirmation that came with recognition for his successes. Mr. Crane felt authentic when he was with Janet. Janet saw him as he believed himself to be or wanted himself to be; when his wife had looked at him, assuming that she had looked at him at all, she had seen only a husband and father.

It is easier to go through life if you have someone that is close to you. Easier if you can share everything with someone. You can be just yourself and be truly loved. Because there has to be at least one person in the world, I think, that you only have to be just the way you are. Someone that you can tell everything that you feel. And if you have that, then you are secure with yourself. It is a wonderful base from which to do anything. You can do almost anything.

I'm just so happy to be able to feel this way about someone. And I feel that I should do all I can to show it. It is not as if I *have* to do things to prove to her how much I love her. It is more that I *like* to talk about it. I like to tell her how I feel. I like her to understand how much I feel for her. If you are conscious of your love for someone, then you are interested in that person. And you can have the kind of relationship you really want.

Leaving his wife, his home, and his children had been extremely difficult for Mr. Crane. He had been tortured by guilt over hurting his children, and over hurting his wife, as well. And he continued to feel guilty.

There were sleepless nights. I think the guilt was the worst part. I felt so guilty! I really did. Still do. That was always the toughest thing to deal with. I mean, there were incidents of yelling and screaming and arguing about this and that. But I don't think I screamed and yelled that much, because my guilt was too much for me. I would rather listen. I did feel very guilty.

Guilt is a debilitating sort of thing. It makes your stomach upset and it makes you feel not very energetic. It is a hard thing to get rid of.

The guilt comes from an action or a decision that is really hurting someone. And you are condemning of yourself. I don't like to think of myself as someone who would do this, but I am doing it.

I don't like to hurt people, I really don't. And I have to recognize I can't avoid it. It hurts to hurt someone. Now I wish I could have done it some other way, where there wasn't so much pain for Gail and for the kids. But I don't know.

Every now and then I have to sort of rationalize it because I just don't want to go around feeling guilty all the time.

There was an interval during which Mr. Crane could neither leave his wife and children and home, nor leave the woman with whom he had fallen in love. He tried being home when he would normally be there, then being with Janet for a few hours. No one found this satisfactory. Finally, Mr. Crane's wife insisted that he choose: Give up Janet or leave the house. He moved in with Janet.

Yet Mr. Crane remained attached to his wife. Despite his new love, his move, and the turmoil in his relationship with his wife, he continued to feel connected to his wife, continued to play the husband, as if from emotional inertia. He bragged to his wife about his achievements and kept silent about his failures; he continued to want her good opinion. It was Mrs. Crane who reported these developments. She said:

He told me that I was really his best friend and even as he was having an affair, he would come over and talk over problems *they* were having. All kinds of very inappropriate things to be telling a wife, he would tell me. And I wanted all the details and information I could get. Now, I think it is really weird. It was weird of him to be telling me these things and weird for me to listen. But I wanted to know, I guess, to understand what had happened.

Even though we are separated, this is still true. I'm a friend to him. He still tells me about, not failures, but successes. Like he's moving into a bigger job and he's going to have a lot more responsibility for people. I can't remember, but he's taking on all of the work for this enormous project. He's taking responsibility for I don't know what. He will still talk about successes. Which seems kind of familiar. That would be the only conversation we would have. He would tell me about his successes, whatever he was proud of. It's still the same.

When we were negotiating about money with our lawyers he told me how successful he was. Which is an ironic thing, to be telling somebody you are negotiating money with about how successful you are. He should be telling me he's got holes in his pockets. I reacted by saying, "That's nice." You know: a wife. But in the back of my mind I was thinking, "He shouldn't be telling me he's successful. He should be pleading poverty."

Mr. Crane, perhaps more than most men, needed the support that came with a woman's recognition of his worth and his effort, along with commitment to his ambitions. When the advent of children removed his wife's attention he was left needful. Yet, even after his needs were met in a new relationship, he could not simply walk away from his wife and children. The bonds to them were strong, and finally leaving the household he shared with them was difficult. Even then he was constantly guilty over having left his children. And aspects of the marital relationship he and his wife had fashioned persisted, much to his wife's bemusement. It was not so difficult for Mr. Crane to take on the new relationship with Janet, but very difficult for him to take off the old relationship with his wife—and, with his children, impossible.

THE HISTORY OF AN AFFAIR

Another story may suggest both the sense of time out provided by an extramarital relationship and the emotional trap it may become.

Mr. Shaw, owner of a middle-sized business, described his marriage as serviceable and sometimes happy, although not ideal. His wife could be inaccessible or unexpectedly critical. But she tried to be a good wife, was energetic in maintaining their home and attentive to their children. She entertained Mr. Shaw's business colleagues without complaint, accompanied him to conventions, and was fun to be with on vacations. Still, Mr. Shaw wished she were more demonstrative, more loving, more indulgent when he was a bit sloppy, less insistent that he drop what he was doing at work so that he could be home for dinner.

Mr. Shaw's marriage, essentially, had settled into a comfortable distance brightened by patches of warmth, with now and again a squall. Mr. Shaw was not manifestly dissatisfied, but he questioned the quality of the marriage:

I know what I feel for my wife certainly isn't love. I don't want to be with her all the time. When we are home together and she is watching television I would just as soon be in a different room reading. Although there are times it makes me feel good. When I wake up at seven in the morning, I love to roll over and hug her before I get out of bed. It makes me feel good that she reaches for my hand.

For me our sexual relationship was real good when she was on the pill when we first got married. Then she got sick from it. And I think that has lessened our interest. It's been good, but it is not what I would like.

Mr. Shaw had established a close, confiding relationship with the woman who had designed the accounting system for his firm. This woman, Ellie Barstow, now returned periodically to supervise the accounting group. During tax season she had a desk in the adjoining office. They had become accustomed to talking with each other about their lives. They thought of themselves as good friends.

Mr. Shaw became seriously ill. During his two weeks of recuperation, lying in a hospital bed, he reviewed his life. Now his marriage seemed to him much less satisfactory than it had earlier. Whatever it was he obtained from it, was that enough?

I developed hepatitis. It was very bad. I went to the hospital and they didn't know how much damage I would sustain. While I was there, I looked at my relationship with my wife. And my relationship was really terrible. A lot of petty arguing. Not a lot of fights, just petty bullshit all the time. Very little affection, virtually no warmth. And I felt a need for some warmth, some understanding, some caring.

Mr. Shaw was visited by both his wife and Ellie Barstow. He was pleased that Ellie would visit him. She told him that she wasn't getting along with her husband and they were thinking of separation.

Out of the hospital, his life restored to him, Mr. Shaw continued to mull over his situation. He felt trapped. He wasn't happy in his marriage, yet he didn't want to leave it. He called Ellie to arrange her next visit to his firm and mentioned that he was depressed. They agreed to meet later that day.

We met for a drink. I was feeling really down. And in the parking lot we were standing and talking and I said, "I think I need a hug." And we hugged and hugged and hugged. Then the next day I called her up and said it was wonderful.

Mr. Shaw had fleetingly imagined, back when Mrs. Barstow first began working with his firm, that the two of them might have an affair. Later, when the two became friends, they discussed the idea in a joking fashion. But they were both married, and it made no sense. Now they both recognized that they had changed their minds.

There was some point along here that it clicked for her and clicked for me. But nothing really happened. When she would come in to work we never really talked about anything.

And then my wife and the kids went to visit my wife's brother. And Ellie's husband was working out of town. They were sort of separating. I called Ellie and said, "My wife is going to be away during the week. Maybe we could go out for dinner." And she said she would love that.

So I picked a restaurant that is a long way from where I live and we went and we had a wonderful dinner. And all the way back we held hands in the car. And we sat and talked and as she was about to leave the car I kissed her. And then she didn't leave.

That is how it got started. It was about as natural to us as anything could possibly be.

Mr. Shaw found himself filled with energy, ebullient and joyful. He felt his life was complete in a way it had never been before. All at once he had gained a sexually rewarding relationship and the affection of a woman to whom he was already close and whom he admired. And the woman made her home available to him as a haven where he could be fully himself, fully loved and loving. Within that home he counted as he did not in his own home. Ellie talked with him about him, concentrated her attention on him. He mattered to her, not as a husband, father, or partner in a home, but as a person, desired only for himself. She brightened his life. Of course he wanted to be with her as much as he could.

My feelings toward Ellie may not be love, but they are a hell of a lot more so than my relationship with my wife. It is not just a physical thing. We enjoy being with each other and doing things together. I even enjoy shopping with her, which I can't stand doing any other time. We want to be together all the time. I would make love with Ellie twenty-four hours a day if I could. I don't care what time of day it is and neither does she.

I know I miss Ellie when I'm not with her. I miss the warmth, I miss the hugging, I miss knowing that there is someone who really cares for me. And I know that she really cares for me. I don't know that with my wife.

Yet in his new relationship, as elsewhere in his life, Mr. Shaw was determined to meet his own standards of behavior: to behave well. No matter what, he wanted to ensure that the affair would not result in harm to this new woman in his life. He did not want to mislead her. He was honest about how little chance there was that he would get a divorce and marry her.

I don't want to see Ellie suffer. I don't want to see her go through difficulty. I wish and hope that she gets her divorce and then finds somebody and gets married again and has children, if she wants to have children.

I told Ellie that, and that chances of my getting a divorce aren't good. I said, "I hope you find someone that will love you and that you will love, because the chances of my wanting to make a change in my life aren't real good. And I wouldn't want to see you go through life just having an affair with me and not having a family of your own."

She was furious with me. She went crazy. But I told her, "I'm telling you this because of my feelings for you. If I didn't have those feelings I wouldn't care."

Mr. Shaw was determined to safeguard his home. His affair with Ellie made him happy, yet he was fearful. He had so much to lose: his home, his children, his standing in his community—his way of life.

I'm sure that if Ellie said to me today, "This is it. You have to make up your mind," I'm sure I would say, "I love you very much, but I'm not leaving."

I don't know why. A million reasons. Because I don't want to leave my kids. Fear.

I would be afraid to get a divorce. I saw a friend get a divorce and watched his wife turn the kids against him. I mean horribly. I couldn't live with my kids feeling that way about me. And I don't think I would want to put my children in the position to hear the kinds of things I know would probably be said.

You hear, "Don't stay married for the kids, because it is not good for them." And Ellie said that my kids are going to leave me before too long. I said, yeah, that is down the road just a little bit. But I don't want to do without my kids. I love my children, I love being with my children.

I really fear for their well-being if they were left. My biggest fear in life is that my kids will be screwed up. And my biggest fear as a parent is that I'm not doing right by my children. I wouldn't want to leave them in the sole care of my wife. I think that would be a disaster at this point. Maybe it would be different in another ten years. Ten years is a large part of my life, but maybe I'm willing to wait and see what happens.

If I didn't like my kids and I didn't like my life-style, if I didn't care about my job or care about money and having nice things, all these different didn't-care-abouts, I'd move to Barbados or some place like that and take Ellie with me. I'd be gone in a flash.

If I got divorced my life-style would have to change. And I like my life-style. I like having four weeks' vacation. I like being able to buy whatever the hell I want, within reason. I like being a member of a country club. I just like my life-style. I really worked my ass off, getting where I am, and I don't want to do without the fruits of my labor.

At the moment my needs are well met. I'm very comfortable having Ellie where she is and having my wife where she is and my home life and my social life and my sexual life. Everything is pretty nice right now.

Mr. Shaw now felt more affection for his wife. Briefly, he had contemplated divorcing her and marrying Ellie. But then he and his wife had a fight that cleared the air, followed by an upsurge of good feeling between them. They went on vacation together and the vacation went well.

Things have been better with my wife lately. The last few months my relationship with my wife has been dramatically improved. It is very strange what is going on, because up until three months ago my relationship with my wife had been pretty shitty.

In the first month I was with Ellie I was very heavily thinking of getting a divorce. As a matter of fact, at one point I was leaving. My wife had criticized me for something that wasn't my fault. We had a fight and I said, "I've had it, I just can't stand it any more." And I was almost out the door when we started talking.

One of the things that I said to her is that I have never been able to know her or get close to her and she has never let me. And she said she didn't want to get hurt. It was a pretty good conversation. Probably the best we have ever had. And I decided to stay the night and think about it. Well, since, my wife has been different.

I dreaded going away on vacation. I thought it would be a disaster. It was wonderful. We had a wonderful time. We didn't have one cross word. I'm sure I could have found some things to get angry at, and she could have found some things to get angry at, which is normal for people together as much as we were.

We made love a few times. Once we made love in the middle of the afternoon. That's only on vacation. Otherwise making love is only before you go to sleep at night.

If my life could go on just the way it is with my wife at the moment, I could be very comfortable, very happy. Happy with my life that way. I'd miss the real highs of sex that I just don't have with my wife, but you can't have everything. We certainly are at peace at the moment.

Mr. Shaw's thought that he might settle down with his wife was partly reactive to the increasing stress imposed by his relationship with Ellie. He felt guilty because of the affair, guilty about lying to his wife, worried that his wife would discover his infidelity and end their marriage. And yet he was always searching for an hour or two when he could be with Ellie.

I figure I've got about as high a moral character as anybody. And I wouldn't go so far as to say what I'm doing is despicable, but it is probably not far from it. It is not nice. It is not fair to my wife. It is not fair to Ellie. It is not fair to my kids. It's not being honest.

Living at home and having an affair means that I am straining for the hours. It is very stressful. I don't want to take time away from my family. I don't like to take time away from work. Where are the hours? I manufacture them. If I have to go away for a week on business, we work it out so that Ellie can come with me, for two or three days anyway.

I think that what I'm doing is unfair to everybody involved. And it isn't right. I don't in general lie. In business I treat people as I would want to be treated. I don't do all sorts of things because I don't think they're right.

I don't like dishonesty. And it is one of the several areas in my relationship with Ellie that really bothers me. It is just a terrible thing. My wife doesn't know. I don't like lying. I don't like untruths, I don't like half-truths. And maybe that's part of what causes me this tremendous anxiety about my relationship with Ellie. I'm really anxious about it.

I'm very confused. Although my life with Ellie in it is much better, if she were to find somebody else it would take a lot of pressure off of me. I feel pressured that she wants me and I feel pressured that if I ever left my wife, or if my wife ever found out about this, it would be a disaster for my children and for me.

I went for a walk this morning and after a couple of miles I was exhausted. That's not like me. So I went for a physical this afternoon. My doctor said that my heart was sound and my blood pressure was good and everything is wonderful. He thought that I was under stress. If I'm not really sick, the only thing that has been added to my life is Ellie.

Mr. Shaw began to feel that he couldn't continue living as he had. He was coming close to breakdown. And yet he could neither give Ellie up nor summon the courage to leave his marriage.

I am trying very hard to make sure, before I go and make any kind of a permanent decision, that it is not a sexual thing that I'm leaving for. And I'm not ready in any way to move. I'm confused.

There are times when I am with my wife and my friends that I wish I was with Ellie. But I don't know if she would be accepted. Somehow, I have become a pillar of the community. I don't know how this has happened other than maybe I've given some time to the town and some money to charity things. I love it when people think I'm a big wheel. I'm not any more important than anybody else, but it makes me feel nice.

My wife fits into my social circle perfectly. I don't know what would happen to my social circle if I were to get a divorce, even if I didn't get married to Ellie but lived with her. I have no idea what it would do to my life.

There are communities where divorce is prevalent and you get one or two and the ball gets rolling and lots of people jump on the bandwagon when they see that it is easier or not easier or whatever. In my town nobody gets divorced.

Mr. Shaw's dilemma was resolved for him. He and Ellie were seen together by, of all people, his wife's sister.

It didn't quite happen the way I anticipated it was going to happen. I had pretty much decided that I was going to leave after my youngest son finished his high school year. Which was in June. I was mulling this over. On the Friday after the end of school my wife's sister saw me walking with Ellie on the beach while my wife was away. She told my wife. And when I was confronted with that, I said I was planning on leaving.

I think it was a relief when my wife confronted me. I had been fence-sitting for a long time. I really wanted to leave, but I was torn. The minute she told me I had been seen, that instant my decision was made. We were kind of a model family in town. And that made it tough. I was a great actor.

Mr. Shaw moved out of his home, first into a hotel room, then into a rented apartment. For a few days he experienced separation distress, the tension and anxiety associated with leaving a setting of security. This is an almost inescapable accompaniment to ending even the most ambivalent relationship of attachment. Nor did it matter that Mr. Shaw had been the one to make the break, nor that he could be with Ellie.

I had a few sleepless nights, probably for a little bit. I didn't sleep so good there, the first few nights I was living in a hotel. But there just weren't any nights that Ellie didn't come over, and I think that cured a lot of problems.

Ellie moved in with Mr. Shaw. The two worked out how they would manage their finances and divide household chores. More difficult was negotiating how they would link their individual emotional economies. Mr. Shaw, it turned out, required more distance than did Ellie, despite his complaints about distance in his marriage.

Ellie and I started living together last week. She sublet her apartment. We have our own place. It is really nice. It is home. And we're looking forward to decorating it. I'm sure that we will be spending lots of time there.

The only thing, sometimes I feel a little smothered. One of Ellie's girl friends told me that when she was married she would want to be with her husband all the time. We had a discussion and I told her I felt a little smothered on occasion. She said, "Well, can you tell me when?" I said, "No." She said, "Well, will you tell me the next time you get those feelings?" I said, "Yes. I'll try. If I can put my finger on when it happens." I try to encourage her to go out with her friends. I said I could stand an evening when I would just sit home and watch television.

Mr. Shaw was required to fashion a new community of friends and acquaintances in which he would have a place.

A lot of people don't talk to me any more. People we were really close with. My wife won't have a relationship with anyone who also has a relationship with me. It is a choice our friends have to make. She has made sure that those people who don't speak to me think that I'm a real bad guy. And maybe I am. But I don't think so.

My wife's friends think that I'm the worst thing that walked the face of the earth. My wife tells everybody that I'm terrible, that I had a girlfriend, and that our life was wonderful until the day I walked out. That's not true. She doesn't recognize the fact that I was miserable, that I told her I was miserable, that I had tried to leave before. These people think I decided overnight.

But lots of people have taken it well. Some of them are people who Ellie and I are close to. And there are going to be a lot of nice neighbors that we'll meet. We have already made a few new friends in the apartment house. *Our* friends.

Mr. Shaw had no problem in maintaining his relationship with his mother, the only one of his relatives he saw with any frequency. She hadn't been terribly fond of his wife anyway—or so she now said:

I haven't had a lot of contact with my family over the last few years. When I left I called them and told them. My mother had known that the marriage was not good for me.

Most of Mr. Shaw's employees knew Ellie, since she had been visiting the firm for years. The employees had speculated about the nature of their relationship. Mr. Shaw thought they took it well when they discovered that he and Ellie were now living together. In any event, it didn't really matter.

It didn't take people at work long to figure it out. A couple of months. As a matter of fact, a lot of people thought we were in love before anything ever started.

The only relationships that Mr. Shaw could neither maintain as they had been nor painlessly drop were with the members of his former family: his wife and his children. He could do his best for his wife, while compartmentalizing his guilt for her state. But his guilt over having left his children could not be suppressed:

I still am loyal to my wife sometimes. I try to be. I try to be very supportive of her position. I understand that she is miserable, and I helped to create it.

I think I did a good thing for myself. I think I hurt my children terribly. That is a terrible feeling, a terrible feeling. I've hurt them and I've made their lives difficult.

Even so, I think this is an improvement. What was I doing to them living in that house as a nonexistent person? I would eat dinner and go in the den because I didn't want my wife crabbing at me.

But it is hard to get that insight when you see the pain and understand that they are doing poorly in school and having trouble for the first time.

When Mr. Shaw left his marriage, he had to reestablish a pattern for living. But his new life was complicated by his continuing responsibilities to his wife and children. Ellie's relationship to the children was also uncertain. She wasn't their mother; how much help with them should he expect? At the moment he was trying to minimize Ellie's contact with the kids, because his ex-wife would otherwise be furious. How much longer could he do that?

In reestablishing a satisfactory life, Mr. Shaw began with the household with Ellie; around it he formed his new community of friends, including some old friends along with new ones. His kin ties remained stable. Although other men whose marriages have ended as his did have found that, in the short run, kin are disapproving, Mr. Shaw's mother and siblings were supportive. But it hardly mattered, because they were so distant from Mr. Shaw's daily life.

In Mr. Shaw's daily life, only the sector of work remained entirely stable. His place at work was unchanged. When he walked through his office door in the morning, his receptionist smiled at him deferentially, just as she had for years. Once his work day began he put everything else out of his mind. He thought he did as well at work as he ever had. Then, in the evenings and weekends, he could go about reconstructing his life.

TIME OUT AND NEW RESPONSIBILITY

Men who are occupationally successful and have achieved the social place that this society makes available to its most effective men do best if they have the emotional and logistical support of marriage and the sense of meaning and purpose that comes with heading a family. And yet the daily meeting of bills, emotional as well as financial, can be wearing and insufficiently gratifying. The man can hardly escape asking: Is this all there is?

And the answer, always, is no, there are other possible partners for affection and for sex, and with them there is the possibility of, at first, being again without responsibility, without a history of small hurts and betrayals, without commitments except to the present. This is clearly the case with a brief adventure, but it can be the case as well with an established affair. Entering the home of the other woman is like walking through a time warp into a world in which there is no wife, no children, no neighbors, no friends, in which no one will call with a reminder of a prior commitment or a prior relationship. The new relationship is wonderfully untouched by disappointments, quarrels, and agreements to disagree. It is free of all the adjustments and compromises that have been necessary to the marital partnership.

With another woman, men can find escape. Yes, there may be anxiety, because outside her door is the world from which he has only temporarily slipped away. And as the new relationship continues, responsibilities will begin to show up in it, too. But for a time the woman's home requires of the man only his presence.

Because a man's relationship with a new woman is free of the burden of the man's past, the man can assume a new self with her. With the new woman he is the person he is today, not, as may be true for his wife, yesterday's person dressed up in a new suit. New understandings begin to be established with the new woman, new ways of seeing himself and the world, that feel to him more true to himself than the understandings he shares with his wife. It begins to be the new woman with whom he is more in tune. Now the person he is for his wife may begin to seem a sham, and his commitments to his home and marriage hostile to his genuine self. He feels truly authentic only with the new woman. And now it can become enormously tempting to the man to escape entirely from the world from which he had, initially, sought only a brief time out.

If he does leave his marriage, he may find himself wanting soon to remarry. He is likely to do best if he has the emotional and logistic support of marriage. He is likely to need a home to serve as a base. He may have become accustomed to the sort of community of friends in which it is most convenient to participate as a member of a couple. And so he will find himself reestablishing the previous organization of his life, with a new person in the role of wife.

If he is lucky, his new wife will devote herself to him as his previous wife did not. His new wife will, after all, have witnessed the consequences of letting him fend for himself emotionally. He may be happier in this new relationship. If the man is less lucky, the new relationship will prove unequal to the challenges of starting over in midlife, especially since the starting over is complicated for the new wife by responsibilities to stepchildren. Then there may be second thoughts and silent or voiced recriminations.

In either case, the man's life will be more complicated than it was previously, for he is likely to continue to love his children, and will worry about them and feel responsible for them, though now they live in another household. For that matter, he may maintain, as well, lingering feelings of responsibility for his ex-wife. Should anything go wrong with his children, he will find it difficult to escape guilt. And he may also feel guilt, though to a lesser degree, should his ex-wife have trouble. Still, men who are as effective as the men of this book tend to be good at focusing their attention on the goals they can achieve, and compartmentalizing off their discomforts about the rest.

CHAPTER ELEVEN

Conclusions

INTERVIEWER   If you could have your life turn out to be just the way you want it, what would you want to have happen?"

YOUNG MAN   I don't know. Be successful. Be happy. Have money. Not to be real rich or something like that. I'd like to be remembered, to be known. Known for something good, not something I did wrong. To have a purpose. Like, I could be a lawyer or something. But I want people to know me as, you know, "There goes Horace Lasslow, I know him." And not like just confined to one.

Everybody wants that, pretty much.

From an interview with a seventeen-year-old recent high school graduate

In this chapter I want to do three things. I want to summarize what has been presented in the book. I want to describe developmental experiences that may contribute to the men of the book being as they are. And I want to consider whether young men should be encouraged to fashion lives different from those lived by these men.

What is the experience of these men? Here is how I think they might describe the lives they lead:

Work may not be the most important part of life—family counts much more—but work is fundamental to the rest. It is fundamental to maintaining your place in your home and fundamental to having enough self-respect so you feel comfortable with your neighbors. Plus, it is truly absorbing. So you give your work whatever it requires. You do as good a job as you can, not worrying about keeping down your hours or whatever.

You need self-confidence for your work, because it is challenging and risky. You get the self-confidence by seeing yourself do well and by having others at work recognize, formally and informally, that you do well. As you get older, you may begin being aware of younger people coming in. If all goes well, the younger people are deferential; if all is not going well, they are threats, ready to shoulder you aside. But your effort is as it has always been, to do the best you can.

You care deeply about your home and your marriage and your children. That is, far and away, the part of your life closest to your heart, although not always the part whose demands you put first. Your wife is your partner, with whom you make a home, and your friend, sometimes, and your lover, although that probably could be better, and the person who knows you best and keeps your world from being empty. You depend on her to make a home for you and the children, just as she depends on you to keep it financed (although she may help). You think she also looks to you to protect your home, should there ever be need, and to ensure that it keeps going. In any event, you believe you have these responsibilities.

Often, it's fun to talk with your wife, but at other times your attention goes elsewhere. So long as you're getting along, it's more comfortable in the house if she's also there. When she's not, when she is away for an evening or is off visiting her parents, you have moments of loneliness.

You care enormously about your children. When they leave home you evaluate yourself as a father: how well did you do in raising them and in launching them? You may feel remorse for not having been with them enough, perhaps for having failed them in another way. But even as adults, your children now and again need you and give you another chance to be a good parent. With luck, there are grandchildren.

You have responsibilities to your own parents, maybe to siblings. You meet these responsibilities as best you can. With siblings, things may not be as you would like them to be. You do what you can.

Your old friends are allies, people on whom you can count. You need not see them regularly; indeed, your lives are likely to have taken you to different parts of the country. But you and they go back a long way, and you don't have to see them frequently to know you can rely on them. Or maybe you don't have friends like that. You have tennis friends and work friends and friends you and your wife go to dinner with. That works for sociability, and maybe you'd be able to call on them for help should you need them. Better that you don't need them.

That's what it's about. Maybe, if you run to that sort of thing, and you're lucky, or unlucky, you may now and again arrange something with a woman with whom, for a bit, you recapture that feeling of being important not for what you do, but for what you are. It can provide a wonderful high of a breather. But real life is somewhere else, and you want to make sure you don't endanger real life.

Real life goes on. That's what it's about.

THE SOURCES OF RESPONSIBILITY

The men of this study want not only to have a good life but to be good men, men they themselves can respect. Being a good man does not mean being in every respect virtuous. As men appraise themselves, being a good man is consistent with having affairs, with occasional loss of temper in the family, perhaps with minor dissimulations at work. Being a good man means being able to maintain a respected place among men, being able to serve as head to a family and as a model for one's children, and being able to raise one's children properly and help them make a life for themselves. Being a good man is not consistent with behavior men cannot respect: at work, falling down on the job or making things harder for others or stealing credit that belongs to someone else; at home, letting down your wife when she's been doing her part or letting down your children. It is inconsistent also with being disloyal to a friend who has a right to expect better.

There may be things along the way about which a man may not be proud: drunkenness, women, and gambling away good money; pettiness, meanness, and the expression of bad temper toward people unable to defend themselves. There may be larger things, too: breaking up your marriage and so inflicting injury on your wife and children; taking a chance on a business or a job that goes bust. Being a fool.

Nevertheless, men expect themselves to be good men, as they understand this. Even in an extramarital relationship, where they might be supposed to be at their most irresponsible, they are likely to want to meet whatever may be their obligations to the women with whom they are involved. Some find it a relief if the obligations are only commercial.

In rare instances there is a white whale—a goal that must be reached, a thing that must be done, if the soul is to have peace, a mission, a dream. Usually there isn't; there is only the desire to be a good man, to do well, to have a good life. Most men like the men of this book are content to move ahead in their work at a reasonable pace, to have a family that's happy enough, to raise their children and see them take their places in the world, to become grandfathers. Equally important to them is the kind of men they are. After all, as they sometimes say when acting to achieve self-respect rather than self-interest, they have to live with themselves.

All this makes the men reliable. They are thoroughly aware of other choices they still could make, thoroughly aware that they still have the freedom to throw it all up. Several of the men we interviewed had contemplated leaving their current work and buying an inn in Vermont or a marina in the Virgin Islands. They had not done it nor was there much likelihood that they would.

Of course, the men with whom we spoke had by definition decided against dropping out, since otherwise they would not have been in our sample. But few men like them drop out. Basically, these men like their lives: the interesting, well-paying jobs with gratifying perks; the attractive families and comfortable family lives. Nor is walking away from responsibility in their character. If there were no other reason for acting responsibly, they would act responsibly because only then could they live with themselves.

They need to demonstrate to themselves as well as to others that they are good men. To be sure, the severity with which men judge themselves varies; some will accept any rationalization they offer themselves for failing to meet their standards, while others take pride in searching self-criticism. Nevertheless, it is ultimately because men like those of the book hold themselves accountable to internalized standards that they can be relied on.[1]

LEARNING TO DO WELL

What are the men's internalized standards? One is meeting the legitimate expectations of others. Another is competence—being good enough. It is wanting to assure themselves of their competence that sometimes makes men like these appear competitive. As Santayana put it, "In what sometimes looks like American . . . jostling for the front place, all is love of achievement, nothing is unkindness."[2] Ultimately these men want to demonstrate to themselves that they have done well, although they often believe they can best accomplish this by doing better than someone else.

Occupationally successful men often are thought to have set out to get to the top. Rarely is this true. Rather, they have set out to do well in their job of the moment. Having done well there, they can move on to additional responsibility. Having done well again, they repeat the process, and so on, until they reach the top. And then they can say, in all honesty, that advancement was a by-product of doing the best they could at whatever they were doing.

Doing well in work requires an ability to focus attention and energy on resolving challenges, and doing so again and again throughout the work day, day in and day out, whatever else may be happening in life. There are personality characteristics that facilitate this kind of steadiness: resilience, determination, competence, self-sufficiency. These are characteristics to which most men have learned to aspire during their growing-up years.

Idealization of resilience, determination, competence, and self-sufficiency are visible in boys of nursery school age—along with idealization of aggressiveness and the other characteristics associated with maleness. Boys of five are put off by what they believe to be sex-inappropriate toys and sex-inappropriate behaviors.[3] By the time they are six or seven, they are well into thinking of the world of girls as entirely foreign. Being thought to like the company of girls would be deeply dangerous to their reputations. And, indeed, the activities and concerns of the girls (as distinct from the girls themselves and their attention) are for most boys without attraction.

Small boys at this time of life idolize sports heroes, manly uncles, and older boys who seem to do everything well—and, of course, their fathers. They may be pleased to be permitted to work alongside their fathers at the fathers' chores or hobbies, to be able to accompany their fathers on hikes, to join their fathers in sports. They are likely to feel thrilled by their fathers' approval.

But peers are the most effective teachers of values. Boys slightly older than kindergarteners—boys fully into latency age—learn from one another, in playground games and in more or less organized sports, to condemn cheaters and showoffs, the clumsy and the incompetent, the cowardly, the egocentric. They learn in confrontations with other small boys to resist aggression, to conquer fear or at least to mask it, to stand up for themselves. In the world of small boys they learn hardihood. They learn not to cry when their feelings have been hurt—but that is the least of it. They learn not to offer alibis for poor performance, not to ask for help,[4] but instead to try again, to hang in there, to respond to failure with renewed determination. They learn not to talk about their uncertainties and fears except, perhaps, as a means of overcoming them. Once they are at bat, once they are required to perform, they must put their fears out of their minds so that they can maximize their effectiveness.

Note here the beginnings of compartmentalization, of suppression of feelings of weakness, of concern for reputation. Note, too, the nature of the standards that are internalized. It is not winning itself that is important; it is being good enough, and winning is only the best way to demonstrate this. That winning is not in itself important is made clear when the victory has been achieved over weak opponents, over opponents who weren't trying, or by a fluke. Then winning, although nice, doesn't really count.

In their internalizations of manliness, latency-age boys are likely to be supported by their fathers. Their fathers will approve as they hold their own with other boys, will applaud when they come through in a sports situation, will admire them when they display judgments and behaviors their fathers think mature. Their fathers will take pleasure in teaching them sailing, carpentry, or other masculine skills. At the same time their fathers will teach them concepts fundamental to adult masculinity, the meaning of work and jobs, the value of doing things well.

The initial temperament of the boy doesn't matter—whether he is bold and outgoing and wonderfully coordinated or possesses interests that those who test such things would call feminine, interests in clothes and colors, art and relationships. So long as the world of other small boys holds attraction for him, so long as it is the world of boys within which he seeks membership, and not the world of girls—from which other small boys have removed themselves—he will internalize the standards and values of the latency-age boy. And all the adults that matter to him will treat him as male and expect him to behave as male.

Later, should the boy now grown to a man fail to act properly by the standards and values of his boyhood, he will have to answer to those internalized standards. And so firmly will he have internalized those standards that he will know, as surely as he knows anything, that he has failed not just the standards but himself. No criticism by others will be necessary; he will criticize himself. One man, explaining why he sometimes was depressed, spoke of failures to behave properly that may not have been observed by anyone else. They had been observed by himself, and that was enough:

> I feel depressed maybe because I haven't done something at work that I should have done or I made a silly mistake. Or I've said something that I shouldn't have said.

Recall Mr. Foster, who went on working despite almost intolerable lower back pain. His explanation for continuing to work was, "I always thought the best way to treat pain is just to pretend it is not there." After seeing a doctor he decided he had been foolish, but he nevertheless displayed a rueful pride in his toughness. He had met his own standard of determination and stick-to-itiveness until given medical permission to acknowledge the pain.

The internalization of latency-age standards is important to cooperative effort. It means that men share with other men a common understanding of the way men should act. The men obtained the same or very similar standards from a common pool.[5] Because men share standards, they can anticipate one another's reactions and, should one man do well, others can join together in approval. On the other hand, if a man unexpectedly behaves badly, those affected by him can find allies to join in his censure.

HOW REPRESENTATIVE OF AMERICAN MEN ARE THE MEN DESCRIBED HERE?

The men on whose reports this book is based live in one of four upper-income suburbs of a New England city or in an upper-income neighborhood within that city. How widely can the implications of the study be generalized beyond this group?

If the men of the study live as they do because of values they internalized in the course of their development and because the structure of their situations provides them with opportunities for implementing these values in particular ways, then any men who have internalized similar values and whose settings provide similar opportunities will lead fundamentally similar lives.

This observation does not tell us whether in Los Angeles or Milan or in a small town or a farm community the culture and social structure will be like those of suburban New England, but it does tell us what to examine. We would look for the goals men are attempting to realize and the opportunities available for realizing them. More specifically, we would consider the meaning and importance to men of participation in work and family and the ways in which it is possible for them to participate. My guess is that we would find that within the great expanse of the American and European urban and suburban upper middle class, culture and social structure are pretty much the same as those described in this book.

But will they remain so? To what extent are the men of this book representative of the men of the future? Aren't we breeding a new kind of man? Aren't differences already evident in men's treatment of women and expectations of marriage? Men must now accept women as co-workers. Will not the men of the future be prepared to understand their wives' careers as no different from their own in importance to the family, in right to respect? How long, then, can they continue to believe that there are "men's tasks" and "women's tasks" in marriage, and that the car but not the kitchen is their domain?

We cannot say what will happen in the future, but insofar as the present is a guide, what seems to be taking place is change in the expression of the principles of the division of marital labor but, after a couple has children, little change in the principles themselves. After a couple has children, men feel, as their fathers and grandfathers did, that their wives are the lead partners in home maintenance and child care and that they are responsible for the resources needed by their families. They feel that their own work—more than their wives' work— is necessary to their families' survival. What has changed is that men seem more likely to believe their wives can legitimately ask their help with home chores, that their responsibilities for child care begin immediately after the children's birth and not a few years later, and that their wives have a right to paid employment. This means that men may do more things in the home, but they are not essentially different things.

Achieving the home of one's own that is the centerpiece of the American Dream helps establish the lives men lead. Because there is no one else in their homes, men's wives have to leave the labor force for a time if they have children. And because there is no one else in their homes, men then understand their own work to be, at least for the time their wives are out of the labor force, essential to their families' survival. But if the men's work is essential at a time of urgent need, then it must be safeguarded all the way through. And so being the man of the house of one's own implies commitment to work.

At the same time, the home of one's own makes the couple heavily interdependent. The absence of adults other than the man and his wife within the home means that all the work of home maintenance and child care that cannot be contracted out must be done by the couple. The man must come home directly from work to help. Furthermore, if the man's wife has stayed home with small children, there is no one else in the home to keep her company, no one else with whom she can talk except by telephone. The man's presence is essential to her. The children, too, can call on no other adults than their parents for aid or nurturance; and here too the man will be expected to help out. In several ways, the home of one's own implies that men will be expected to give a good deal of time to their families—and, even so, may end by feeling that they have not given enough.

All this means that in marriages in which there are growing children, so long as the couple live in a house of their own, the traditional bases for the household division of labor are likely to remain intact. This is not to say that the changes thought to have taken place in men as husbands and fathers are illusory. The increased use of the principle of equity in deciding the household division of labor, the more skeptical view of men who contribute nothing to their families beyond their physical presence and a standard of living—these changes matter. But despite them, the man remains the breadwinner, the woman the homemaker, although they each get help and may expect help from the other.

The underlying structure of men's lives remains as it has. Work remains the sector in which men establish social place and feelings of worth; marriage remains a relationship to which men look for emotional and logistic support; and friendships between men continue to be more or less affectionate alliances in which self-disclosure, unless handled properly, is dysfunctional. The emotional meanings of work, marriage, and friendship remain what they were. And within the home, once there are children, men understand their responsibilities as they always have, although now to meet them requires that they do more.

IMPLICATIONS FOR CHANGE

The way of life described in this book is complex, coherent, and stable. A man's functioning in any sector is dependent on his functioning in other sectors. If work takes precedence over other responsibilities, it nevertheless requires family and, to a lesser degree, community, to have meaning. Change anywhere requires change everywhere. And so attempts at change in one sector only are likely to encounter resistance. All this should be recognized when considering the likelihood of success in efforts to change men's lives piecemeal.[6]

In what follows my values and my beliefs, of necessity, enter. My values lead me to respect these men as they strive to meet their standards for themselves. And my beliefs are such that while I do not think of myself as a biological determinist, I do think that the plasticity of human nature is limited. I do not believe that the right childraising and the right spirit will produce people such as have never been seen before. But readers with other values and other beliefs may see social policy pointed down different paths by the discussion of the book.

Work

Men treat their work community as the community within which effort truly matters. That this is the case should not be surprising. Membership in a community of work both assures their security and validates their social worth, while loss of work produces vulnerability, the threat of social isolation, and loss of support for feelings of worth. For men in the age range of the men of this book, loss of the community of work is not compensated by membership in neighborhood communities, in church groups, or in activity-focused associations. Only in the community of work do men have activities that they can be assured matter to others, since they are paid for them.

We as a society must be aware that work, for men in their middle years, is not only a source of income but also a basis for their functioning. Families, especially those in which there are dependent children, require the income that men produce by their work. But a program of income support for unemployed men would not meet all the men's needs. The men require, as well, that they have work.

Still, it is not the case that any employment is good enough. Rather, the employment must provide opportunity for contribution and demonstration of worth. Only in this way can it engage men's energies. In addition, men need to have their work provide them with enough support and enough freedom from conflict so that they can deal effectively with its challenges. Particularly productive of stress are supervisors who are critical or verbally assaultive. On the other hand, supportive supervisors can help men manage formidable challenges.

All this is well known. But in the absence of empirical materials like those presented earlier in the book, it is easy to imagine that the wealthy have no need for work and that other men must live under threat if they are to be motivated to work effectively. Social policy should recognize how critical to men's well-being are feelings of successful performance in socially valued work.

Marriage

Men rely on their wives for much that is critical to the quality of their lives. They rely on them to help maintain emotional equilibrium, to care for the children, to provide the men with a home, to help them maintain a social life. Should a man's marriage come to an end, he may discover himself emotionally and socially bereft.

And yet the way of life described here burdens marriages by subjecting both husbands and wives to overload and by ensuring that men are often preoccupied and sometimes severely stressed. Should men's wives have careers as demanding as the men's, there is the further problem that both the men and their wives will often be unavailable to respond to the partner's needs. The enormous importance to these men of their marriages, together with the burdens they place on the marriages because of their way of life, constitutes a most serious vulnerability. Two issues may deserve special attention: the work–family conflict and the issue of equity in the division of household labor.

The work–family conflict. Men's work is necessary as a foundation for their lives, but their families have an ultimate, irreducible emotional importance to them that their work cannot have. Nevertheless, among the paradoxes with which men live is that their work may demand most of their time and energy.

Work tends to be a greedy institution, taking as its due whatever time is given to it and wanting more. Nor can men easily defend themselves. Prodded by their own ambitions and anxieties, by the pure attractiveness of their work, and by the many rewards and penalties of the workplace, men accede to work's demands. They then give their families residual time, time not required by their work, or time when fatigue prevents them from going on with their work. Their wives may complain that the men treat their homes as hotels. The men may themselves fear that they have become absentee fathers. They feel guilty for having neglected the people most important to them.

It seems to me that men might do well to treat their marriages as partnerships that are fundamental to everything else, and to work out with their wives plans and schedules with which both can live. But while this may seem little enough, it implies that the needs of the couple, or of the family as interpreted by the wife, will have some right to limit the demands of the job. There are many lines of work—science, medicine, journalism—in which deadlines or competition with peers or sudden crises are likely to require men to give what should be family time to their work. And in almost any line of work the achievement of excellence requires more than full time. Men who want to be with their families evenings and weekends and holidays (not to mention workdays when one of the children is sick) may have to sacrifice some career choices.

If their wives work, many men feel that equity—and just plain practicality—requires that they take on a larger share of the domestic division of labor. But in any line of work, even the academic with its flexible schedules, there is a cost to men as they approach nearer to sharing equally the tasks of home maintenance and child care. The demands at home will constrain what they can do at work. Others may see their investment in their work as limited. A man who must leave a meeting to pick up the children at the daycare center may feel embarrassed when he leaves the meeting and insecure later.

I imagine a woman reader saying, "Yes, and the same is true for a woman!" But that is the problem: Two parents, each committed to a career, who are raising children without additional help are likely to be overloaded. The solution may be to find help with child care, or it may be to agree that sometimes the husband will give up work and sometimes the wife will, or it may be to agree to protect the work time of one of the partners. None of these solutions is without new problems.

In any event, it will not be easy for men to reduce the hopes and ambitions they bring to their work, and their need to do their work well. If men are asked to do more at home, they are likely to add the new home responsibilities to their existing work responsibilities, and to try to meet them all. When they run out of time they will let friendships slide and dispense with talk with the neighbors. Although eventually they may congratulate themselves on being closer to their children than their fathers were to them, they are likely to feel beset by having more to do than they can manage.

Equity as a basis for deciding the division of household labor. Couples, like other partners, sometimes dispute the division of labor between them and the division of their enterprise's rewards. Occasionally, to ensure fairness, a couple will decide that each partner must do half of every task; he must do half the cooking, she half the yard work, and the two must alternate picking up the kids at the child care center. But appeals to equity tend to be divisive. They assume a zero-sum situation: What is good for him is bad for her, and vice versa. "If I do this disagreeable task, you do that one." The possibility that a task disagreeable to one is acceptable to the other is not explored, because it makes possible collusion in exploitation. And the very real advantages of complementarity and specialization may be sacrificed to achieve what seems like a more equal sharing of the work.

It seems to me that disputes over equity are the worst kind of marital disputes, because their premise is that the tasks of the relationship are intrinsically disagreeable. Husband and wife are encouraged to emphasize how arduous and generally unpleasant everything they do is. If going to pick a child up at nursery school is a pleasant drive, it can't be balanced off against the other partner's doing laundry. But if it is a miserable slog through frazzling traffic, it can be a bargaining chip.

Furthermore, disputes over equity are undecidable. Arguments the husband may find compelling may be thought by the wife to be irrelevant, and vice versa. And new arguments can always be brought in. Take, for example, a couple who have agreed that the woman will drive their daughter to child care, the man will pick her up. The man says that this week he has to work late. The woman says that's not fair. The man says he can't help having to work late, and besides, he is supplying most of the family's income. The woman says that's because the society is tilted in his direction and also she had to take time out for pregnancy and childbirth. The man says that's irrelevant, that right now he's supplying most of the income and it's not fair that he should have to leave the office before his work is done. His wife says they both wanted the child, they should share the work of child care. And so on.

Nor is there any standard by which to decide when equity has been achieved. There is simply no way to ensure an objectively equitable arrangement. Trading off tasks isn't certain to work, because it may be easier for him (or for her) to sweep and mop and move the furniture around. Giving the same number of hours to home maintenance may not work, because one partner may be more efficient than the other or may be working harder or bringing in more money. Nor is it always clear what is a task and what is pure pleasure: Reading to the children in the evening, for example, could be either.

Best is if instead of trying to achieve equity each partner simply pitches in wholeheartedly, doing what needs doing. With this commitment the traditional division of labor, liberally modified by the principle of helping out, and adapted to the tastes and skills of the husband and wife, can be satisfactory to both partners. I like the comment made by one of our staff members just after her marriage: "I don't want a fifty-fifty marriage. I want to put in a hundred percent and I want my husband to put in a hundred percent." Unstinting investment in the marital enterprise by both partners is a better recipe for marital success than is vigilant refusal to be misused.

Community

One of the ways in which men like those of this book have been criticized is that they are unable to let down, to reveal themselves, to share intimacy. They lack the kind of warm, intimate friendships that seem common among women. Men's best friends may live at a distance, and meetings, when they occur, rarely involve an exchange of confidences. Men are likely to think of their wives as the people in whom they confide, but they often prefer to keep their worries to themselves. Reasons for these behaviors are given in several places in the book. Especially important are men's tendency to compartmentalize potentially painful experiences and their need to present themselves as people worthy of respect.

Men sometimes delegate responsibility for social warmth to their wives. They often rely on their wives to maintain their linkages with family and with the couples they and their wives think of as friends. Should they have to maintain their social linkages themselves, as would happen after a marital separation, they may be at a loss.

But under ordinary circumstances it works perfectly well for men to have friends who are allies rather than confidants. And it is fine with them if they are linked through their wives to the networks of sociability in which they participate. And though the men may sometimes be troubled by recognition that, except for their wives, they don't really confide in anyone—and they don't confide in their wives that much, either—by and large they appear satisfied with the way they organize their social lives. For most men, when contemplating a recommendation that they change their social styles so that they can have deeper, more meaningful, relationships with others, it may be well to adhere to the principle, "If it's not broke, don't fix it."

IN GENERAL

It seems to me that we cannot predict the changes that will actually occur in men's lives. Undoubtedly change will take place. But we cannot know, for example, whether we will continue to disparage the traditional bases for the division of household labor (even while following them) or will launch upon a counterreformation.

For reasons I have given, I do not believe that there will be change in the underlying structure of the lives of men who are doing reasonably well in their work. I would be surprised if men who have been able to obtain challenging work were to reduce commitment to that work. Nor do I believe they will reduce commitment to their families; that commitment, I believe, has biological as well as social bases. I would therefore be surprised if they were to stop being troubled by conflict between their commitments to work and to home.

Nor do I believe that there will be fundamental changes in the division of marital labor, at least among those couples who are parents or intend to become parents. I think that no matter how much men do in the home, child care will remain within the woman's domain. Accompanying responsibility for child care will be responsibility for the functioning of the home, for the furnishing of common space within the home, for the maintenance of this common space, and for relationships within the home. Given that women remain the lead partners in these areas, men will of necessity be the lead partners in income production.

Of course, in the future, as now, there will be men whose lives are differently organized. In the future, as now, there will be artists whose commitment to self-expression leads them to devalue familial responsibilities and there will be men of a domestic bent for whom paid work is no more than a regrettable necessity. But these will not be the men who provide the society's energy, who maintain the society's functioning, who give it direction. The men who keep the society going will continue to be men for whom both work and family are of enormous importance, each in its own right and each because it supports the other. They will continue to be men who, despite stresses at work and tensions at home, show up, day after day, both at work and at home, determined to do what needs doing. And they will continue to have lives like those described in this book, lives whose mission is to do well at work and at home.

Nor is it evident, at least to me, that the lives of these men should be changed even if they could be. This is not to say that their way of life has no costs. When their children leave home the men may regret not having spent more time with them. And after the men retire many of them are likely to wonder if so many years of devotion to work made any sense. But some of the men of our sample did find the time and energy to be close to their children when the children were growing up, without doing any the less at work. And most of the men of the sample, during their working years, had lives that fully engaged them, fully used their best efforts, and that rewarded them not only with an enviable standard of living but with self-respect and the respect of their communities. That's not bad.

In any event, this book is neither a call for change nor an argument against it. It is, primarily, an anatomy and physiology of the lives of men who have done well by the standards of contemporary society. Its primary aim is to make evident how such lives are organized and how they work. Anyone who would seek to modify them would need to know at least this.

Appendix on Methods

"CONTEMPORANEOUS" RATHER THAN "DEVELOPMENTAL" STUDY

The aim of the study was to learn how successful men lived their lives right now, rather than how they became the men they are. The study therefore required a "contemporaneous" approach, an examination of how men function at a moment in time, rather than a "developmental" approach that would concern itself with changes in men's lives over a substantial number of years.

The social-psychological outlook that underlies the idea of "contemporaneous" study is that the object of study can be understood as having a structure, a particular pattern of organization. Men's lives can be seen as organized in work relationships, familial arrangements, and community linkages. Objects of study can also be understood to have functions, including behaviors aimed at achieving something in the outer world, and other behaviors aimed at maintaining internal coherence. The former are said to be behaviors in pursuit of "action aims," the latter behaviors in pursuit of "maintenance aims." The action aims of men's lives include achieving at work, raising children to take their places as adults among other adults, and contributing to a larger society. The maintenance aims include continuing to feel secure and effective despite inescapable challenges, reversals, and losses.

Had this been a developmental study, it might have considered instead the phases in men's lives, the tasks of each phase, the ways the tasks are managed, and the problems of transition to the next phase. Valuable developmental studies include Daniel Levinson's *Seasons of a Man's Life*[1] and George Vaillant's *Adaptation to Life*.[2]

SAMPLING

Because we wanted our sample to be one of men who had achieved a place in the social world and were no longer struggling to find that place, we sought men aged thirty-five to fifty-five.[3] We also wanted men who had achieved a "good enough" place, which we defined as a middle-class occupation and a home in either an upper-income suburb or an upper-income metropolitan district.

Seven men served as a pilot group. Two of these were married to women who had participated in a colleague's study of women of an appropriate age. Three were recruited from a large manufacturing firm. Two were recruited because they were in a high-stress occupation. As further preparation for the study I participated as I could in conferences on "men's issues" and interviewed some of the men I met. Materials from only one of these interviews appears in the book: the quotations attributed to "Mr. Gilbert" in Chapter Ten.

We obtained the Street Lists for four upper-income suburbs and one upper-income metropolitan district. We randomly selected from the Street Lists men aged thirty-five to fifty-five, in occupations that seemed both middle-class and likely to entail responsibility for the work of others—occupations that were administrative or managerial, or professional with supervisory responsibility. We did not seek men who were members of a political or financial elite, so we recruited from districts that were upper-income but not the very richest.

We sent all the randomly chosen men a letter describing the study and, after looking their names up in the telephone directory, called them to ask them to participate. We first selected men from the suburbs, and when sixty-five men had agreed to participate in the study, selected ten additional men from a metropolitan neighborhood. At this point we had decided to interview men's wives as well. We also returned to ten of the men we had interviewed in the suburbs to request permission to interview their wives. One of the men had by that time separated from his wife but gave us permission to ask her if she would be interviewed.

About sixty percent of the suburban men whom we approached who were eligible for the study agreed to participate. This high participation rate was largely to the credit of one of the interviewers who proved an extraordinarily effective recruiter. No one else on the study's staff could match her in effectiveness. About forty percent of the men contacted in the metropolitan neighborhood agreed to participate; the lower rate was probably due to our request that their wives also agree to participate in the study.

We found in our interviewing that six of the randomly chosen men did not meet all our selection criteria. One man, identified in the street list as a warehouse manager, told us in our telephone conversation that he did indeed have supervisory responsibilities. It turned out that he could have been called a stock clerk with equal accuracy. Subordinates were sometimes assigned to him, but his pay was little more than theirs. He, together with a foreman of a construction crew and two owners of very small businesses, were designated "contrast cases." The other two men who did not meet our selection criteria included one man who had never really worked at his occupation, although he resisted calling himself "unemployed," and a man who had just sold one business and had not yet bought another. Although these six contrast cases were selected in error, their reports proved extremely instructive.

Our interviewing took place between 1983 and 1987. We initially planned to be in touch with each of the men of our study for only a year of their lives. As it happened, we were in touch with many for more than two years and with some for more than three. In addition to interviewing the men, we interviewed twenty of the women to whom they were married. Two of the men divorced during the data collection phase of the study, and, as was noted earlier, we interviewed one of the ex-wives.

All of our respondents were white, and all but three or four were born in the United States. More were Protestant than Catholic; eight or nine were Jewish. Several had Ph.D.'s, two had law degrees, all but a very few had B.A.'s. All but five were married; three of the unmarried men were divorced.

DATA COLLECTION

The interviews we held with respondents were free and conversational, although disciplined by an interview guide. We asked respondents to give us as much concrete detail as they could about the issues we wanted to learn about. One of the interviewers hit on the phrasing, "Could you walk me through that?" and all the interviewers adopted it in their interviewing because it so effectively communicated the level of detail we wanted.

The interviewing guide identified the sectors of respondents' lives about which we wanted to learn and certain issues in each sector we thought should be addressed. The interviewers were instructed to permit respondents to develop their thoughts, asking for expansion or elaboration if there seemed to be more to be told. The aim of the interviewing was to obtain full, detailed reporting of the experiences shaping respondents' current emotional and relational lives. Our premise in our interviewing was that respondents should be treated as if they were observers of the events of their lives who were providing us with field reports of those events.

The study staff had seven interviewers over its course: four graduate students from Harvard's School of Education, a former student of mine who had conducted most of the interviews in a study of single parents, a woman whose previous experience was in survey interviewing but who was willing to learn a new approach (and who was our most effective recruiter of respondents), and me. I interviewed all of our pilot subjects and was the male half of the male–female interviewing team that interviewed our ten suburban couples and the one former wife.

Our plan was to conduct three two-hour interviews with each respondent, spaced about two weeks apart, and then a follow-up interview a year after the third. In pilot interviewing I had from one to four sessions with respondents. In the study proper, we had only one interview with each of four respondents. Three of them had said beforehand they had time for only a single extended interview. One said, following the first interview, that he had not anticipated talking so much about his work and did not want to continue. One respondent did not want to continue after the second interview; we never understood why. Another respondent, after two interviews, pleaded the press of work. We had at least three interviews with all remaining respondents. With about half we also had at least one follow-up interview, and with several we had two or three follow-up interviews. We had from six to eight hours of interview with each of the twenty wives and four hours of interview with the single ex-wife.

Respondents usually found being interviewed a positive experience. Some told us they looked forward to the interviews. Several told us that they found the interviewing personally valuable because it gave them an opportunity to review their situations. Among these were men whom we interviewed in their offices who instructed their secretaries to turn off the telephone so that they could devote themselves to the interview. Two men volunteered to continue as respondents indefinitely, as long as we should want them, because of the value to them of participation. A third man requested copies of our tapes of his interviews so he could discuss the material with his wife. All the women we interviewed, without exception, were helpful and cooperative and appeared to find value in the experience of serving as respondents.

We talked with the men who were our respondents first about their work. That seemed the easiest place to begin. Sometimes the first two-hour interview was about nothing else. In the second interview we ordinarily shifted to family life: marriage and fatherhood. Sometimes the man's social commitments outside work and the family were already evident. They might now be explored. In the third interview we would further develop the man's relationships with his family of origin, his social community, his experience with psychotherapy or counseling, his experiences of tension and depression, his aims for his life. All the interviews were tape-recorded.

Although we tried to ensure that in every case there was examination of the critically important relationships of work, home, and community, we did not require that interviewers cover exactly the same issues with all respondents. Virtually every respondent had significant developments in his or her life that were different from those in the lives of other respondents. These could be a troubled child or a partnership problem or a deeply held religious belief. We were happy to learn about these, because they provided us with the opportunity to extend our understandings.

Our interview guide went through several modifications over the course of our interviewing. It is partly for that reason that the sample size for our coded responses varies. Some issues did not become evident to us until we were well into our interviewing. This was the case for materials on marital quarrels, on depression as a consequence of what was perceived as irretrievable failure, on extramarital relationships, and on the various meanings of income.

The issue of candor is a difficult one. To what extent were we told the truth and the whole truth? Our style of interviewing made it extremely difficult—I would say virtually impossible—for respondents to concoct events that hadn't happened. Nor would there have been any reason for them to do so. But there is no way we could obtain information respondents preferred us not to have. In consequence, we may well underestimate the incidence of violence in marital quarrels. The three instances where we were given information, in a gingerly fashion, may fall well short of representing the actual incidence of violence. We may also underestimate the incidence and the emotional significance of extramarital relationships. Some interviewers felt much more comfortable than others in discussing men's sexual experiences and did better interviewing in this area. Also, men interviewed in their offices were probably more candid than those interviewed in their homes. Two men told us flatly that they would prefer not to discuss this area. Other men, however, gave what seemed to us to be full reports.

DATA ANALYSIS

We transcribed all the tapes of all the interviews. We finished with from 85 to 150 pages or more of single-spaced transcript for each respondent.

We conducted two analyses more or less simultaneously, one qualitative, the other quantitative. The qualitative was by far the more important and is essentially the basis for the book. We used for the qualitative analysis interviews with five pilot study respondents who had provided full materials and with all seventy-five of the randomly chosen respondents. We used for the quantitative analysis only the seventy-five randomly chosen respondents.

The qualitative analysis began with a tentative outline of the areas to be reported on. For each area, what seemed likely to be representative interviews were chosen and relevant materials excerpted. I developed summaries of these materials and integrated them into "chapter drafts," which also contained more theoretical speculations. At the same time Carolyn Bruse, who was the administrative director of the project, was reading transcripts of other interviews and, with them in mind, would review my chapter drafts. When chapter drafts seemed developed enough to be presented as papers, they were reviewed with the interviewers and transcribers. In effect, the entire staff of the project contributed to the analysis of materials.

Our aim was to take into account everything told us by everyone we interviewed. Needless to say, I have fallen short of this ideal, but not for want of trying. We did not accept as a reason for dismissing data that the person was an exception. We attempted to describe not only the "main line" of the materials—the developments most typical in the materials—but also the developments that diverged from the main line. Since we were analyzing materials while still interviewing, the analyses had to be kept open, with revision of ideas always possible. But analyzing alongside interviewing made it possible for us to ask interviewers to explore issues that were promising or problematic in interviews they were about to do.

About three-fourths of the way through the interviewing we developed codes for issues about which we were fairly sure we wanted counts: for example, how many men reported relational stress at work. These initial codes were integrated into a draft code book. Members of the interviewing staff then used the code book to code a set of interviews. When we compared results, we discovered, as might have been expected, that our reliability wasn't very good. Discussion of coding decisions with the interviewers of the respondents being coded suggested that our validity wasn't very good either. I thereupon rewrote the codes, with the help of the coding team, and we repeated the exercise with a new group of interviews. And then we did it again and, for some items, still again. Eventually the code book seemed to have good enough reliability and validity to be used for systematic coding of materials.

Coding of the interview materials was time-consuming. Because issues could be discussed anywhere in a transcript, coders had to become familiar with the entire transcript when making judgments. Area coding, of the sort we were doing, is notoriously unreliable. Because we thought we might want to review coders' decisions, we asked the coders to write the transcript page numbers of the materials that supported each judgment that was not absolutely clearcut. Furthermore, if there might be any question about the basis for their judgment, they were to quote the supporting material. We did not insist that the coders do this for each judgment, because we thought it would make coding impossibly tedious. However, we later found the supporting quotations given by coders so valuable, both in telling us what the coders had in mind and in directing us to useful quotations, that I regret not having had coders always list supporting quotations.

When the coding of materials was complete, the codes were entered into a database program. We were then able to print out not only totals—how many men shared housework, for example—but also the page numbers of evidence for judgments and, often, quotations from those pages. This permitted us to work back and forth between the qualitative and quantitative. Often the qualitative and quantitative assessments were entirely in concordance. Where they were not, we both reconsidered the qualitative assessment and checked on the quantitative assessment by looking up the pages in the transcripts that had led to it.

The quantitative assessments based on the codes were invaluable. They permitted us to check on whether a qualitative formulation could stand up against the total sample. Often they directed us to just the right interviews from which to learn about some issue. Often, too, they provided a kind of skeleton around which a qualitative argument could be developed. And they were our ultimate safeguard, our assurance that we had listened to each of the reports of each of our respondents.

Notes

INTRODUCTION

1 "The mass of men lead lives of quiet desperation. What is called resignation is confirmed desperation. . . . A stereotyped but unconscious despair is concealed even under what are called the games and amusements of mankind. . . . It appears as if men had deliberately chosen the common mode of living because they preferred it to any other. Yet they honestly think there is no choice left . . . ." Henry David Thoreau, *Walden* (Princeton, N.J.: Princeton University Press, 1971; first published, 1854), p. 8.

2 Dair L. Gillespie writes, in her much republished article, "Who Has the Power? The Marital Struggle," *Journal of Marriage and the Family,* 33 (1971):445–58, that "professional men . . . demand deference because of their work, thus enabling them to accept the doctrine of equality while at the same time undermining it for their own benefit as males. If this is the effect of that much touted egalitarian ideology which will bring about better conditions for women and racial and ethnic minorities . . . it seems we will have a long, long wait for . . . justice." In this vision, occupationally successful men have power that properly should be shared with women and racial and ethnic minorities.

1. THE PROVISIONS OF WORK

1 An example of the way in which failure at work can damage self-confidence and ability to deal with challenge was provided in an interview with a pilot study respondent, Mr. Gordon, a highly skilled air traffic controller. A year earlier Mr. Gordon had received an award for outstanding performance. He said later that he had enjoyed the challenge of difficult assignments "because I had a lot of confidence in my ability." But then Mr. Gordon made a serious mistake on the job: He permitted two planes to come into what air traffic controllers call "close proximity." This means the planes were closer to each other than they should have been, although not close enough to qualify as a near miss. Mr. Gordon said:

> With the instructions I had given the pilots, they should never have come in close proximity. But they did. And what goes through my mind is, "God, how did that happen?" I'm trying to think, "How did I descend the guy?" And I'm trying to replay in my mind what had transpired in the last ten minutes. I'm still working airplanes, but in between transmissions I'm trying to think, "Did I create this? Did I go back and change one of those guys' headings?" I couldn't believe it.

The dramatic failure at work was devastating to Mr. Gordon's self-confidence. But without trust in his own competence he could not take responsibility for other people's lives. He said:

It was traumatic. I went home on sick leave that afternoon and I stayed home for three days. Because what had happened was like a loss in my confidence in my ability. I started doubting myself. And I couldn't go back to work. It's like your ego's so fragile, the slightest little crack in it and you start doubting yourself. And if you don't trust yourself, you can't do something like our profession.

After three days of sitting at home, Mr. Gordon was visited by a co-worker whom he liked and respected. The co-worker brought a six-pack of beer, and the two talked through the evening about sports, fishing, their children—everything but work. The next day Mr. Gordon returned to his job. He asked his supervisor to assign him to easy sectors. Gradually, as he watched himself perform well, he regained self-confidence. But for a few months after his return, he said, "I was always overcautious, always making sure that I wasn't doing anything wrong."

2   A review of research on job satisfaction reports that for work to be satisfying it is most important that (1) it be challenging and (2) its challenges permit the exercise of job skills. See Gordon E. O'Brien, *Psychology of Work and Unemployment* (New York: John Wiley & Sons, 1986). Work that is at the right level of challenge seems to foster increase in both skill and self-esteem. See also Gordon E. O'Brien, "The Relative Contribution of Perceived Skill-utilization and Other Perceived Job Attributes to the Prediction of Job Satisfaction: A Cross-validation Study," *Human Relations*, 35 (1982): 219–23.

3   Work can be engaging enough to serve as a distraction from troubles elsewhere in life. The playwright Neil Simon has said that his work has, at times, been a refuge from a painful personal life. He has been able to block everything else out when he worked. *New York Times*, Sunday, November 13, 1988. One of the men in this study's sample said that during the time when an earlier marriage had been breaking up he could give his work his full attention and so gain relief from worrying about his marital problems. Still, at the end of the day he was utterly depleted by doing his job while fending off awareness of his domestic troubles.

4   Henry Mintzberg, in a review of jobs containing managerial responsibilities, reports that the job pressures that constitute challenges for managers exist at all levels and not only at the top. Henry Mintzberg, *The Nature of Managerial Work* (New York: Harper & Row, 1973), p. 113. But there are many nonmanagerial jobs, and undoubtedly some managerial ones, where the primary challenge is sticking it out. On demoralizing work, see Kai Erikson, "On Work and Alienation," *American Sociological Review*, 51 (February, 1986): 1–8.

5   Oriana Fallaci, *Interview with History* (New York: Liveright, 1976).

6   Discussions of work motivation often distinguish between "intrinsic motivation" (wanting to do the job for the good feelings engendered by doing it) and "extrinsic motivation" (wanting to do the job because it will lead to pay, promotion, or other reward). Intrinsic motivations for working appear primarily to be work's contributions to enhanced feelings of worth. A brief review is given by William W. Notz, "Work Motivation and the Negative Effect of Extrinsic Rewards," *American Psychologist*, 30 (September 1975):884–91; see also Frederick Herzberg, *Work and the Nature of Man* (Cleveland: World Publishing, 1966.) The Meaning of Work research group found that those who had done well in their careers appeared to care more about the intrinsic

values of working, while those who had done badly focused more on income and other extrinsic benefits of working. MOW International Research Team, *The Meaning of Working* (New York: Academic Press, 1987), p. 193.

7 Just as the daytime television that is directed toward women focuses on relational developments, so the sports programs that are directed to men provide settings in which professional players demonstrate their ability to perform under pressure. Although there may also be pleasure in witnessing athletic skill, the thrill of sports seems to consist more of identifying with players who carry one's banner as they meet well-defined challenges before an attentive audience. Casey failed in his critically important turn at bat, but his situation was one that sporting events are designed to produce. Michael Novak writes, "What I have learned from sports is respect for authenticity and individuality . . . ; for courage and perseverance and stamina; for the ability to enter into defeat in order to suck dry its power to destroy; for harmony of body and emotions and spirit." *The Joy of Sports: End Zones, Bases, Baskets, Balls, and the Consecration of the American Spirit* (New York: Basic Books, 1976), p. 43. Character seems to be the issue more than athletic skill.

But if watching sports offers the passive pleasures of identification and assessment, discussing sports provides men with opportunity for performance. Discussing sports, men can display their worth as evaluators. Sports discussions are often competitions in knowledge and probity that take place before an audience that will evaluate the *discussants'* performance.

Twenty-five percent of our randomly chosen sample of seventy-five men at least occasionally attended professional sports events. Most other men now and again watched an event on television.

8 One study found recognition to be one of the most often cited causes of job satisfaction and the absence of recognition one of the most often cited causes of dissatisfaction. E. A. Locke, "The Nature and Causes of Job Satisfaction," in M. D. Dunnette, ed., *Handbook of Industrial and Organizational Psychology* (Chicago: Rand McNally, 1976), pp. 1297–349.

9 Gruneberg has made the same observation. "It is not necessarily actual level of pay which is related to job satisfaction, but relative levels, that is, the amount of pay received relative to others with whom one is comparing oneself." He reports that those at higher levels can be dissatisfied with their pay because they believe it is not sufficiently better than that of subordinates. See Michael M. Gruneberg, *Understanding Job Satisfaction* (London: Macmillan, 1979). Away from work a good many factors influence men's satisfaction with pay. Men compare their pay with that received by people like themselves who work in other settings, with what they themselves could earn elsewhere, with what their fathers earned, or with what their siblings, wives, or children now earn. In addition, men are thoroughly aware of the exchange value of their pay, and their absolute level of income most certainly matters. See Herbert G. Henemann and Donald P. Schwab, "Pay Satisfaction: Its Multidimensional Nature and Measurement," *International Journal of Psychology*, 20 (1985): 129–41.

10 Many firms keep salaries and bonuses secret. One possible reason is that senior executives hope that by doing so they will make it less likely that people will feel inadequately valued in comparison with others. An instance of this practice is described in Rosabeth Moss Kanter, *Men and Women of the Corporation* (New York: Basic Books, 1977).

2.   THE IMPORTANCE OF WORK

1   On the basis of a study of almost 700 men classified as "lower middle class" and "upper working class"—men who were clerks, salesmen, technicians, low-level managers, or employed in the building trades—Harold Wilensky writes: "Chaotic experience in the economic order fosters a retreat from both work and the larger communal life." Harold L. Wilensky, "Orderly Careers and Social Participation: The Impact of Work History on Social Integration in the Middle Mass," *American Sociological Review*, 26 (August 1961): 521–39. A vivid statement of the importance of work to men is given by Robert Coles, "Work and Self-respect," *Daedelus*, 105 (Fall 1976):29–38. The importance of work even for men who are at the very bottom of the occupational ladder is documented by Elliot Liebow in *Tally's Corner* (Boston: Little, Brown, 1967).

2   Nancy C. Morse and Robert S. Weiss, "The Function and Meaning of Work and the Job," *American Sociological Review*, 20, no. 2 (April 1955): 191–98. A survey study of representative samples of men and women living in eight industrialized nations found that 86 percent of the combined national samples "say they would continue to work even if they had enough money to live comfortably for the rest of their life without working." MOW International Research Team, *The Meaning of Working* (New York: Academic Press, 1987), p. 251.

3   An extensive review of the literature on the social and psychological effects of unemployment is given by Gordon E. O'Brien, *Psychology of Work and Unemployment* (New York: John Wiley & Sons, 1986). Unemployment has been shown repeatedly to have disastrous consequences for men's psychological, social, and physiological functioning. Its impact on physiological functioning can, indeed, be immediate. Men may feel so beleaguered and despairing that they become impotent or, at least, lose interest in sex. For one report, see Alan Harrington, *Life in the Crystal Palace* (New York: Knopf, 1959). A discussion of the health effects of unemployment is given in Ronald C. Kessler, James S. House, and J. B. Turner, "Unemployment and Health in a Community Sample," *Journal of Health and Social Behavior*, 28 (1987): 51–59.

The destructive effects of unemployment on men's morale have been recognized since Marie Jahoda's 1933 study of an Austrian village, republished in Marie Jahoda, Paul F. Lazarsfeld, and Hans Zeisel, *Marienthal: The Sociography of an Unemployed Community* (London: Tavistock, 1972). In a later comment on that study, Johoda wrote: "The apparently obvious fact that in the Depression unemployment was not the fault of an individual became less and less obvious to those who looked for work without success; irrational self-doubt and depressive mood took over." Marie Jahoda, "The Impact of Unemployment in the 1930s and the 1970s," *Bulletin of the British Psychological Society*, 32 (1979): 309–14. For more recent work, see Paula Goldman Leventman, *Professionals Out of Work* (New York: Free Press, 1981), which describes the experience of scientists and engineers who lost their jobs during a recession in the computer industry. For a description of unemployment in England, see Peter Kelvin and Joanna E. Jarrett, *Unemployment: Its Social Psychological Effects* (Cambridge: Cambridge University Press, 1985).

Men's unemployment can be almost as destructive to the morale of their wives as it is to their own. See Lili Penkower, Evelyn J. Bromet, and Mary Amanda Dew, "Husbands' Layoff and Wives' Mental Health: A Prospective Analysis," *Archives of General Psychiatry*, 45 (November 1988): 994–1000.

4   The extent to which work contributes to feelings of worth largely determines whether work is satisfactory. On the basis of a study of two hundred engineers

and accountants chosen to be representative of their fields, Frederick Herzberg writes: "Five factors stand out as strong determiners of job satisfaction—achievement, recognition, work itself, responsibility, and advancement." With the possible exception of "work itself," a difficult term to interpret, these are all ways in which the job supports feelings of worth. Other aspects of the job—easy duties, lots of time off, or friendly people at work—are comparatively unimportant. Frederick Herzberg, *Work and the Nature of Man* (Cleveland: World, 1971).

A number of investigators have assumed that the basis of "job involvement" is the job's support for self-esteem. Lodahl and Kejner *define* job involvement as the extent to which self-esteem is affected by job performance. See Thomas M. Lodahl and Mathilde Kejner, "The Definition and Measurement of Job Involvement," *Journal of Applied Psychology*, 49, no. 1 (1965): 24–33. Samuel Rabinowitz and Douglas T. Hall do much the same in "Organizational Research on Job Involvement," *Psychological Bulletin*, 64, no. 2 (1977): 265–88. A historical and critical review of the concept of involvement and its polar opposite, alienation, is offered by Rabindra N. Kanungo, "The Concepts of Alienation and Involvement Revisited," *Psychological Bulletin*, 86, no. 1 (1979): 119–38. See also, for a discussion of the related issue of "work involvement," *The Meaning of Working* by the MOW International Research Team (New York: Academic Press, 1987), p. 81.

5   The time clock is a misleading image for work. It suggests that working is an exchange in which an employer pays for a certain amount of an employee's time and energy and effort, whereas the employee wants to retain as much as he can of his supply. If the employer is not alert, he will receive short weight. Rarely do these assumptions hold. Often enough, workers do cheat on the time they work, or would if they could, but not because they think their time and energy are in limited supply. Rather, they cheat because they are alienated from their work, and cheating increases their income or lets them engage in an activity—such as talking—more rewarding and more social than their work. Furthermore, cheating is one way they can exert control over what they do in jobs where their control is otherwise minimized. When men care about their work and control its procedures, they are as likely to work overtime without recompense as they are to fiddle. See Gerald Mars, *Cheats at Work: An Anthropology of Workplace Crime* (Boston: Allen & Unwin, 1982).

6   Heckscher and de Grazia, in a discussion of the way executives use leisure, note that many of the men to whom they had spoken liked to mull over problems at home. They quote one man, a company president, as saying, "I don't know whether I'm working or fishing." A similar comment could be made by most men. August Heckscher and Sebastian de Grazia, "Executive Leisure," *Harvard Business Review*, 37, no. 4 (July–August 1956):6–12.

7   George E. Vaillant and Caroline D. Vaillant, "Natural History of Male Psychological Health: X. Work as a Predictor of Positive Mental Health." *American Journal of Psychiatry*, 138 (1981): 1433–40.

8   Young and Willmott found in a representative sample of Londoners that fifteen percent of married men did not have regular work hours; nevertheless, on average, they devoted a large part of their week's hours to their work. Managers were especially likely not to have formal work hours and were also likely to devote sixty hours a week or more to work. But lengthy hours of work were not a strictly middle-class phenomenon; skilled and semiskilled manual workers were the next most likely occupational grouping to work sixty hours a week or more. As is suggested in the text, manifest work time is an imperfect measure of devotion to work. Young and Willmott

quote a number of respondents who say they often are focused on work when they appear not to be. One manager said he worked best when he was apparently doing nothing. Michael Young and Peter Willmott, *The Symmetrical Family* (New York: Pantheon Books, 1973).

9   Rosabeth Kanter points out that uncertainty about evaluation generates a pressure for total loyalty and devotion to the organization. Kanter, *Men and Women of the Corporation.*

10   Lewis A. Coser. *Greedy Institutions: Patterns of Undivided Commitment* (New York, Free Press, 1974).

11   Hannah Arendt, in reviewing meanings of "labor," writes: "Labor, finally, is man's confirmation of himself." Hannah Arendt, *The Human Condition* (Chicago: University of Chicago Press, 1958). This accurately describes the relationship to their work of the men of our study.

3.   WORK STRESS AND ITS MANAGEMENT

1   Investigators of stress have meant by the term (1) the events that put pressure on the individual, (2) the state of the individual experiencing pressure, (3) the symptoms that develop as a result of the pressure, or (4) some amalgam of two of these. See, for one discussion, John W. Mason, "A Historical View of the Stress Field—Part II," *Journal of Human Stress*, 1,no. 2: (1975) 22–36.

The earliest definitions of stress were concerned with effects. Selye, who introduced the concept of stress, proposed that an organism was stressed if its response to challenge produced wear and tear on its vital organs. See Hans Selye, *The Physiology and Pathology of Exposure to Stress* (Montreal: Acta, 1950), and Hans Selye, "The Stress Concept: Past, Present, and Future," in Cary L. Cooper, ed., *Stress Research* (New York: John Wiley & Sons, 1983), pp. 1–20. Much current research on stress uses "life events" scales to measure stress; implicitly this identifies stress with potentially disturbing impacts. See, for a review, J. G. Rabkin and E. Struening, "Life Events, Stress, and Illness," *Science*, 194 (1979): 1013–20, and for examples of the work, Bruce S. Dohrenwend and Bernice P. Dohrenwend, eds., *Stressful Life Events: Their Nature and Effects* (New York: John Wiley, 1974).

I here identify as stress the state of the organism following unresolvable challenge but preceding the development of symptoms. This approach has the advantage of permitting independent identification of stress states, potential stressors and consequences of stress. A similar approach appears in Marianne Frankenhaueser, "Coping with Job Stress—A Psychobiological Approach," in B. Gardell and B. Johansson, eds., *Working Life,* (New York: John Wiley & Sons, 1981), pp. 213–33.

2   Meyer Friedman and Ray H. Rosenman, *Type A Behavior and Your Heart* (New York: Alfred A. Knopf, 1974). People displaying the Type A syndrome were reported to have an unusually high incidence of cardiovascular failure. Rosenman and Chesney offer this description of the Type A personality: "Individuals who are engaged in a relatively chronic struggle to do and achieve more and more in less and less time, often in competition with other people or opposing forces in the environment." See Ray H. Rosenman and Margaret A. Chesney, "Stress, Type A Behavior, and Coronary Disease," in Leo Goldberger and Shlomo Breznitz, eds., *Handbook of Stress: Theoretical and Clinical Aspects* (New York: Free Press, 1982), pp. 547–65.

3   The stress research program of the University of Michigan's Institute for Social Research has offered a detailed classification of sources of occupational stress. Their classification includes: (1) role ambiguity, by which is meant the clarity of responsibilities and relationships; (2) role conflict, including conflicts with other people and internal conflicts over job activities the person does not want to perform; (3) role overload, being required to meet what seem to be unattainable standards of performance; (4) issues of territoriality, including not only being able to control one's own space but also being required, by the job, to enter other people's; (5) responsibility for other people's work, which can mean responsibility without control; (6) troubled relationships with others in the organization; (7) marginality, especially to decision-making; and (8) personality characteristics, especially Type A characteristics, but including any characteristics that fail to fit the requirements of the job. See John R. P. French, Jr., and Robert D. Caplan, "Organizational Stress and Individual Strain," in Alfred J. Marrow, ed., *The Failure of Success* (New York: AMACOM, 1972), pp. 50–66. The ISR list of stress sources emphasizes threats to place, except for (3), which is another way of phrasing task difficulty, and (8), which combines Type A character with ability to do the work.

4   The process here referred to as "compartmentalization" has been noted by others, under other names. Vaillant, in describing it as a defense against anxiety, calls it "suppression." See George Vaillant, *Adaptation to Life* (Boston: Little, Brown, 1977).

5   This is a further specification of the definition of social support as "resources provided by other persons." See Sheldon Cohen and S. Leonard Syme, "Issues in the Study and Application of Social Support," in Cohen and Syme, eds., *Social Support and Health* (New York, Academic Press: 1985), pp. 3–22. The definition in the text draws on the "open systems" idea that individuals need to maintain themselves and also desire to achieve goals.

6   Kasl and Wells, in a review of studies of workplace support, write: "Work-related psychological outcome measures, such as job satisfaction or boredom, show very low correlations with home support, moderately low . . . with coworker support, and somewhat higher correlations with supervisor support." In other words, a man's relationship with his boss counts more than his relationship with anyone else in deciding how he feels about his job. Stanislav V. Kasl and James A. Wells, "Social Support and Health in the Middle Years: Work and the Family," in Cohen and Syme, eds. *Social Support and Health,* pp. 175–98, esp. p. 182.

7   On the basis of a study of support, stress, and health in twenty-three occupations, LaRocco, House, and French report that men who had high levels of social support were much better able than those with lower levels of social support to avoid somatic expressions of stress (especially illness) while within potentially stressful work situations. James M. LaRocco, James S. House, and John R. P. French, Jr., "Social Support, Occupational Stress, and Health," *Journal of Health and Social Behavior,* 21 (September 1980): 202–18. See also the discussion of this finding in James House, *Work Stress and Social Support* (Reading, Mass.: Addison-Wesley, 1981). In a chapter on work stress, support, and health, House summarizes research suggesting that in general the support of supervisors and co-workers is especially important.

8   Men who are in the position of boss very often are the recipients of transference feelings. Mr. Andrade, who moved from being in charge of research in a large firm to being president of a smaller one, described this situation:

You know, they have this view that a president's not a normal being, that the person's like God. You suddenly can't be a normal being. People don't want you to be. They want you to play their model of what a president is.

The wife of our Western representative shared with my wife, "When we were driving here I said to my husband, 'What am I going to say to the company president?' And then I found out he's really a human being." But people have these sorts of expectations of what you are. It's like you are Prince Charles. Even though you really are a human being, they don't want that.

4.   UNMANAGED STRESS

1   Somatic consequences of unrelieved stress have been well documented. Using questionnaire data, House and his colleagues have shown that job situations likely to produce stress include having too much to do, having more responsibilities than resources, and worrying about being able to do acceptable work. Men whose job situations had these characteristics were more likely than other men to report symptoms of angina and of gastrointestinal ulcer. Among workers exposed to noxious agents, those also subject to stress were most likely to report respiratory problems. James S. House, Anthony J. McMichael, James A. Wells, Berton H. Kaplan, and Lawrence R. Landerman, "Occupational Stress and Health Among Factory Workers," *Journal of Health and Social Behavior*, 20 (June 1979): 139–60. In a study of air traffic controllers, a group whose members experience severe occupational stress, Cobb and Rose found hypertension to be significantly more frequent than in a comparison group of pilots. The controllers also had a somewhat greater incidence of peptic ulcer. Sydney Cobb and Robert Rose, "Hypertension, Peptic Ulcer, and Diabetes in Air Traffic Controllers," *Journal of the American Medical Association*, 224 (1973): 489–92.

2   Specific questions regarding symptoms of depression were asked of sixty of our seventy-five randomly chosen respondents. Symptoms and the proportions saying that the symptoms had occurred during the preceding year were: (a) not wanting to get up and face the day, 26 percent; (b) feeling tired all the time, 49 percent; (c) feeling down or depressed, 70 percent.

3   A good deal of research has examined the connection between stressful life events and depression. The argument of this section is that it is not stress that makes someone depressed but rather his belief that he is unable to master whatever demand led to the stress. A review of findings regarding the connection between stress and depression is given by Judith G. Rabkin, "Stress and Psychiatric Disorders" in Leo Goldberger and Shlomo Breznitz, eds., *Handbook of Stress: Theoretical and Clinical Aspects* (New York: Free Press, 1982), pp. 566–84.

Some psychiatrists would argue that Mr. Daniels was suffering from an understandable low mood, not from a real depression. But except for the difference in hopefulness, the symptom picture is indistinguishable.

4   One psychotherapist who has commented on the functional value of brief depression is Emmy Gut. See her *Productive and Unproductive Depression: Success or Failure of a Vital Process* (New York: Basic Books, 1989).

5   Perlman and Hartman provide a summary of research on burnout between 1974, when the term first appeared in the research literature, and 1980. They suggest that the burnout syndrome includes: (1) exhaustion, (2) lowered productivity, and (3)

withdrawal of emotional investment in the work. Baron Perlman and E. Alan Hartman, "Burnout: Summary and Future Research," *Human Relations*, 35, no. 4 (1982): 283–305. Burnout seems especially likely in jobs characterized by unrelenting pressure, uncontrollability, and absence of support. See, e.g., Diane McDermott, "Professional Burnout and Its Relation to Job Characteristics, Satisfaction, and Control," *Journal of Human Stress*, 10, no. 2 (Summer 1984): 79–85.

5.   BRINGING WORK STRESS HOME

   1   Burke and Weir, in a review of their own questionnaire-based research, suggest that men who talk easily about their problems at work find their wives more helpful to them than do men who talk less easily, but that talking about the problems of work is more likely in early marriage. Marriages, as they continue, tend to be seen by both husbands and wives as less helpful. Ronald J. Burke and Tamara Weir, "Husband–Wife Helping Relationships as Moderators of Experienced Stress: The 'Mental Hygiene' Function in Marriage," in Hamilton I. McCubbin, A. Elizabeth Cauble, and Joan M. Peterson, eds., *Family Stress, Coping and Support* (Springfield, Ill.: Charles C. Thomas, 1982), pp. 221–38.

   2   It is not only middle-class men who try not to bring home their troubles at work. Mirra Komarovsky described blue-collar men as also excluding their wives from knowledge of their work, and for very much the same reasons. Indeed, Komarovsky concluded that blue-collar men were less likely to talk about their work than were men more highly placed occupationally. Mirra Komarovsky, *Blue-Collar Marriage* (New York: Random House, 1962), pp. 148–55.

   3   Janet Finch writes that there are three ways in which events at work "spill over" into life at home. The men may be preoccupied by the work events, may express at home behaviors responsive to the events (displacing anger, for example), or may attempt to counteract the effects of the events, as by moving quickly to the liquor cabinet on arrival at home. Janet Finch, *Married to the Job: Wives' Incorporation in Men's Work* (London: George Allen & Unwin, 1983).

   4   Kasl and Wells, in a summary of research on the marital support of men experiencing work-based stress, report findings that suggest that men's wives are aware of men's stress and are themselves negatively affected by it. Stanislav V. Kasl and James A. Wells, "Social Support and Health in the Middle Years: Work and the Family," in Sheldon Cohen and S. Leonard Syme, eds., *Social Support and Health* (New York, Academic Press: 1985), pp. 175–98, esp. p. 187.

   5   A good deal of attention has been given to men's "inexpressiveness." Actually, men are often willing and quite regularly able to express certain feelings: anger and triumph, to name two. It is the "weak" feelings men seem unwilling or unable to express: uncertainty, dependency, need, and, when it implies any of these, love. See Jack Balswick, *The Inexpressive Male* (Lexington, Mass.: Lexington Books, 1988), Ch. 8.

   6   Of the sixty-nine respondents who were currently married, about a third talked with their wives about what they were doing at work and a fifth about the people at work. Only one in twelve gave evidence of talking about dissatisfactions or problems. Most had such dissatisfactions or problems but didn't talk about them at home. They did, of course, talk with their wives about feelings and concerns apart from those in the occupational sphere: Of the fifty-three respondents where inference could be justified,

almost half were coded as frequently talking with their wives about feelings and concerns and a slightly smaller proportion as occasionally talking with their wives about feelings and concerns. What they seemed to talk to their wives about most was children and home life: Of the fifty-eight respondents where inference could be justified, seventy percent frequently talked with their wives about children and home; all talked with their wives at least occasionally about children and home.

Of the fifty-nine respondents where inference could be justified, eighty-three percent said their wives were usually supportive and ten percent that their wives were sometimes supportive. Only seven percent believed that their wives were rarely or never supportive. In two cases the coder thought that the respondent exaggerated the extent to which his wife was supportive. Seventy-two percent of the men thought they were usually supportive of their wives. In four cases the coder thought the men were exaggerating.

7   Kirsty McLeod, *The Wives of Downing Street* (London: William Collins Sons, 1976). For example, she writes (p. 14) of Lord Salisbury: "Unworldly and retiring by nature, he married a forceful, ambitious wife, who gave a sense of purpose to his aspirations, urging him on 'to play the great game' of politics whenever his resolution flagged."

6.   MARRIAGE

1   Blood and Wolfe, who give a good deal of attention to "the mental hygiene" function of marriage, report that much of marriage's contribution to the emotional well-being of the partners goes unnoticed by them. Robert O. Blood, Jr., and Donald M. Wolfe, *Husbands and Wives: The Dynamics of Marital Living* (Glencoe, Ill: Free Press, 1960).

2   Although partnership concerns absorb the bulk of marital energy, men's reasons for marrying emphasize companionship and attachment. On the basis of an interview study of seventy-one men, Bruce Nordstrom reports that two of the words men use most often to explain why they married are "companionship" and "security." By "companionship" men meant having a partner who would share their lives; by "security" they meant having a partner who could be counted on to provide a home, to be loyal, to be *there*—an attachment figure. See his "Why Men Get Married: More and Less Traditional Men Compared," in Robert A. Lewis and Robert E. Salt, eds., *Men in Families* (Beverly Hills Calif.: Sage, 1986), pp. 31–53.

3   Carol Tavris and Carole Offir, *The Longest War: Sex Differences in Perspective* (New York: Harcourt Brace Jovanovich, 1977).

4   These principles have been stated many times. An influential formulation—husbands specialize in the instrumental, wives in the expressive—was given by Talcott Parsons and Robert Freed Bales in *Family, Socialization, and Interaction Process* (Glencoe, Ill.: Free Press, 1955). For a general discussion of men's responsibilities in households, see David Gutmann, *Reclaimed Powers* (New York: Basic Books, 1987).

5   Implementation of the principle of equity is considered by Elaine Hatfield, Jane Traupmann, Susan Sprecher, and Julia Hay, "Equity and Intimate Relations: Recent Research," in William Ickes, ed., *Compatible and Incompatible Relationships* (New York: Springer-Verlag, 1985), pp. 91–117.

6   Seventy of the seventy-five randomly chosen respondents were currently married. Three were divorced, two of them with custody of the children. (It should be remembered that the sample was drawn from family neighborhoods.) Only two of the

men in the sample had never been married. Of those married, fifty-four men gave enough information about how they and their wives did things to permit coders to assess the principles underlying their marital division of labor. Fifty-seven percent of the men described marital divisions of labor that fully conformed to traditional principles. Nineteen percent were believed by the coders to introduce the modification that self and wife were jointly responsible for child care. In sum, about three-quarters of the sample conformed to traditional principles in income production and home maintenance. My own belief is that the coders several times erred in the direction of imputing shared responsibility when there was rather a great deal of helping out.

7   Cynthia Fuchs Epstein notes that a study of voting behavior found husbands defining discussions about politics with their wives as "telling their wives what politics was all about." Cynthia Fuchs Epstein, *Deceptive Distinctions: Sex, Gender and the Social Order* (New Haven: Yale University Press, 1988), p. 157.

8   See the persuasive, empirically based criticism, from the woman's perspective, of the traditional division of domestic labor in two-job families by Arlie Hochschild with Anne Machung, *Second Shift: Working Parents and the Revolution at Home* (New York: Viking, 1989). A statement acknowledging women's right to complain and advocating flexibility in the organization of domestic work, yet at the same time offering a defense of men, is provided by Mark Hunter, *The Passions of Men: Work and Love in the Age of Stress* (New York: G. P. Putnam's Sons, 1988). A very strong defense of men's outlook by a man who has also been an advocate of feminist efforts to improve women's situations is Warren Farrell, *Why Men Are the Way They Are: The Male–Female Dynamic* (New York: McGraw-Hill, 1986).

9   This is a critical issue in relation to the idea, sometimes proposed jokingly or bitterly, that the husband pay his wife for her cooking and cleaning. It would change the wife from lead partner to employee. On the other hand, when couples separate, wives should be able to gain recognition as having been partners to their husbands in the marital enterprise and therefore having a right to a share in its capital accumulation. For a discussion of the husband's income as a marital income, see Lenore Weitzman, *The Divorce Revolution* (New York: Free Press, 1986).

10   It is a mistake to believe that men of an earlier generation held themselves aloof from the work of the home. Men have always helped out at home. Pahl quotes the 1908 account of a district nurse in England: "There are really no bounds as to what a mere ordinary father will do . . . for the sake of his young children. To spend his half holiday at the wash-tub, or to finish up his day's work with the hardest part of the house cleaning, is by no means unusual." See, for an extended discussion of the history of the marital division of labor in England, Raymond E. Pahl, *Divisions of Labor* (Oxford: Basil Blackwell, 1984), pp. 57–62. The quotation is from M. E. Loane, *From Their Point of View* (London: Edward Arnold, 1908).

11   On the basis of a careful analysis of national sample survey data, Kessler and McRae reported that husbands display increased distress—especially depression and reduced self-esteem—if their wives work. They find no evidence that this is related to increased home responsibility; if anything, men who take on more responsibility for their children are less distressed. The increase in men's distress produced by working wives is greatest among men in the age range of our respondents: thirty-five to fifty-five. One possible explanation is that men in this age range are especially needful of their wives' support. Ronald C. Kessler and James A. McRae, Jr., "The Effect of Wives' Employment on the Mental Health of Married Men and Women." *American Sociological Review.* 47 (April 1982):216–27.

Huber and Spitze, on the basis of a telephone survey, say: "The longer a wife was employed, the more the spouses thought about divorce." Joan Huber and Glenna Spitze, *Sex Stratification: Children, Housework and Jobs* (New York: Academic Press, 1980), p. 216. The problem may not be conflicts over division of household labor (as the authors suggest) but rather an increased likelihood that each spouse will have unmet need for emotional support.

12   It might be worth noting how unusual is marital companionship on the human scene. Katz and Konner note that the expectation in Western industrial society that "the husband–wife relationship is outstanding among all other social relationships" is in striking contrast to "the separately defined spheres of male and female" displayed in many—I would say in all but a few—non-Western societies. Katz and Konnor give the example of women observed in rural Fiji: "A wife's interactions with her husband were a minor portion of her social interactions in general; most of her interactions were with other women, her children, and other children." Mary Maxwell Katz and Melvin J. Konner, "The Role of the Father: An Anthropological Perspective," in Michael E. Lamb, ed., *The Role of the Father in Child Development*, Revised Edition (New York: John Wiley & Sons, 1981), pp. 155–86.

13   Robert Louis Stevenson, *Travels with a Donkey in the Cevennes*, Everyman's Classic edition (London: Dent & Sons, 1984; first publ. 1879), p. 158.

14   See C. Murray Parkes and Robert S. Weiss, *Recovery from Bereavement* (New York: Basic Books, 1983).

7. MARITAL UPSET

1   As is noted in the text, the most frequent topic of disagreement reported by the sixty-nine married respondents was the children. Sixty-three of the sixty-nine had children or stepchildren; fifty-four had children living at home. As reported by the men, about two couples in five of those who had children had some disagreements about the children. Issues giving rise to disagreement included how to deal with the children's misbehavior, the man's performance as a father and the wife's performance as a mother. Among all married couples, almost one couple in five was reported by the men to have had disagreements over the amount of time the man was available to his wife; only one in fifteen over the amount of time the wife was available to the man. Other reported issues of disagreement included communication (eleven couples), in-laws (nine couples), and social life (seven couples). A few couples were reported to have disagreed about the use of money. In one, the husband wanted his wife to spend more on herself.

These findings concur with a 1981 survey of about six hundred couples living in a city in Western Canada. Jarmila L. A. Horna reports that by far the most frequent source of disagreement was the way the children were dealt with. Older children more frequently produced disagreement than preschool children. Among the less frequent sources of disagreement, money ranked highest, followed by irritating personal habits, the use of free time, time spent with friends and not showing love. Jarmila L. A. Horna, (University of Calgary, Alberta). "The Dual Pattern of Marital Conflict," paper presented to the XI World Congress of Sociology, New Delhi, India, 1986.

2   Sixty men in our random sample were asked to say whether they had experienced any of a list of symptoms of both stress and depression in the recent past. Of the thirty-five men who reported stress-provoking incidents in their work and also in

their family lives, fifty-one percent said that there were times when they felt low or depressed. Of the twenty-five men who reported stress-provoking incidents in their work but not in their family lives, twenty-four percent said that there were times when they felt low or depressed. No men reported stress-provoking incidents in their family lives but not in their work. It appears that stress-provoking incidents both in the home and at work makes depressive reaction more likely than does the experience of stress-provoking incidents only at work.

3   To say that women tend not to forget injury is not to say that they insist on reviewing it. Women, as well as men, regularly avoid discussing potentially conflictual issues. Harold L. Raush and his colleagues asked forty-six young couples to deal with a set of conflict situations. About fifteen percent of the time, couples distorted the instructions and avoided confrontation. Sometimes the avoidance constituted punishment by withdrawal, but often it seemed to be a choice for good feelings over interpersonal clarity. Harold L. Raush, William A. Barry, Richard K. Hertel, and Mary Ann Swain, *Communication, Conflict and Marriage* (San Francisco: Jossey-Bass, 1974). The authors write: "The marriages of those who avoid and deny interpersonal involvement are, so far as we can see, no less stable, no less compatible, no less comfortable than other marriages" (p. 82). They find that these couples are more likely than other couples to describe their marriages as happy.

4   Robert S. Weiss, *Going It Alone* (New York: Basic Books, 1979).

5   Theodore Reik, a psychoanalyst trained by Freud, provides a detailed description of the man's experience of this sort of blowup in his *Fragment of a Great Confession: a Psychoanalytic Autobiography* (New York: Citadel Press, 1965). Reik's wife had mistakenly suspected him of infidelity. Note, in his account, the feeling of being shattered, the sense of loss of self, the conviction that the assault was unjust, and then the discovery, on rejoining his wife, that the blowup had cleared the air. He writes:

> My wife . . . reproached me severely. . . . She got more and more excited the less I had to say, and what was there to be said . . . ? At the end she was carried away by her fury and shouted, "You are a scoundrel!" It was like a blow on the head. I left the room silently and walked into the garden that surrounded the cottage.
>
> There had been arguments between us before, tiffs and disharmonies. . . . There had never been any name-calling, never a scene like this one. I felt as in a daze. I still remember it was a beautiful summer afternoon and everything was flowering. The air was so quiet and the landscape presented its most beautiful view. . . .
>
> I walked around the big flower-bed for hours and there was, it seemed to me, not a single thought in my head. I did not feel depressed, nor was I sad. There was apparently a heavy load on my breast because I could not breathe freely. It seemed nothing mattered any more. I was far away from myself, walking there, and in a kind of depersonalization, in one of these states of mind in which one is a stranger to oneself. I do not know any more how long I walked around the small garden paths automatically and unthinking. . . . Suddenly I heard myself say: "I am not a scoundrel. . . . "
>
> . . . I returned to the apartment and spoke to Ella in a quiet and very friendly way. . . . Our conversation was friendly and it did not concern the subject of our discussion a short time before. . . . We both now felt that we belonged together.

6   Among the sixty-nine married men in our randomly chosen sample of seventy-five, fourteen reported at least one occasion on which his wife blew up at him, and seven at least one occasion when he attempted to intimidate his wife either verbally or physically. However, as is noted above, we became aware of the importance of blowups only after completing most of our interviews and made systematic inquiries only with the last twenty or so respondents.

7   Displaced violence can take many forms. One woman said of her husband:

> He'll do whatever he has to do to get his point across. So he'll start small and build. He'll start off kind of pleading, wheedling, build to a little bit of self-righteous indignation and escalate into "You can't do this to me. If you really loved me, you wouldn't!"

> He will get mad enough that he will hop in his car and take off one hundred miles an hour for a while.

8   One study has found that men who are prone to violence tend to feel humiliated by marital conflict and to be made anxious by it. Donald G. Dutton and James J. Browning, "Power Struggles and Intimacy Anxieties as Causative Factors in Wife Assault," in Gordon W. Russell, ed., *Violence in Intimate Relationships* (New York: PMA Publisher, 1988), pp. 163–75.

8.   FATHERHOOD

1   This is true for men, but less so for their wives. Huber and Spitze report that the presence of young children in the home deters fathers' thoughts of divorce but does not deter mothers'. Joan Huber and Glenna Spitze, *Sex Stratification: Children, Housework and Jobs* (New York: Academic Press, 1980), p. 106. Undoubtedly fathers fear that they will lose their children should their marriages end; mothers do not.

2   David Gutmann, an anthropologist who has studied the effects of becoming a father on men in several cultures, writes:

> Males are almost universally socialized toward achievement and self-reliance in a world they never made, the lands beyond the perimeter. . . . Whether as trader, hunter, soldier, rebel, itinerant merchant, or worker, the candidate for manhood moves from the inward, central location of the mother's world to the outward perimeter of his father's world.

David Gutmann, *Reclaimed Powers* (New York: Basic Books, 1987), p. 193

Young people, both males and females, move from their mother's world in the interior of the family to the wider world outside, but the young male ordinarily moves farther, sooner, and with more freedom. In most societies, the young male's efforts are sponsored by an already adult male, usually the young male's father.

3   However, fathers seem to spend about the same amount of time with children just entering latency or not quite there as they do with older children. Lamb observes: "Fathers may know more about older children than about younger children, they may feel more comfortable and competent, and they may appear more interested, but they do not appear to spend more time with their older children. In part, this may be because older children no longer want to interact with parents as much." Michael E. Lamb, "Introduction: The Emergent American Father," in Lamb, ed., *The Father's Role: Cross-Cultural Perspectives* (Hillsdale, N. J.: Erlbaum, 1987), p. 10.

4   This uncertainty can result in what appears to be a preference for the sons. Lamb reports: "Fathers are indeed more interested in and more involved with their sons than with their daughters. They tend to spend more time with boys than with girls." It seems to me unlikely that fathers are more concerned about their sons than their daughters. Indeed, they are so concerned about both that comparisons make no sense. But fathers often believe they have more to offer their sons and can do more with them. See Michael E. Lamb, "Fathers and Child Development: An Integrative Overview," in Lamb, ed., *The Role of the Father in Child Development*, Rev. Ed. (New York: Wiley, 1981); pp. 1–9. Lamb's chapter offers a comprehensive review of research prior to 1980 on the father's role in child development. The book also includes two other useful reviews: Henry B. Biller, "The Father and Sex Role Development," pp. 319–58, and Martin L. Hoffman, "The Role of the Father in Moral Internalization," pp. 359–78.

5   Some men share nurturant responsibilities with their wives, although very rarely do they approach their wives' level of investment in nurturing, and ordinarily whatever they do is only with their wives' endorsement. Men who do act in a nurturant fashion tend to think less well of their wives as mothers; what is cause and what effect is not known. Grace K. Baruch and Rosalind C. Barnett, "Correlates of Fathers' Participation in Family Work: A Technical Report," *Working Paper No. 106* (Wellesley, Mass.: Wellesley College Center for Research on Women, 1983).

6   I have been told by colleagues whom I respect that they have had as clients or respondents men whom they believe never can have cared about their children, given how easily they walked away from them. I myself have not met such men, although at one time much of my work was with couples whose marriages had ended. (This section of the chapter is based on that work and on my continued work with men experiencing marital separation.) For the behavior and experience of men after divorce, see Judith S. Wallerstein and Sandra Blakeslee, *Second Chances: Men, Women and Children a Decade After Divorce* (New York: Ticknor & Fields, 1989); Judith S. Wallerstein and Joan B. Kelly, *Surviving the Breakup: How Children and Parents Cope with Divorce* (New York: Basic Books, 1980); and Robert S. Weiss, *Marital Separation* (New York: Basic Books, 1975).

9.   COMMUNITIES

1   Our seventy-five respondents were coded as reporting the following social linkages: one or more old friends, from college or earlier, 60%; a male friend or colleague who is a confidant (usually about work issues), 49%; a female friend or colleague who is a confidante (usually about life issues), 13%; a group of friends, none especially intimate, 75%. Two of the men were coded as having no social linkages at all outside their families and working relationships. For only ten percent of the sixty-seven men from whose reports inference was possible did coders believe their social linkages approached their families and work in importance. For twice as many, twenty-one percent, coders believed their social linkages to be emotionally unimportant. Only nineteen percent of the men were coded as turning frequently to friendships outside the workplace for support. Nine percent had no such friendships. Twenty-three percent had such friendships but never turned to them for support. In sum, about a third of the men interviewed never seek support from friends.

On the other hand, about four-fifths of the men interviewed belonged to voluntary organizations of some sort: a church, a governmental committee, a social organization. Coders thought that of these organizational members, four-fifths found the membership emotionally important.

Forty-nine men had living parents and, in addition, provided enough information to make it possible for coders to judge their parents' emotional importance to them. Of this group, eighty-three percent remained emotionally linked to both parents; just two men remained emotionally linked to only one. Only twelve percent were no longer linked emotionally to their parents.

Forty-nine men also had siblings and provided enough information to make it possible for coders to judge the quality of their relationships with the siblings. For not quite three-quarters of this group, at least one brother or sister was important in ongoing life; for a bit more than a quarter, no brother or sister was important in ongoing life. Several men were estranged from one or more siblings while linked to other siblings.

2   Since liking and respect and loyalty are not present in every relationship we would like to call friendship and when they are, can vary over time, we should not define friendship as a relationship necessarily containing these qualities. A better definition is that friendship is a residual category, containing relationships that are not obligatory, as are kinship ties, or required by the tasks of making a living, as are relationships with supervisors and subordinates and clients, or required by domestic or personal needs and goals, as might be relationships with professionals or tradesmen. Friendships are relationships maintained for themselves; they have no other justification.

3   Jacobson, on the basis of work with unemployed engineers, reports that former friends who did not come through when needed were retrospectively redefined as never having been real friends. David Jacobson, "Fair-Weather Friend: Label and Context in Middle-Class Friendships," *Journal of Anthropological Research*, 31, no. 3 (Autumn 1975.): 225–34.

4   For a review of research and a program for reducing men's caution with other men, see Robert A. Lewis, "Emotional Intimacy Among Men," *Journal of Social Issues*, 34, no. 1 (1978): 108–21.

5   Belle, on the basis of a review of research, reports that men are much less likely than women to respond to a problem by seeking the help of friends. Men are also more likely to believe that talking is beneficial only as it contributes to problem-solving. Women are more inclined to think of talking as beneficial in itself. Deborah Belle, "Gender Differences in the Social Moderators of Stress," in Rosalind Barnett, Lois Biener, and Grace Baruch, eds., *Gender and Stress* (New York: Free Press, 1987), pp. 257–77.

6   This is a variant of the "self-handicapping" explanation that drinking can be used to protect the self from blame for poor performance: "I would have done better, except that I'd had a drink." See Thomas A. Kolditz and Robert M. Arkin, "An Impression Management Interpretation of the Self-handicapping Strategy," *Journal of Personality and Social Psychology*, 43 (1982): 492–502.

7   Belle reports that research consistently finds that for both men and women, women are more supportive friends. Belle, "Gender Differences in Social Moderators," pp. 257–77.

8   A perceptive and detailed discussion of differences between the friendships formed by men and by women is given by Lillian Rubin, *Just Friends: The Role of*

Friendship in Our Lives (New York: Harper & Row, 1985). See also Peter Willmott, *Friendship Networks and Social Support* (London: Policy Studies Institute, 1987). Willmott, on the basis of a study of residents of a London district, corroborates the observation that women's friendships require more frequent meetings and involve more self-disclosure.

10. TIME OUT

1   In a study by Frank and her colleagues of one hundred couples (average age of husbands 37) who believed that their marriages were working, about a fifth of wives and about a third of husbands complained of sexual dissatisfaction in the marriage. About a third of the sample reported a frequency of intercourse of less than once a week; ten percent reported a frequency of less than once a month. The men in the present study are on average about ten years older than those in the Frank study, and their marriages about ten years longer in duration. See Ellen Frank, Carol Anderson, and Debra Rubinstein, "Frequency of Sexual Dysfunction in "Normal" Couples," *New England Journal of Medicine*, 299 (July 20, 1978,): 111–15

2   Terman reported that almost three-quarters of a sample of married men said that they had at some point wanted an extramarital partner. His study was done in the 1930s, when an admission of this sort was more difficult to make than it would be today. Lewis Terman, *Psychological Factors in Marital Happiness* (New York: McGraw-Hill, 1938).

3   Neither Kinsey nor Hunt had a probability sample, and their estimates might best be treated as informed guesses. Alfred Kinsey et al., *Sexual Behavior in the Human Male* (Philadelphia: W. B. Saunders, 1948), and Morton Hunt, *Sexual Behavior in the 1970's* (Chicago: Playboy Press, 1974). In an earlier work Hunt estimated a sixty percent lifetime incidence for American men, perhaps forty percent for American women, based on guesses made by therapists and sociologists, augmented by his own informal sampling. Morton Hunt, *The Affair: A Portrait of Extramarital Love in Contemporary America* (New York: Signet Books, 1969).

A review of incidence estimates is given by Philip E. Lampe, "Adultery and the Behavioral Sciences," in Philip E. Lampe, ed., *Adultery in the United States* (Buffalo, N.Y.: Prometheus Books, 1987), pp. 165–98.

The proportion of married men *currently* involved, continuously or sporadically, with other women would be much less than a lifetime incidence figure. In our data, there is indication that about ten percent of the men we interviewed included an extramarital relationship of some sort in their current lives, most often in the form of occasional brief relationships, perhaps one-night stands, during a conference or business trip. However, a true value as low as five percent or as high as twenty percent would be consistent with our materials.

4   A discussion of the reasons men hire prostitutes is given in Lewis Diana, *The Prostitute and her Clients: Your Pleasure Is Her Business* (Springfield, Ill.: Charles C. Thomas, 1984), pp. 180–205. Diana suggests that the commercial character of the transaction is an attraction: The man need not feel he is emotionally unfaithful to his marriage and need not worry about his responsibilities to the woman. He says of the men who employ prostitutes, " . . . among the married majority, most are satisfied with their marriages but dissatisfied with their sexual expectations within them" (p. 187).

The variety of meanings an upper-middle-class man may impart to an encounter with a call girl are discussed in Martha L. Stein, *Lovers, Friends, Slaves* (New York: Putnam's, 1974).

11.   CONCLUSIONS

1   Thoreau recognized that men can be driven by the desire to obtain their own good opinion, and thought it regrettable. He wrote:

> Look at the teamster on the highway, wending to market by day or night; does any divinity stir within him? . . . See how . . . vaguely all the day he fears, not being immortal nor divine, but the slave and prisoner of his own opinion of himself, a fame won by his own deeds. Public opinion is a weak tyrant compared with our own private opinion. What a man thinks of himself, that it is which determines, or rather indicates, his fate.

Henry David Thoreau, *Walden* (Princeton, N.J.: Princeton University Press, 1971; first pub., 1851), p. 7. Thoreau was himself responsive to the scrutiny of an internal appraiser. He did not spare himself in his effort to get his manuscript right.

2   George Santayana, *Character and Opinion in the United States* (New York: Charles Scribner's Sons, 1921), p. vii.

3   See the brief discussion of research on children in Virginia E. O'Leary and James M. Donoghue, "Latitudes of Masculinity: Reactions to Self-role Deviance in Men," *Journal of Social Issues*, 34, no. 1 (1978): 17–28.

4   An exploratory study of a small sample of children by Belle, Burr, and Cooney suggests that latency-age boys, much more than latency-age girls, dislike showing themselves in need of help. The adult male unwillingness to ask directions when lost, so trying to their wives, is already visible in latency. Deborah Belle, Robin Burr, and James Cooney, "Boys and Girls as Social Support Theorists," *Sex Roles*, 17, nos. 11–12 (1987): 657–65.

5   The latency-age standards which men have internalized have often proven easy targets for criticism. See the papers in Deborah S. David and Robert Brannon, eds., *The Forty-Nine Percent Majority: The Male Sex Role* (Reading, Mass.: Addison-Wesley, 1976).

6   Another implication of this observation is that difficulties in one sector are likely to diffuse to other sectors. On the interrelationships of events in the sectors of work and family see David N. Ulrich and Harry P. Dunne, Jr., *To Love and Work: A Systemic Interlocking of Family, Workplace, and Career* (New York: Brunner/Mazel, 1986). But see, for another view, Joseph H. Pleck, *The Myth of Masculinity* (Cambridge: MIT Press, 1981).

APPENDIX ON METHODS

1   Daniel Levinson, et al., *Seasons of a Man's Life* (New York: Knopf, 1978).

2   George Vaillant, *Adaptation to Life* (Boston: Little, Brown, 1977).

3   We anticipated that men in this age interval would have established a fully adult way of life. Super has proposed that between the college years and about age thirty men are still establishing themselves in a line of work. Donald E. Super, *The Psychology of Careers* (New York: Harper, 1957). In Schein's terms the men we interviewed are beyond the "early career" stage of establishing themselves in a line of work. They are in the stage of "middle career," when they are performing at their highest levels, or "later career," when they may include, in their mix of activities, more than are managerial and instructional. Edward H. Schein, "The Individual, the Organization

and the Career: A Conceptual Scheme," *Journal of Applied Behavioral Science* 7 (1971): 401–26. Lorence and Mortimer demonstrate that these "career stage" models are correct in their anticipation that the years of our study are a time of stability of work involvement and, presumably, of social involvement. Jon Lorence and Jeylan T. Mortimer, "Job Involvement Through the Life Course: A Panel Study of Three Age Groups," *American Sociological Review*, 50 (October 1985): 618–38.

Bibliography

Arendt, Hannah. *The Human Condition*, Chicago: University of Chicago Press, 1958.

Balswick, Jack. *The Inexpressive Male*. Lexington, Mass.: Lexington Books, 1988.

Baruch, Grace K., and Rosalind C. Barnett. "Correlates of Fathers' Participation in Family Work: A Technical Report." *Working paper No. 106*. Wellesley, Mass.: Wellesley College Center for Research on Women, 1983.

Belle, Deborah. "Gender Differences in the Social Moderators of Stress." In Rosalind C. Barnett, Lois Biener, and Grace K. Baruch, eds., *Gender and Stress*. New York: Free Press, 1987. Pp. 257–77.

Belle, Deborah; Robin Burr; and James Cooney. "Boys and Girls as Social Support Theorists." *Sex Roles*, 17, nos. 11–12 (1987): 657–65.

Biller, Henry B. "The Father and Sex Role Development." In Michael E. Lamb, ed., *The Role of the Father in Child Development*. Revised Edition. New York: John Wiley & Sons, 1981. Pp. 319–58.

Blood, Robert O., Jr., and Donald M. Wolfe. *Husbands and Wives: The Dynamics of Marital Living*. Glencoe, Ill.: Free Press, 1960.

Burke, Ronald J., and Tamara Weir. "Husband–Wife Helping Relationships as Moderators of Experienced Stress: The 'Mental Hygiene' Function in Marriage." In Hamilton I. McCubbin, A. Elizabeth Cauble, and Joan M. Peterson, ed., *Family Stress, Coping and Support*. Springfield, Ill.: Charles C. Thomas, 1982. Pp. 221–38.

Cannon, Walter G. *Bodily Changes in Pain, Hunger, Fear and Rage: An Account of Recent Researches into the Function of Emotional Excitement*. Second Edition. New York: Appleton, 1929.

Cobb, Sydney, and Robert Rose. "Hypertension, Peptic Ulcer, and Diabetes in Air Traffic Controllers." *Journal of the American Medical Association*. 224 (1973): 489–92.

Cohen, Sheldon, and S. Leonard Syme. "Issues in the Study and Application of Social Support." In Sheldon Cohen and S. Leonard Syme, ed., *Social Support and Health*. New York: Academic Press: 1985. Pp. 3–22.

Coleman, Karen H. "Conjugal Violence: What 33 Men Report." *Journal of Marriage and Family Therapy*, 6 (1980):207–13.

Coles, Robert. "Work and Self-respect." *Daedelus*, 105 (Fall 1976):29–38.

Coser, Lewis A. *Greedy Institutions; Patterns of Undivided Commitment*. New York: Free Press, 1974.

Crouter, Ann C., "Spillover from Family to Work: The Neglected Side of the Work–Family Interface." *Human Relations*, 37, no. 6 (1984): 425–42.

David, Deborah S., and Robert Brannon, ed. *The Forty-Nine Percent Majority: The Male Sex Role*. Reading, Mass.: Addison-Wesley, 1976.

Diana, Lewis. *The Prostitute and Her Clients: Your Pleasure Is Her Business*. Springfield, Ill., Charles C. Thomas, 1984.

Dohrenwend, Bruce S., and Bernice P. Dohrenwend, ed. *Stressful Life Events: Their Nature and Effects*. New York: John Wiley, 1974.

Dutton, Donald G., and James J. Browning. "Power Struggles and Intimacy Anxieties as Causative Factors in Wife Assault." In Gordon W. Russell, ed., *Violence in Intimate Relationships*. New York: PMA Publishers, 1988. Pp. 163–75.

Erikson, Kai. "On Work and Alienation." *American Sociological Review*, 51 (February 1986):1–8.

Fallaci, Oriana. *Interview with History*. New York: Liveright, 1976.

Finch, Janet. *Married to the Job: Wives' Incorporation in Men's Work*. London: George Allen & Unwin, 1983.

Finn, Jerry. "The Relationship Between Sex Role Attitudes and Attitudes Supporting Marital Violence." *Sex Roles*, vol. 14, nos. 5–6, 1986.

Frank, Ellen; Carol Anderson; and Debra Rubinstein. "Frequency of Sexual Dysfunction in 'normal' couples." *New England Journal of Medicine*, 299 (July 20, 1978):111–15.

Frankenhaueser, Marianne. "Coping with Job Stress: A Psychobiological Approach." In B. Gardell and B. Johansson, eds., *Working Life*. New York: John Wiley & Sons, 1981. Pp. 213–33.

French, John R. P., Jr., and Robert D. Caplan. "Organizational Stress and Individual Strain." In Alfred J. Marrow, ed., *The Failure of Success*. New York: AMACOM, 1972. Pp. 50–66.

Friedman, Meyer, and Ray H. Rosenman. *Type A Behavior and Your Heart*. New York: Alfred A. Knopf, 1974.

Gillespie, Dair L. "Who Has the Power? The Marital Struggle." *Journal of Marriage and the Family*, 33 (August 1971):445–58.

Gruneberg, Michael M. *Understanding Job Satisfaction*, London: Macmillan, 1979.

Gut, Emmy. *Productive and Unproductive Depression: Success or Failure of a Vital Process*. New York: Basic Books, 1989.

Gutmann, David. *Reclaimed Powers*. New York: Basic Books, 1987.

Haney, Thomas L., and James A. Blumenthal. "Stress and the Type A Behavior Pattern." In Susan R. Burchfield, ed., *Stress: Psychological and Physiological Interactions*. New York: Hemisphere, 1985. Pp. 207–21.

Harrington, Alan. *Life in the Crystal Palace*. New York: A. A. Knopf, 1959.

Hatfield, Elaine; Jane Traupmann; Susan Sprecher; and Julia Hay. "Equity and Intimate Relations: Recent Research." In William Ickes, ed., *Compatible and Incompatible Relationships*. New York: Springer-Verlag, 1985. Pp. 91–117.

Heckscher, August, and Sebastian de Grazia. "Executive Leisure." *Harvard Business Review*, 37, no. 4 (July–August 1959):6–12.

Heller, Joseph. *Something Happened*. New York: Knopf, 1974.

Henemann, Herbert G., and Donald P. Schwab. "Pay Satisfaction: Its Multidimensional Nature and Measurement." *International Journal of Psychology*, 20 (1985): 129–41.

Herzberg, Frederick. *Work and the Nature of Man*. Cleveland: World Publishing, 1966.

Hoffman, Martin L. "The Role of the Father in Moral Internalization." In Michael E. Lamb, ed., *The Role of the Father in Child Development*. Revised Edition. New York: John Wiley & Sons, 1981. Pp. 359–78.

Horna, Jarmila L. A. "The Dual Pattern of Marital Conflict," paper presented to the XIth World Congress of Sociology, New Delhi, India, 1986.

House, James. *Work Stress and Social Support.* Reading, Mass.: Addison-Wesley, 1981.

House, James S.; Anthony J. McMichael; James A. Wells; Berton H. Kaplan; and Lawrence R. Landerman. "Occupational Stress and Health Among Factory Workers." *Journal of Health and Social Behavior,* 20 (June 1979): 139–60.

Huber, Joan, and Glenna Spitze. *Sex Stratification: Children, Housework and Jobs.* New York: Academic Press, 1980.

Hunt, Morton. *The Affair: A Portrait of Extra-Marital Love in Contemporary America.* New York: Signet Books, 1969.

———. *Sexual Behavior in the 1970's.* Chicago: Playboy Press, 1974.

Jacobson, David. "Fair-Weather Friend: Label and Context in Middle-Class Friendships." *Journal of Anthropological Research,* 31, no. 3 (Autumn 1975):225–34.

Jahoda, Marie. "The Impact of Unemployment in the 1930s and the 1970s." *Bulletin of the British Psychological Society,* 32 (1979):309–14.

Jahoda, Marie; Paul F. Lazarsfeld; and Hans Zeisel. *Marienthal: The Sociography of an Unemployed Community.* London: Tavistock Publications, 1972.

Janis, Irving L. *Psychological Stress: Psychoanalytic and Behavioral Studies of Surgical Patients.* New York: Academic Press, 1974.

Kanter, Rosabeth Moss. *Men and Women of the Corporation.* New York: Basic Books, 1977.

Kanungo, Rabindra N. "The Concepts of Alienation and Involvement Revisited." *Psychological Bulletin,* 86, no. 1 (1979):119–38.

Kasl, Stanislav V., and James A. Wells. "Social Support and Health in the Middle Years: Work and the Family." In Sheldon Cohen and S. Leonard Syme, eds., *Social Support and Health.* New York, Academic Press: 1985. Pp. 175–98.

Katz, Mary Maxwell, and Melvin J. Konner. "The Role of the Father: An Anthropological Perspective." In Michael E. Lamb, ed., *The Role of the Father in Child Development.* Revised Edition. New York: John Wiley & Sons, 1981. Pp. 155–86.

Kelvin, Peter, and Joanna E. Jarrett. *Unemployment: Its Social Psychological Effects.* Cambridge: Cambridge University Press, 1985.

Kessler, Ronald C.; James S. House; and J. B. Turner. "Unemployment and Health in a Community Sample." *Journal of Health and Social Behavior,* 28 (1987):51–59.

Kessler, Ronald C., and James A. McRae, Jr. "The Effect of Wives' Employment on the Mental Health of Married Men and Women." *American Sociological Review,* 47 (April 1982):216–27.

Kinsey, Alfred, et al. *Sexual Behavior in the Human Male.* Philadelphia: W. B. Saunders, 1948.

Kobasa, Suzanne C. "Stressful Life Events, Personality, and Health: An Inquiry into Hardiness." *Journal of Personality and Social Psychology,* 37, no. 1 (January 1979):1–11.

Kolditz, Thomas A., and Robert M. Arkin. "An Impression Management Interpretation of the Self-handicapping Strategy." *Journal of Personality and Social Psychology,* 43 (1982): 492–502.

Komarovsky, Mirra. *Blue-Collar Marriage.* New York: Random House, 1962.

Kriegel, Leonard. *On Men and Manhood.* New York: Hawthorn Books, 1979.

Lamb, Michael E. "Fathers and Child Development: An Integrative Overview." In Michael E. Lamb, ed., *The Role of the Father in Child Development*. Revised Edition. New York: John Wiley & Sons, 1981. Pp. 1–70.

————. "Introduction: The Emergent American Father." In Michael E. Lamb, ed., *The Father's Role: Cross-Cultural Perspectives*. Hillsdale, NJ.: Lawrence Erlbaum Associates, 1987.

Lampe, Philip E. "Adultery and the Behavioral Sciences." In Philip E. Lampe, ed., *Adultery in the United States*. Buffalo, N.Y.: Prometheus Books, 1987. Pp. 165–98.

LaRocco, James M.; James S. House; and John R. P. French, Jr. "Social Support, Occupational Stress, and Health." *Journal of Health and Social Behavior*, 21 (September 1980): 202–18.

Leventman, Paula Goldman. *Professionals Out of Work*. New York: Free Press, 1981.

Levinson, Daniel, et al. *Seasons of a Man's Life*. New York: Knopf, 1978.

Lewis, Robert A. "Emotional Intimacy Among Men." *Journal of Social Issues*, 34, no. 1 (1978): 108–21.

Lewis, Sinclair. *Babbitt*. New York: Harcourt, Brace, 1922.

Liebow, Elliot. *Tally's Corner*, Boston: Little, Brown, 1967.

Locke, E. A. "The Nature and Causes of Job Satisfaction." In M. D. Dunnette, ed., *Handbook of Industrial and Organizational Psychology*. Chicago: Rand McNally, 1976. Pp. 1297–349.

Lodahl, Thomas, and Mathilde Kejner. "The Definition and Measurement of Job Involvement." *Journal of Applied Psychology*, 49, no. 1 (1965): 24–33.

Lorence, Jon, and Jeylan T. Mortimer. "Job Involvement Through the Life Course: A Panel Study of Three Age Groups." *American Sociological Review*, 50, (October 1985): 618–38.

Mars, Gerald. *Cheats at Work: An Anthropology of Workplace Crime*. Boston: Allen & Unwin, 1982.

Mason, John W. "A Historical View of the Stress Field (Part II)." *Journal of Human Stress*, 1, no. 2 (1975): 22–36.

McDermott, Diane. "Professional Burnout and Its Relation to Job Characteristics, Satisfaction, and Control." *Journal of Human Stress*, 10, no. 2 (Summer 1984): 79–85.

McLeod, Kirsty. *The Wives of Downing Street*. London: William Collins Sons, 1976.

Mead, Margaret. *Male and Female*. New York: Morrow, 1949.

Mintzberg, Henry. *The Nature of Managerial Work*, New York: Harper & Row, 1973.

Morse, Nancy C., and Robert S. Weiss. "The Function and Meaning of Work and the Job," *American Sociological Review*, 20, no. 2 (April 1955): 191–98.

MOW International Research Team. *The Meaning of Working*. New York: Academic Press, 1987.

Nordstrom, Bruce. "Why Men Get Married: More and Less Traditional Men Compared." In Robert A. Lewis and Robert E. Salt, eds., *Men in Families*. Beverly Hills, Calif.: Sage, 1986. Pp. 31–53.

Notz, William W. "Work Motivation and the Negative Effect of Extrinsic Rewards." *American Psychologist*, 30 (September 1975):884–91.

Novak, Michael. *The Joy of Sports: End Zones, Bases, Baskets, Balls, and the Consecration of the American Spirit*. New York: Basic Books, 1976.

O'Brien, Gordon E. *Psychology of Work and Unemployment*. New York: John Wiley & Sons, 1986.

————. "The Relative Contribution of Perceived Skill-Utilization and Other Perceived Job Attributes to the Prediction of Job Satisfaction: A Cross-Validation Study." *Human Relations*, 35 (1982): 219–23.

O'Leary, Virginia E., and James M. Donoghue. "Latitudes of Masculinity: Reactions to Self-Role Deviance in Men." *Journal of Social Issues*, 34, no. 1 (1978): 17–28.

Pahl, Raymond E. *Divisions of Labor*. Oxford: Basil Blackwell, 1984.

Parkes, C. Murray, and Robert S. Weiss. *Recovery from Bereavement*. New York: Basic Books, 1983.

Parsons, Talcott, and Robert Freed Bales. *Family, Socialization, and Interaction Process*. Glencoe, Ill.: Free Press, 1955.

Penkower, Lili; Evelyn J. Bromet; and Mary Amanda Dew. "Husbands' Layoff and Wives' Mental Health: A Prospective Analysis," *Archives of General Psychiatry*, 45 (November 1988): 994–1000.

Perlman, Baron, and E. Alan Hartman. "Burnout: Summary and Future Research." *Human Relations*, 35, no. 4 (1982): 283–305.

Pleck, Joseph H. *The Myth of Masculinity*. Cambridge: MIT Press, 1981.

Rabinowitz, Samuel, and Douglas T. Hall. "Organizational Research on Job Involvement." *Psychological Bulletin*, 64, no. 2 (1977):265–88.

Rabkin, Judith G. "Stress and Psychiatric Disorders." In Leo Goldberger and Shlomo Breznitz, eds., *Handbook of Stress: Theoretical and Clinical Aspects*. New York: Free Press, 1982. Pp. 566–84.

Rabkin, J. G., and E. Struening. "Life Events, Stress, and Illness." *Science*, 194 (1979): 1013–20.

Rausch, Harold L.; William A. Barry; Richard K. Hertel; and Mary Ann Swain. *Communication, Conflict and Marriage*. San Francisco: Jossey-Bass, 1974.

Rcik, Theodore. *Fragment of a Great Confession: A Psychoanalytic Autobiography*. New York: Citadel Press, 1965.

Rosenman, Ray H., and Margaret A. Chesney. "Stress, Type A Behavior, and Coronary Disease." In Leo Goldberger and Shlomo Breznitz, eds., *Handbook of Stress: Theoretical and Clinical Aspects*. New York: Free Press, 1982. Pp. 547–65.

Rubin, Lillian. *Just Friends: The Role of Friendship in Our Lives*. New York: Harper & Row, 1985.

Santayana, George. *Character and Opinion in the United States*. New York: Charles Scribner's Sons, 1921.

Schein, Edgar H. "The Individual, the Organization, and the Career: A Conceptual Scheme." *Journal of Applied Behavioral Science*, 7 (1971): 401–26.

Selye, Hans. *The Physiology and Pathology of Exposure to Stress*. Montreal: Acta, 1950.

————. "The Stress Concept: Past, Present, and Future." In Cary L. Cooper, ed., *Stress Research: Issues for the Eighties*. New York: John Wiley & Sons, 1983. Pp. 1–20.

Stein, Martha I. *Lovers, Friends, Slaves*. New York: G. P. Putnam's Sons, 1974.

Stevenson, Robert Louis. *Travels with a Donkey in the Cevennes*, Everyman's Classic edition. London: Dent & Sons, 1984. First published 1879.

Super, Donald E. *The Psychology of Careers*. New York: Harper, 1957.

Terman, Lewis. *Psychological Factors in Marital Happiness*. New York: McGraw-Hill, 1938.

Thompson, Anthony P. "Extramarital Sex: A Review of the Research Literature." *The Journal of Sex Research*, 19, no. 1 (February 1983): 1–22.

Thoreau, Henry D. *Walden*. Princeton, N.J.: Princeton University Press, 1971. First printed in 1854.

Ulrich, David N., and Harry P. Dunne, Jr. *To Love and Work: A Systemic Interlocking of Family, Workplace, and Career*. New York: Brunner/Mazel, 1986.

Updike, John. *Rabbit Redux*. New York: Knopf, 1971.

Vaillant, George E. *Adaptation to Life*. Boston: Little, Brown, 1977.

Vaillant, George E., and Caroline D. Vaillant. "Natural History of Male Psychological Health: X. Work as a Predictor of Positive Mental Health." *American Journal of Psychiatry*, 138 (1981): 1433–40.

Wallerstein, Judith S., and Sandra Blakeslee. *Second Chances: Men, Women and Children a Decade After Divorce*. New York: Ticknor & Fields, 1989.

Wallerstein, Judith S., and Joan B. Kelly. *Surviving the Breakup: How Children and Parents Cope with Divorce*. New York: Basic Books, 1980.

Weiss, Robert S. *Going It Alone*. New York: Basic Books, 1979.

———. *Marital Separation*. New York: Basic Books, 1975.

Weitzman, Lenore. *The Divorce Revolution*. New York: The Free Press, 1986.

Whyte, William H. *The Organization Man*. New York: Simon & Schuster, 1956.

Wilensky, Harold L. "Orderly Careers and Social Participation: The Impact of Work History on Social Integration in the Middle Mass." *American Sociological Review*, 26 (August, 1961): 521–39.

Willmott, Peter. *Friendship Networks and Social Support*, London: Policy Studies Institute, 1987.

Young, Michael, and Peter Willmott. *The Symmetrical Family*. New York: Pantheon Books, 1973.

Acknowledgments

Many people have contributed to this study during its six years of life from first concept to final manuscript.

Jack Fowler helped design the sample and sampling approach. Sue Gore provided useful advice in drafting the proposal that led to the study. Emily Hancock provided referrals to pilot interview respondents.

Interviewers in the study proper were Sharon Spector, Nancy Marshall, Ruth Paradise, Philip McArthur, and Claire Mitchell, assisted by Anna Wexsler and Marjolein de Jong. In addition to serving as interviewers, Ruth Paradise was invaluable as a recruiter of respondents and Sharon Spector contributed to the development of the coding manual. Important contributions to the development of interview guides were made by Sharon Spector, Nancy Marshall and Philip McArthur.

Mary Coffey and John Drabik were the study's transcriptionists. Each contributed in many other ways as well. Coders included Dennis Firedler, Emily Schultz, and Amber Keshishian. Amber Keshishian, Roseann Torre, Margaret Amara, and Miriam Caldwell all helped locate relevant literature.

The study's administrator, field director, and director of coding was Carolyn Bruse. She also responded to chapter drafts and helped think through the underlying conceptual scheme of the study. In the final months of the study her administrative duties were ably assumed by Anna Sant'Anna.

I was aided in planning the study by a professional advisory committee whose members were Sue Gore, Karen Lewis, Lee Rainwater, and Martin Rein. Judith Wallerstein made me aware of areas not sufficiently developed in our early interviewing guides.

Early drafts of this book were read by Carol Baxter, Arlene Daniels, Sophie Freud, Gay Kitson, Mary McCrae, Lisa Peattie, Stuart Pizer, Joseph Pleck, Martin Rein, Marion Sanders, Blanca Silvestrini, and Carol Stack. All contributed helpful comments and criticisms.

Stuart Pizer joined me in presenting materials during eight weekly meetings to a men's group at Lexington's Temple Israel. I also found helpful my participation in the Grant Foundation continuing seminar on stress and support chaired by John Eckinrode and Susan Gore.

I have been fortunate to have had Erwin Glikes's editorial advice at critical junctures. I have also benefited from the editorial help of Kathleen Much, Muriel Bell, Ketura Persallin, Douglas Weiss and Gina Prenowitz. Maxine Groffsky, my agent, has been supportive throughout the project.

My closest colleague throughout the years of the study has been my wife, Joan Hill Weiss. She has helped me think through ideas and manage stresses and has tolerated evenings and weekends during which I was preoccupied with writing.

Data collection and analysis of materials were supported by two grants from the National Institute of Mental Health, Numbers: 5-R01 MH36708 and 5-R01 MH39353.

I completed the book during a year as a Fellow at the Center for Advanced Study in the Behavioral Sciences in Palo Alto. I am grateful for the year and for the financial support provided by the John D. and Catherine T. MacArthur Foundation.

I feel a special debt to the study's respondents. I cannot acknowledge them by name, but I am grateful to each. I hope they approve of the way in which I have told their stories.

Index

Accessibility to marital partner, marital disagreement over, 143

Achievement
of children, father's contribution to, 123–24
pride in business, 9–11

Action aims, 267

Adaptation to Life (Vaillant), 267

Administrative assistant, support of, 66

Adopted children, 166

Affairs: *see* Extramarital relations

Alcohol use, 144, 149, 283*n*3, 290*n*6
confiding in friends and, 212
tension relief through, 69
by wife, 178

American Dream, 258

Analysis, data, 272–74

Anderson, Carol, 291*n*1

Anxiety, limiting one's work hours and, 43–44; *see also* Stress, work

Arendt, Hannah, 279*n*11

Arkin, R. M., 290*n*6

Attachment
loneliness and, 138–39
love and, 139–40
in marriage, 119, 136–40, 284*n*2
in place vs. in formation, 136–37, 139–40

Attention
blowups to compel, 154–58
mobilization of, 45–46

Babbitt (Lewis), xi

Barnett, Rosalind C., 289*n*5

Barry, William A., 287*n*3

Baruch, Grace K., 289*n*5

Belle, Deborah, 290*n*5, 292*n*4

Bereavement, conjugal, 137

Best friends, 217

Bickering, 142, 153

Birth of children, experiencing, 163–66

Blood, Robert O., Jr., 284*n*1

Blowups, marital, 154–60, 287*n*5, 288*n*6
to compel attention, 154–58
to intimidate, 158–60

Bonus, judging organizational meaning of, 24–25

Boss
being the, 53–55, 281*n*8
hostile, 51–53
support from, 63–64, 281*n*6

Boys, standards internalized by, 255–58, 292*n*5

Browning, James J., 288*n*8

Bruse, Carolyn, 272

Burke, Ronald J., 283*n*1

Burnout, 75, 85–86, 88, 282*n*5

Burr, Robin, 282*n*4

Caplan, Robert D., 281*n*3

Challenge in work, 2–5, 261; *see also* Task difficulties, stress from
introducing 4–5
involvement and, 3–5

Wife/wives *(cont.)*
reliance on, to help with children, 152, 182–83
reluctance to talk about work
with, 92–93
sharing success with, 93–94
shielding work stress from,
98–99
support from, 100–102, 107–8,
283*n*4, 284*n*6
working, xiv, 17–18, 117–18,
129–33, 216, 262, 285*n*11
Wilensky, Harold, 278*n*1
Willmott, Peter, 279*n*8, 290*n*8
Withdrawal from children, 191–93
Wolfe, D. M., 284*n*1
Work, 1–26; *see also* Challenge in
work; Community of work
as basis for functioning, 260
being fired from, xvi, 32, 34–36
cheating at, 279*n*5
compartmentalization and, 44,
192–93
as escape, 44, 276*n*3
evaluation at, xv, 16–21
fantasy substructure of, 5–11
fatherhood and, 233–34
friendships made through, 216
importance of, xvi, 251–52,
260–61
job involvement, 3–5, 279*n*4
motivations to, 28–31, 276*n*6
persisting preoccupation with,
46, 94–96
recognition and emblems of
worth at, 21–26, 277*n*8
reduction of, during family crisis,
184

relationships at
with bosses, 51–53, 63–64,
281*n*6
with partners, 51, 67–68
as source of stress, 49, 50,
51–55
with subordinates, 51, 64–67
reputation and standing at,
12–16
self-esteem and, 27
single fathers and, 177–78
social place and, 27–31
as source of support against
stress, 62–68
support at, 62–68, 281*n*6, 7
time given to, 39–44, 261–62,
279*n*5, 6, 8
unemployment, effects of,
28–36, 278*n*3
unsatisfactory, 36–39
volunteer, 30–31
Workaholics, 44
Work-family conflict, 261–63
Working wives, xiv, 17–18,
117–18, 129–33, 216, 262,
285*n*11; *see also* Dual-career
marriage
Work stress: *see* Stress, work
Worth, emblems of, 23–26
Worth, feelings of
contribution of work to, 278*n*4
fantasy substructure of work and,
7–8
importance of place to, 31–36

Young, Michael, 279*n*8

Zeisel, Hans, 278*n*3

ABOUT THE AUTHOR

ROBERT S. WEISS, Ph.D., is Research Professor at the University of Massachusetts (Boston), where he is director of the Work and Family Research Unit. He is also a lecturer in sociology in the department of psychiatry at the Massachusetts Mental Health Center, Harvard Medical School. The author of *Loneliness* (1973) and *Marital Separation* (1975), he lives in Brookline, Mass.